Gustave Trouvé

For Richard & Amanda Kay,

Gustave Trouvé
French Electrical Genius
(1839–1902)

KEVIN DESMOND

Foreword by John Devitt

Inviting you discover a remarkable & forgotten inventor & many things you use today. Thank you so much for your kind hospitality in October 2018.

Kind Regards,

Kevin Desmond...

McFarland & Company, Inc., Publishers
Jefferson, North Carolina

This is an expanded edition of a book originally published in French as *À la recherche de Trouvé: La quête d'un génie française oublié* (Paris: Éditions Pleine Page, 2012).

LIBRARY OF CONGRESS CATALOGUING-IN-PUBLICATION DATA

Desmond, Kevin, 1950–
[À la recherche de Trouvé. English]
    Gustave Trouvé : French electrical genius (1839–1902) /
Kevin Desmond ; foreword by John Devitt.
        p.   cm.
    Includes bibliographical references and index.

    ISBN 978-0-7864-9709-6 (softcover : acid free paper) ∞
    ISBN 978-1-4766-1968-2 (ebook)

    1. Trouvé, Gustave, 1839–1902.   2. Electrical engineers—
France—Biography.   3. Inventors—France—Biography.
4. Electrical engineering—France—History—19th century.
5. Inventions—France—History—19th century.   I. Title.
TK140.T7D4713 2015
621.3092—dc23
    [B]   2015018139

BRITISH LIBRARY CATALOGUING DATA ARE AVAILABLE

On the cover: Gustave Trouvé, frontispiece of *L'Histoire d'un Inventeur* by Georges Barral (1891), engraving made from a painting by Fernand de Launay

Printed in the United States of America

McFarland & Company, Inc., Publishers
  Box 611, Jefferson, North Carolina 28640
   www.mcfarlandpub.com

To all those who are helping
to rediscover and to rehabilitate
Gustave Trouvé

Table of Contents

Acknowledgments

The author wishes to thank the following for their help in this book: Dominique Sentagnes (*L'électrolyse*), Bernard Guellard (President of the French Electric Boat Association), Michel Couture (Directeur de la Direction Mobilité Électrique d'EDF), and Didier Périz (Pleine Page) for their generous patronage, which enabled publication of the original French edition. And a big thank you to Carlo Galluzzo for his help with indexing the book. The following is a list of institutions and individuals that proved to be invaluable to my research.

Académie des Sciences de l'Institut de France, Archives Service
Académie royale de Médecine de Belgique
Archives of the City of Paris, Christiane Filloles
Archives de l'Assistance Publique des Hôpitaux de Paris
Archives départementales de Maine-et-Loire, Angers
Archives départementales d'Indre et Loire, Nelly Marquet
Archives municipales de la Ville de Tours
Archives municipales de la Ville de Chinon
Archives of Alexander Graham Bell, Nova Scotia, Canada
Association européenne des Musées d'Histoire des Sciences
    Médicales, Marie-Véronique Clin
Association de Sauvegarde du Patrimoine de l'Art Dentaire,
    Dr. Gérard Braye
Association des Amis des Archives diplomatiques, Nantes
Bibliothèque interuniversitaire de Médecine (Paris)
Bibliothèque nationale de France
Bibliothèque-musée de l'Opéra, Paris
Bibliothèque nationale de Luxembourg

Bibliothèque historique des Postes et des Télécommunications
Bibliothèque de Bordeaux, Dominique Quercioli-Duqueroix
Bibliothèque interuniversitaire de Médecine et d'Odontologie,
    Bernadette Molitor
Bibliothèque interuniversitaire de la Sorbonne, Isabelle Diry
Bibliothèque d'Étude et du Patrimoine de Toulouse, Angeline
    Lavigne
Centre historique des Archives nationales
Château royal de Blois, Yvan Boukef, Chargé des collections
    d'archéologie et de magie
Chatou, François Casalis
Conservatoire national des Arts et Métiers
Georgia State Archives, USA
Gilbert and Sullivan Archive
INPI-Aquitaine Valérie Brethes, INPI-Courbevoie
Irving Society
Mairie de La Haye-Descartes
Maison de la Chasse et de la Nature, Claire Maillard
Musée Carnavalet, Catherine Tamburn
Musée de la Marine, Cristina Baron
Musée de l'Air et de l'Espace, Le Bourget
Musée Grévin, Marie Vercambre
Muzej Nikole Tesle, Belgrade
Sammlungen der Medizinischen Universität, Vienna, Austria
Science Museum, Kensington, London
Shakespeare Centre Library, Shakespeare Birthplace Trust
Société d'encouragement pour l'industrie nationale
SNCF, Centre d'Archives historiques
Victoria and Albert Museum, London
Wellcome Museum, London

   And also Jean-Louis Aucouturier, Jacques Calu, Daniel Charles, Olivier Hellé, Bennet Maxwell, Jean-Marie Oms, Alain Ségal, Jean-François Trouvé, and John Devitt.
   Very special thanks to Damien Kuntz at the EDF Museum Electropolis in Mulhouse for his patient assistance; and to my wife Alex and our two children for their unswerving support.

Foreword
by John Devitt

It must stand out as a major anomaly in the history of science, and in particular of electrical progress, that for the past century and more our world has remained largely ignorant of the crucial role played by Gustave Pierre Trouvé, nineteenth century Parisian electrical engineer. In 1881, telephone inventor Alexander Graham Bell encouraged the far-from-business-minded Trouvé to bring his electrical instruments and gizmos to the USA. Had the ingenious Parisian done so, he would have become a household name like Tom Edison and Nicola Tesla. These latter two certainly knew of the Frenchman's "modest" contributions to a fledgling electrical world.

It is not my task in this foreword to cite all of Trouvé's seventy-five inventions and improvements. This is ably done by Kevin Desmond in the pages that follow. But from now on, as I continue my research with new batteries and ultra-capacitors which follow my invention of the first oxygen cycle lead battery in 1971 at Gates in Colorado, I can fully appreciate Monsieur Trouvé's key innovations and empathize with the challenges he faced in the 1870s.

Whenever I climb into an electric vehicle, switch on its headlamps, and sound its horn, from now on the name Trouvé may well come to mind. As I see disaster workers, underwater divers, speleologists and others wearing useful headlamps, I may again recall "Trouvé de Paris." As a lover of jazz, I can marvel at his patent for an electric piano. Then, too, there are a growing number of artistes wearing LED light-embroidered clothing, and electrical fountains—another two of Trouvé's children.

Kevin Desmond, a Briton residing in Southern France, is admirably suited for the task of bringing Trouvé back to his deserved high stature in electrical engineering history. Coming from a medical family, for over 40 years Kevin has earned a fine reputation with a succession of books about powerboats, cars and even airplanes. I first appreciated his painstaking approach when we worked together on a biographical feature about my own life and work for a series in the magazine *Batteries International*. Since then Kevin has continued to write a highly respected series of biographies of battery pioneers, both in the distant past and on today's cutting edge from all over the world.

Kevin's 25 years of unstinting research, still ongoing, into Trouvé, the Eureka man, is evidenced in this rich and fascinating volume.

I sincerely hope, like Kevin, that from now on, you in our English-speaking world, be it the United States or beyond, will start telling both friends and colleagues about G. Trouvé, whose name is translated from the French as "I have found"!

In the late 1960s John Devitt, an electrical engineer, innovated a maintenance-free, valve-regulated, lead-acid, sealed-cell battery (VRLA). Originally manufactured by the Gates Rubber Company of Denver, Colorado, more than 100 plants internationally now produce VRLA batteries. In 1986 Devitt received the Research Award of the Electrochemical Society, and in 2007 the International Lead Award in Shanghai, recognizing that the VRLA battery produced the largest single boost to total lead sales of any invention in the twentieth century.

Preface

The twenty-first century. The year is 2009. Paris by night. Paris illuminated. In a square by a canal, changing colored lights play with the water jets of a fountain. On a screen opposite is publicity for 30 years of *Star Wars*, complete with light sabers. People pass by, most of them talking or listening to their battery-powered phone or iPod, its colored lights reflected on their cheeks. If they so wished they could take a sequence of photos, or a film, using the same battery-powered device. A klaxon sounds. Someone rides past me on her tricycle. She is not pedaling; it makes little noise, so it is an electric tricycle, the fashion. A ferryboat silently cruises up the canal, again electric, its headlamps lighting the water in front of it. Lights, lights. One of the passengers reminds me of the specialist whom I went to see this morning with problems of vision.

Taking his battery-powered ophthalmoscope, he looks into my eyes.

"Have you been using your eyes a lot for work?" he asks me.

"Yes," I reply. "I've been researching into the life of a French inventor and it has involved studying a lot of documents."

"Oh, really?" he asks. "What was his name? Science history is one of my hobbies."

"His name was Gustave Trouvé." I reply.

"Trouvé, you say—like the past participle of to find, found? No, I can't say that I have heard of someone of that name."

"This doesn't surprise me," I reply.

"What did he invent?"

"Well, your ophthalmoscope, for a start," I reply. "And many other things which surround us today..."

London Meeting

In 1977, I was researching for a book about the history of motor boating in the Library of the Science Museum, South Kensington, London: a

3

somewhat challenging task. But the Scottish librarian was proving very helpful.

"Would motor boating history include electric boats?" he asked.

"Yes," I replied. "But I don't exactly know what electric boats are…"

"Then you'd better take a look at this," he suggested.

It was a slim beige folder, marked "electric boats." Turning through its contents, fragile old news cuttings, I learned about battery-powered launches in the early 1900s—on the River Thames, on the Austrian lakes, in the United States, and in France. Two of the articles mentioned a French engineer called Trouvé. Apparently as long ago as 1881 Monsieur Trouvé had ingeniously fitted his electric engine to the back of a punt and run it between the steamboats on the River Seine. It also mentioned that Trouvé had been the first to fit electric motors to a pedal tricycle, again in Paris.

I was intrigued, but at the time, I was attempting a daunting overall appreciation of motor boating history that had to include steam, petrol, diesel, and outboards. So I duly photocopied the pages to insert in my growing ring files.

A few weeks later, searching for pictures to illustrate my book, I found myself at the Mary Evans Picture Library.

"Have you any illustrations of someone called Trouvé?" was just one of my questions.

Positive result: The first engraving showed a portrait of a bearded man experimenting with some electric coils with what seems to be an electric lamp alongside. The second showed the electric boat, named *Le Téléphone*, with two men aboard in top hats.

Eighteen years later. I was in Bordeaux, southwest France, and part of a team creating a pleasure-boat museum. Our main goal was to find, bring together and present historic boats and engines to the public in a converted former wartime submarine base. In our temporary library, there was a series of bound volumes of *Le Yacht*, France's main pleasureboating magazine for a century. In a spare moment, I took down some of the volumes to look for Gustave Trouvé. One or two articles surfaced.

Soon after, I paid a visit the Bordeaux public library to check out the dictionaries and encyclopedias. To my disappointment, he did not appear in the main French reference works of the twentieth century, such as *Larousse, Hatchette,* and *Robert*.

I also found a tantalizing reference to a biography, *History of an Inventor: Exposition of the Discoveries and the Works of M. Gustave Trouvé in the Field of Electricity*, written by Georges Barral and published in Paris by Georges Carré in 1891.

Encouraged and counseled by my friend and colleague Daniel Charles,

I now made researches into the places where Gustave Trouvé had been educated: Chinon College in 1850 (Chinon Town Archives) and the Angers Technical College in 1854–55 (Indre et Loire Departmental Archives). In an older publication, also from his home country, *The Illustrated Dictionary of the Indre et Loire*, which had two editions, one in 1895 and the other in 1909, he is given several pages, not merely as the inventor of electric boats and trikes, but also of a whole range of electrically powered precision instruments for use in transport, medicine and the theatre. I found out that he died sometime in 1902, but when exactly and how—he was only 63—would elude me for yet another 12 years.

In 1996, I was able to publish an article about him in *Neptunia*, the journal of the Friends of the Naval Museum in Paris. But even with this, I remained sure that there was more to find, much more.

This intuition became a conviction when, via an Internet bookseller, I was finally able to locate and purchase on-line a faded copy of Georges Barral's biography, running to 610 pages, with countless engravings. But despite poring over this tome for many an hour, I realized that, if Gustave Trouvé died in 1902, there were still 12 crucial and missing years of his inventions.

So I contacted the town hall of Descartes, the place where he was born and spent his childhood and indeed where there is a "Rue Gustave Trouvé." But I was in for some very bad news indeed. After Trouvé's death, his archives and possessions had been transported by train from his Paris workshop back to his hometown. When that home became the town's secondary school, they were then transferred to the town hall. But then in the late afternoon of Saturday, 19 February 1980, a fire ravaged Descartes Town Hall. The civic archives, kept in the loft, including those of Trouvé, perished in the flames.

Since that discovery, it has become a researcher's challenge for me to fill in the gaps, to complete the pieces of the jigsaw, which would enable this tribute. Looking for the elusive life crumbs of this inventor has proved the hardest challenge that I have taken in half a lifetime of international researching.

I, as an Englishman resident in France, only hope that, with this American edition, my still incomplete findings will bring back to luminescence this modest and genial Frenchman, "the Gallic Edison," to whom our modern electrical world owes so much.

Let the search continue…

ONE

A Boy from the Touraine

In the year one thousand eight hundred and thirty-nine, on the second of January, at ten hours in the morning, in the room of the Commune of La Haye–Descartes, in front of us, Olivier Mascarel, mayor, officer of the civil state of the aforementioned commune, has appeared Monsieur Jacques Trouvé, cattle dealer, aged thirty-seven years, living in this commune, who has presented to us Gustave[1] Trouvé,[2] child of masculine sex, born this morning, at two o'clock, by the present and by Marie Clarisse Granger, his legitimate wife.

The said declaration and affirmation having been made, as well as the presentation, in the presence of Messieurs Antoine François Delaunay-Caillault, owner, fifty-two years old, and Louis Alphonse Cesvet, clerk of the justice of the peace, twenty-six years old—both living in this commune, witnesses who have thus that the said Monsieur Trouvé, signed with us after reading this.

This register of births in the Commune of La Haye–Descartes for 1839 is signed "Trouvé Granger, Cesvet, Delaunay-Caillault, and Mascarel."

Gustave Trouvé came from a middle-class or bourgeois background. His father Jacques was born on 21 October 1801 at La Haye Descartes, the son of Augustin Trouvé, a merchant, and Françoise Girault, his wife. Jacques' wife Marie Clarisse Granger was born on 15 October 1811, at Sepmes, a staging post for the carriage of mail, a few miles from La Haye. She was the daughter of Pierre Granger, a proprietor. Jacques Trouvé was 10 years older than his wife, who was 19, hence a minor, when they married on 23 February 1831.

In 1839, the year of Gustave Trouvé's birth, while King Louis Philippe I had been king of France for nine years, Martin Van Buren was in his second year as president of the United States of America, and the 20-year-old Queen Victoria had been monarch for just over a year. The French were fighting a brief war with Mexico.

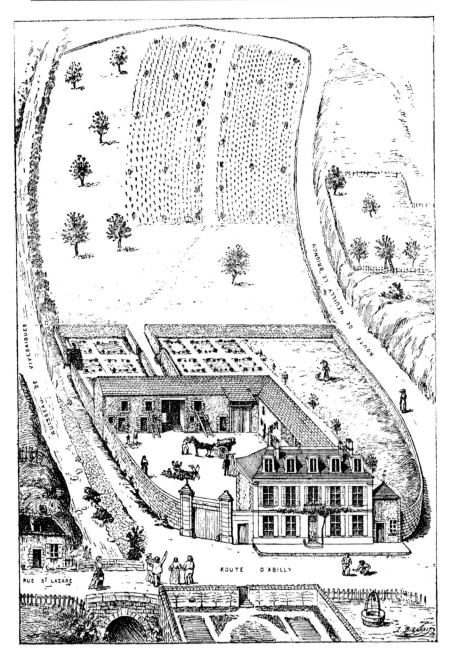

1839. As a wealthy cattle dealer, Trouvé's father Jacques was well off: the family home at La Haye–Descartes in the Indre-et-Loire region (from Georges Barral, *L'histoire d'un inventeur*, 1891).

Trouvé's birthplace, the commune of La Haye–Descartes, 180 miles southwest of the capital, Paris, is in the central region of the Indre-et-Loire. At the time, it had a population of only 1,400. Its proud claim to fame was that René Descartes, the great philosopher and mathematician, had been born there over two centuries before. This was the reason why, in 1801, his name had been officially coupled with that of La Haye. In physics, Monsieur Descartes is considered the founder of mechanics, particularly in his defining the optical laws of refection and refraction.

In France, the inhabitants of a town are called after its name. For Paris, it is *parisien*, or *parisienne* for woman. For Tours it is *tourangeaux* and for La Haye–Descartes, it is *lahaisien*.

Very little happened in this sleepy rural community. On 14 and 18 June 1839, when Gustave was just five months old, hailstorms of a rare violence fell on the town, damaging the roofs of church and belfry of St. Georges. The wind that accompanied the hail blew with such force that it staved in the stained glass windows. The entire town suffered enormously from this hail, as did the surrounding countryside.

Electricity was learning to walk. Primitive batteries were modifications of the Voltaic pile. Michael Faraday, an English chemist residing in Hampton Court near London, had invented an electric motor in 1821, while six years later Georg Ohm, a 38-year-old science teacher at the Jesuit Gymnasium of Cologne, Germany, had published his research in a paper called *Die galvanishe Kette, mathematisch bearbeitet* (*The Galvanic Circuit Investigated Mathematically*). Using equipment of his own creation, Ohm had found that there is a direct proportionality between the potential difference (voltage) applied across a conductor and the resultant electric current. Also in 1827, Hungarian Benedictine monk Anyos Jedlik started experimenting with electromagnetic rotating devices that he called lightning-magnetic self-rotors, and in 1828 he demonstrated the first device to contain the three main components of practical direct current motors: the stator, rotor and commutator. Following experiments by André-Marie Ampère and François Arago, Samuel Morse was developing an electric telegraph system using a system of dots and dashes.

It was also in 1839 that a 27-year-old Scottish blacksmith, Kirpatrick MacMillan of Courthill, Dumfrieshire, invented the first rear-wheel-driven wooden bicycle, which included iron-rimmed wooden wheels, a steerable wheel in the front and a larger wheel in the rear that was connected to the pedals via connecting rods. Its furthest distance travelled was 40 miles. Anyone proposing the idea of an electric bicycle might have been put in a mental asylum.

And yet, over in Imperial Russia, a Professor Moritz von Jacobi, financed by Tsar Nicholas of Russia, built the *Eleketrokhod*, an electric paddleboat. Nine meters long, powered by a 220-watt electromagnetic motor, this boat transported 14 passengers at a speed of 2.5 km/h (1.5 mph) against the current of the River Neva. Jacobi's non-rechargeable battery used zinc and platinum, very expensive. But the motor gave out nitrous fumes in as big a quantity as smoke from a steam train. Jacobi and his volunteer passengers, choked and asphyxiated by these sickening and suffocating fumes, were obliged to temporarily halt their observations.

The Trouvé children, Gustave, his two older brothers, Jacques Augustin and Jules, and an older sister Marie-Clarisse, were ignorant of such pioneer developments. Perhaps the only mechanical device the children might have seen was the local watermill, powered by the River Creuze. There, they may have marveled at how the speed of its wooden paddle wheel from the river flow could be adjusted by the sluice gate, then by going inside, have watched how the power from its horizontal shaft was transmitted through a series of toothed wheels and belts to one or more grindstones.

Due to the French inventor's personal archive being destroyed in an accidental fire in 1980, much of what we know about Trouvé comes from an extensive biography published in 1891: *History of an Inventor: Exposition of the Discoveries and the Works of M. Gustave Trouvé in the Field of Electricity,* researched and written by Georges Barral in close collaboration with Trouvé, then in his fifties.

Translating this, we learn that Gustave's father Jacques Trouvé

> was a wealthy middle-class cattle merchant, good at heart, but severe and inflexible, jealous of his authority, only understanding father-son relationships as superior to inferior, wishing to be obeyed, not suffering observations. As a child, Gustave had an outgoing and sensitive nature. He had to withdraw into himself, and in not finding in this paternal household the echo necessary to his vibrant soul, he fell in love with study and exclusive isolation.
>
> From his youngest years, perhaps in the shadow of Descartes, he showed the greatest tendencies for drawing and mathematics. He was passionate above all about mechanical works that occupied his thoughts and hands. He little involved himself in the games of children of his age. From morning to evening, armed with a knife, a hammer, or some nails, he was only thinking of building little chariots, telegraphs, mills, rabbits, or automata moved by wings filled by the wind. He gave all these ingenious toys to his astounded comrades. A little man of genius, he spent his time amusing the companions of his age and was the admiration of his mother, Clarisse Granger, who did her best to defend him against the taunting and harshness of his father.

In 1845, the seven-year-old boy decided to build a steam engine. He used a huntsman's powder box as boiler, hairpins for connecting rods and han-

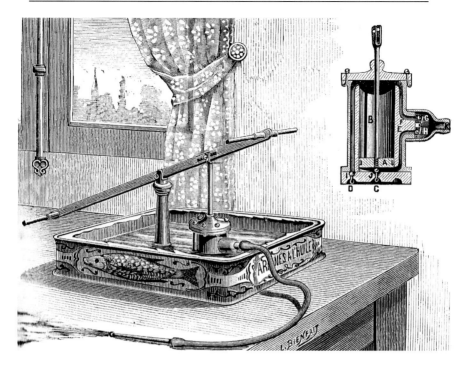

1845. Despite his father's criticism but with his mother's encouragement, Trouvé began to construct small inventions from a very early age, such as this fire pump. L. Bienfait is the pseudonym invented by Trouvé as an artist (from Georges Barral, *L'histoire d'un inventeur*, 1891).

dles, and a little lead for welding. The machine was entirely built of wood, lead and tin. Despite the small size of its parts, it worked. Trouvé would nostalgically keep it with him in years to come. Next he built a fire pump out of a sardine tin.

His next creation was a wind-powered puppet show, with connecting rods and gearwheels of wood and wire. Once built and working, it was placed on the left pillar of the entry gate of Trouvé's home, situated at the intersection of the Abilly and Neuilly-le-Brignon roads, beside a country stream called Vivesaigues. It was the beginning of his love of making small but crowd-pulling machines, a love that would stay with him for the rest of his life, despite his often turning his attention to more important devices.

Over in the United States, a boy was born on 11 February 1847 in Milan, Ohio, who would later revolutionize the world of electricity. His name was Thomas Alva Edison. Although they would never meet, their lives would run parallel.

It is perhaps interesting to observe that only half a day's carriage ride north of La Haye–Descartes is the Château of Clos Lucé, in the town of Amboise. It was here in the beginning of the sixteenth century that the aging Italian-born inventor Leonardo da Vinci spent the final three years of his life as the guest of French king François I as his painter, engineer and architect. Leonardo's copious deciphered notebooks show how brilliantly fertile the mind of an inventor can be. But in Trouvé's youth, this château was privately owned by the Amboise family, and the only trace of da Vinci's brief residence there was a single portrait. It is unlikely that the young boy would have visited it.

Between October and December 1850, Gustave, 11 years old, began his studies with his brother Jules at the nearby College of Chinon, some 20 miles from Descartes. He served his apprenticeship as a locksmith, learning the intricacy of tumble locks, pins, and keys.

Four years later, because Gustave wanted to devote himself to mathematical and mechanical studies, his parents decided that it would be a good idea for him to go study at the Imperial School of Arts and Trades at Angers, some 80 miles away. While he was preparing to take the stiff entry exam, he almost burned down the College at Chinon when a small steam engine that he had left running on his desk developed too much pressure and blew up.[3]

The curriculum of the Arts and Trade School was like other colleges in France: to train engineers ready to specialize rapidly in all branches of industry. The duration of the studies lasted four years, of which three were in Angers, the fourth in Paris. It was a boarding school. Teaching included theoretical lessons, general mathematics, differential calculus, practical mechanics, thermodynamics, and chemistry. The practical teaching given in the workshops was very thorough. Trouvé spent much time in the foundry. Trouvé received mixed grades for his first half-year:

Theoretical Education

Mathematics:	Mediocre
Drawing:	Good
Language:	Fair
Writing:	Fair
Application to his studies:	Mediocre

Practical Education

Enthusiasm:	Fair
Final mark:	Good
Rank of merit:	127

Behavior:	Fair
Punishments:	9 times in the guardroom[4]

In the second half-year, Trouvé did not attend because of illness; in his class notes he was "sent home because of a weak constitution." He would have to repeat. However, he did not appear in the student results tables for the years 1856 or 1857, so there are three missing years.

On 10 July 1856, in the village of Smiljan in the Austrian Empire, a little boy was born to a Serbian Orthodox priest Milutin Tesla and his wife Duka. They christened him Nikola Tesla.

Two

Paris!

In 1859, aged 20, Trouvé arrived in Paris of the Second Empire and obtained a job with one of the main clock and watch manufacturers in France. He was still in the world of precision engineering—the intricacy of interrelated gears and cogwheels, pendulums and hairsprings.[1] He impressed his manager and workshop staff with the marvelous skillfulness of his fingers and his drawing ability. Full of humor, he drew cartoons to make them laugh. In his spare moments he started to study architecture, math, precision engineering, physics, chemistry—and electricity.

At this time, one hundred percent of the French capital's traffic was horse-drawn or man-pushed. There were more than 80,000 horses jostling for position in its narrow streets, while the horse-drawn passenger cabs plying their trade numbered about 15,000. There were regular steam-powered trains in service between Paris and Orléans, Rouen and Lille. Water transport along the River Seine was mostly sail, occasionally steam-powered, and for most people, flight, known as aerostation, was by Montgolfière hot-air balloons, although within recent memory, an engineer called Henri Giffard had astonished the world with his steam-powered aerial ship. The streets were gas-lit, the theaters were gas-lit, and most buildings used a combination of gaslight and candles.

In the same city, working at the Conservatoire des Arts et Métiers, a 26-year-old electrician and geologist called Raymond-Louis-Gaston Planté, while researching into voltmeters and secondary batteries, had discovered the remarkable properties of the lead acid battery. He delivered a learned paper about this to the Academy of Sciences in 1859, the first of a succession. But the breakthrough came the following year when Planté announced that he had produced "a secondary battery of great power"—*one that could be recharged*. It was the first in the world. His early model had consisted of a spiral roll of two sheets of pure lead separated by a linen cloth, immersed in a glass jar of sulphuric acid solution. But the one he presented was a nine-cell, lead-acid battery.

Such an invention led to Planté's obtaining the post of professor of physics at the Polytechnic Association for the Development of Popular Instruction. During the next six years, he went full out with research concerning electrolytic deposits; he had been pushed by observations that he had been able to make during his previous work in the laboratories of the Maison Christofle, to which he belonged for some years, at first in his capacity as electro-chemist, then administrator. Planté's key discovery would help to make Gustave Trouvé a pioneer in the introduction of electricity into the French capital.

Like many a young man arriving in a big city, Trouvé began by renting a flat; his was on the fifth floor of a boarding house, the Montesquieu Hostel, N° 5 rue Montesquieu, in the first arrondissement (district). He was a short walk from the Louvre Museum and the River Seine.[2] Indeed he would live and work in this arrondissement for the rest of his life.

The Barral biography, sometimes taking poetic license in its narrative, but based on Barral's interview with Trouvé, paints the following picture:

January 1864: It is a bitterly cold winter's morning. The tenants of a boarding house are assembled in the ground-floor lounge around an excellent fire. One of them is missing. This is a big young man, with dark and deep eyes, meditative, always working, ceaselessly preoccupied, with a simple and sympathetic appearance, come to Paris to learn precision watch making.

"Go look for Monsieur Trouvé," says the owner, a fine woman, with a maternal and delicate heart, talking to one of her sons. "Invite him to come and warm up."

After several minutes' waiting, not seeing her tenant appear, the hotel-keeper, worried and astonished, decides to climb the five floors that separate her from the attic room occupied by her recalcitrant client. Arriving at the door, she knocks by established conscience and as the key is already in the lock, she immediately enters, as much curious as frightened by this unusual silence.

To her great surprise, she then notices, seated in front of a little table covered with tiny tools, in shirtsleeves, sponging his forehead, her guest, so absorbed in constructing a Lilliputian[3] mechanism that he is feeling neither cold nor hunger, that he hears no call, that he is not even aware that somebody has entered his room.

"Monsieur Trouvé, I beg you, you will fall ill, cover yourself up, leave your inventions and come down for a moment into our room which is really warm."

"Oh, it's you, dear lady! You are really good to come and take an interest in me this way. But don't be alarmed. I am not even dreaming of being cold, I am too absorbed. I believe I am on the certain path of a little motor which will work wonders, if my hand is skilful enough to build it as my mind is to conceive it."

"It's not about that, Monsieur Trouvé. You are a foolhardy person and you will get a chest infection. It's madness to stay without warmth and hardly clothed, while they are skating on the Seine."

"But I am not cold, Madame Carré. You see, science and discovery liven the brain and the body so much that one doesn't even feel the biting frost. My blood is inflamed in my fingers, like my ideas are burning in my head!"[4]

Sometime during the mid–1860s, Trouvé was introduced to Viscount Gustave du Ponton d'Amécourt and his two colleagues, Gabriel de la Landelle and a young journalist photographer called Félix Nadar.[5] Nadar had set up the Society for the Encouragement of Aerial Locomotion by Means of Heavier Than Air Machines—with him as president and a certain Jules Verne as secretary. Verne, 35 years old, had just published his first book, *Five Weeks in a Balloon*.

In 1863, the viscount published a 40-page monograph in Paris, entitled *The Conquest of the Air by Propeller: Account of a New System of Aviation*.[6] In this he put together the Greek words *helico* and *pteron*, meaning "spiral" and "wing," to make the word *hélicoptère* (helicopter). For d'Amécourt and his friends were among those very few who were passionately convinced that the future of flying was with heavier-than-air machines.

To prove their point, having built a fragile flying-machine model driven by clockwork springs, they watched it ascend vertically for a few seconds to a height of less than 3 meters (10 feet), only to crash back to the ground. Stimulated by the brief success of his clockwork models, in 1868, the Viscount d'Amécourt built a *hélicoptère* powered by a small steam engine with an aluminum boiler. This model proved a failure inasmuch as it only lifted a third of its own weight. But it would convince the 29-year-old Trouvé that, ultimately, "heavier-than-air" must be the way ahead, if only a lightweight and long-running motor could be built. Trouvé would not make his own attempt for another couple of years.

Once established in Paris, Trouvé would doubtless have heard about Jean-Eugène Robert-Houdin, the famous clockmaker, illusionist and electrical inventor. Between 1845 and 1852, the "Fantastic Evenings of Robert-Houdin," presented at 11 rue Valois, at the Palais-Royal, were immensely successful. Robert-Houdin presented his magic automata, such as *The Wonderful Orange Tree*, *The Cakemaker of the Palais-Royal* and *The Soldier on the Trapeze*.

Having made his fortune, leaving the theater that in the meantime had been installed on the Boulevard des Italiens to his brother-in-law Hamilton, Robert-Houdin went back to live at Saint-Gervais-la-Forêt close to Blois, in a property called the Priory, whose garden he then rigged with electro-mechanical commands and devices he had invented to surprise his visitors. From the 1850s, Robert-Houdin became interested in the applications of electricity, at first for use in his automata and his clocks. As a magician he also used many scientific innovations for his magic tricks. He took out several patents concerning electricity, including a patent for a "plunging" electric battery (1855) and a patent for a "regulating type" clock mechanism (1855). He also invented the ancestor of the electromagnetic motor (1855), adapting an electromagnet that he was using for one of his magic tricks. Robert-Houdin also worked on other applications that he did not patent. For example, from 1851, he was interested in electric-arc lighting. In 1863, he constructed electric light bulbs whose filament was of bamboo but whose short lifespan did not enable him to take out a patent. Finally, for his property, the Priory, Robert-Houdin used electric bells and equipped the gateway of his property, which was located 400 meters (437 yards) from his house, with an electric opening system. His house was fitted with a certain number of inventions that today are part of home automation. Distressed by the death of one of his sons killed during the 1870 war, Robert-Houdin died in 1871.

Monsieur Yvan Boukef, in charge of collections of archaeology and of magic at the Château Royal de Blois, reports: "Concerning Monsieur Gustave Trouvé, I believe that we have no traces of this gentleman in our documentation or of a possible link with Jean-Eugène Robert-Houdin. But the closeness of researches by the one and the other is sufficiently noticeable to think that Gustave had, at least, a good knowledge of the works of his senior."[7]

On 8 May 1865, Trouvé took out his first patent:

Monsieur Trouvé (Gustave), watchmaker, living in Paris, rue and hotel Montesquieu, 5, has conceived of animating jewelry, clockwork and other objects d'art by the application of electricity and he has invented a wearable Lilliputian battery especially for this application. Here is the specification for his industrial application.

This electric battery is cylindrical. It is made up of a tube whose length is double that of the piece of zinc and carbon used inside the upper part. This device enables that in the vertical position, the liquid placed in the lower part has no contact with the carbon and zinc, while in the horizontal position, on the contrary, with the immersion taking place, the battery immediately starts to work. With this device, the battery does not wear out and lasts as long as it is not working, while in general, other systems of battery wear out without even being used.

Another advantage of this battery is that Mr. Trouvé reduces it as required to the infinitely small, and hence easily transportable. In addition, it can be placed in a hardened rubber pouch, which completely encloses the cylindrical tube, in such a way that if it has just broken, the liquid in the battery cannot escape.

> …As each object carries an engine in itself in an annex, it is easy to under-
> stand how the inventor succeeds in animating, by this process, birds, flowers
> and general objets d'art, from the moment they are in contact with his battery.
> These objets d'art being either for hanging, office ornaments, etc.
>   Patent Granted July 1, 1865   N° 67294   Duration: fifteen years.
>   *Ministry of Agriculture, Commerce and Public Works. For the Minister. The
> Associate Director.*[8]

Although Trouvé may have been inspired by a catalogue issued in 1866 by Jean-Charles Dubosq, offering electrical playthings to the rich, he did not know that over in Brussels, a Belgian inventor called Georges Leclanché, exactly the same age as our Parisian, was working in a shed on a battery based on zinc and carbon activated by a solution of ammonium chloride. It was extremely similar to that of Trouvé. Leclanché patented his battery just six months after Trouvé. The Belgian telegraph service and the Netherlands Railways soon made use of it, and Leclanché opened a factory for its production—unlike Trouvé, disinterested in business potential. Leclanché's battery became known as the forerunner of today's dry cell battery and his name entered into history. Trouvé is not remembered for having invented the ubiquitous AA-sized battery in use throughout the world today.

Twenty years later, Carl Gassner of Mainz, Germany, took the Leclanché wet battery and replaced the liquid with a porous bonding agent, namely plaster, and add water-absorbing ammonium chloride so that the energizing agent remained damp: in other words, the first dry cell battery.

Alongside his battery, Trouvé modified the bichromate primary cell (today's chromic acid cell), invented by German Johann Christian Poggendorff in 1842, by creating a model he called a "winch cell." The cell was set up in a long-necked glass bottle with a zinc plate located between two carbon plates. The electrolyte and depolarizer were mixed. But the mixture would continue to dissolve the zinc plate even when the cell was not in use, so Trouvé developed a more economic winch for lifting the zinc plate out of the liquid and storing it in the neck of the bottle, so varying the output. His studies on the performance of these batteries, showed that they could deliver up to 8 A (amps) for four hours.

Also in 1865, the 26-year-old inventor developed an electro-medical kit. This kit would become indispensable to doctors in both town and country. It was a leather case like an ordinary surgeon's bag. But in addition, there was Trouvé's protected battery, the handles of the induction coil, a sulphate tube, an exciter in olive or birch, a comb, two sponge collars, and cords. It gave the practitioner a choice of either a current that acted on the muscles with little effect on the nerves, or a strong current to stimulate the nerves.

In 1866, Trouvé left his lodgings at the rue Montesquieu and moved a couple of streets away to rent rooms on the second floor of N° 6 rue Thérèse, a property owned by a widow called Adelaïde Geneviève Marion de Tiville. His apartment overlooking the courtyard was made up of a kitchen, two heated rooms, a dining room and toilets. He described himself as a "made-to-order mechanic, electrical appliances."[9]

This is when Trouvé decided to register his brand name. The initial of his first name added to his family name to produce G. Trouvé, translated as *j'ai trouvé* ("I have found [it]," Archimedes' famous exclamation in Greek, εὕρηκα *heúrēka*), would from now on be engraved on almost all the instruments he would conceive and make.

His materials of construction included wood, iron, copper, tin, porcelain and glass. To give them a touch of class, most of these instruments would be contained in boxes lined with purple velveteen with his brand name in gold.

That year, at the Academy of Sciences, Saint Petersburg, Russia, Professor Moritz Jacobi presented members with an extraordinary invention: the electro-gyroscope of a young French inventor, Monsieur Trouvé. Some 15 years before, Léon Foucault had achieved fame when he hung his 68-meter (223-foot) pendulum under the dome of the Pantheon in Paris, to demonstrate the Earth's rotation. But because this pendulum was cumbersome, in 1852 Foucault replaced it by inventing the gyroscope. This was made up of a metal core animated by a rapid movement of rotation using a tower and gears. But even then, because of the passive friction, the observations were limited to only a few minutes. Henri Tresca, assistant director at the Conservatoire des Arts et Métiers, suggested Foucault meet Trouvé, 20 years his younger. Foucault asked the young clockmaker with a talent for electricity if he could solve the problem. Trouvé built an electro-motor core and solved a problem hitherto considered insurmountable.

It was inevitable that Trouvé's innovative work would be brought to the public's attention. Initially this appeared in French periodicals. For example, Abbé François Moigno was a French mathematician, known as a popularizer of science. Every week since 1862, the abbé had been publishing his weekly science review *Les Mondes (The Worlds)*. As he explained to his readers: "I present my work with a certain pride. The science for which I have made myself the echo is real and stimulating progress whose banner I have courageously flown by defining it as an upward and increasing walk towards all that is True, Good and Beautiful."

In an August 1877 edition of *Les Mondes*, Abbé Moigno recorded with some pride, "We think we were the instrument for which Providence used us to give flight to the inventive genius of M. Trouvé. He was only a

In his weekly journal *Les Mondes*, Abbé François Moigno was the first to praise Trouvé for his genius in reducing electrical instruments to compact and usable dimensions, which he nicknamed "Lilliputian" (Musée EDF Electropolis, Mulhouse).

modest worker watchmaker in a room when we had the chance to discover and to encourage his first successes.... Is there not here, in fact, a name predestined, the real name which belongs to an inventor?"

To "give flight," Moigno published a pamphlet about Trouvé in which he wrote:

> The spirit breathes where it wishes. Nothing truer that this evangelical adage; invention is a real inspiration which, at a given moment, invades the improvising mind of the one who had been predestined to sow it and bring it to the daylight. M. Trouvé is a worker watchmaker who would have been tempted to smile if one had told him to him, a few years ago, that he would be called on to tame and to put into play, with an incomparable skill, the

most elusive of all the agents, electricity, to as to obtain new and really unexpected effects. The electrical world of M Trouvé is the world of the infinitely small: his induction coils, his electromagnets, his switches, his battery, are all restricted to Lilliputian dimensions; and everything works, however, with extraordinary regularity; each of these organs is a real masterpiece.

Abbé Moigno

The same pamphlet explains a series of electric jewels realized by M. Trouvé, "with the assistance of a very skilful jeweler, M. Cadet-Picard":

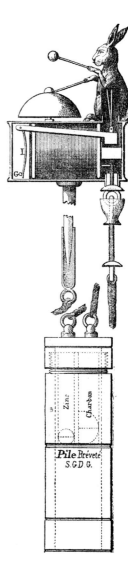

(1) Grenadier beating a drum.
(2) Monkey, playing the violin.
(3) Turcos under his skull cap.
(4) Death's head with a jockey's hat: eyes and jaw move up and down vertically. Height 9.2 cm × width 1.5 cm × depth 1.6 cm.
(5) Rabbit playing with sticks on a little drum.
(6) Electro-spherical doorbell.
(7) Theatre scene: Harlequin and Columbine dance a ballet.
(8) Monkey with spectacles, making faces.
(9) Decapitated head on a table—speaks and moves its eyes.
(10) Bird in diamonds—moves its wings and tail.
(11) Butterfly flaps its wings.

We know that in 1860, Auguste-Germain Cadet-Picard had made a silver, gold and enamel stickpin depicting Joan of Arc, the face revolving to show an enameled skull. Her helmet also closed. (Cadet-Picard later moved to Geneva, where he made Art Nouveau and Art Déco watches in gold, platinum and diamonds. The Clock and Watch Museum of Geneva has an example of his work: a watch mounted on a ring that was worn on the finger—ingenious as ever.)

Between April and November 1867, Trouvé, age 28, first showed his inventions at a major exhibition. This was at the Exposition Universelle, at Champs-de-Mars, Paris. This was the second world's fair to be held in Paris, and 42 nations were repre-

1865. Trouvé adapted his miniaturized "Lilliputian" battery to power his range of gadgets, such as this electro-mobile rabbit (from Georges Barral, *L'histoire d'un inventeur*, 1891).

sented. To launch the exposition, Emperor Napoleon III offered a brilliant reception in his private garden in the Tuileries. Among the guests were Tsar Alexander III of Russia, Wilhelm I of Prussia, Chancellor Otto von Bismarck of Germany, the sultan of the Ottoman Empire and the viceroy of Egypt.

It helped that Trouvé's friend Gaston Planté was a member of the Admission Committee and of the Reunion of Offices of the Tenth Group at the Exposition. Trouvé exhibited his electric rifle, fitted with two of his Lilliputian zinc-carbon batteries inside the butt, protected by hardened rubber. Whenever the firearm was vertical the batteries were out of operation. But the moment the marksman brought the gun up to his shoulder, the batteries went into operation. Press the trigger, the circuit was closed and a platinum wire running from the batteries to the shell started to glow. This ignited the powder which exploded. Emperor Napoleon III, visiting the exposition, was shown the Trouvé rifle. His Imperial Majesty admired its simplicity.

The first gun whose gunpowder was set off by electricity had first been tested in 1859 by the Vicomte de Dax. He was followed in 1867 by two arquebusiers, Le Baron and Delmas, and then almost half a century later by Tépin and d'Ogny, who would make their prototype in 1913. In 1893, an American, Doctor Richard Gatling, further adapted his machine gun to be powered by electric motor and belt to drive the crank.

Trouvé also exhibited his miniature, double-movement, electro-spherical motor, spinning at 12 to 15 revolutions per minute, and the Foucault-Trouvé electro-gyroscope. Sadly, Foucault had died some months before from consumption. Trouvé was awarded a Mention with Distinction at the show.

Cadet-Picard exhibited the *"bijoux électriques lumineux"* (electro-luminous jewels). One is still conserved today at London's Victoria and Albert Museum (M.121–1984).

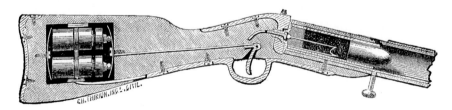

1867. Among those admiring Trouvé's electric rifle, exhibited at the Exposition Universelle, was the Emperor Napoleon III (from Georges Barral, *L'histoire d'un inventeur*, 1891).

Among those visitors to the exhibition who may well have admired Trouvé's inventions were the Tissandier brothers, Gaston (29 years old) and Albert (27 years old). The following year, the Tissandiers made their first aerial voyage in a balloon over Calais, publishing *Aerial Voyages* soon after. Before long, Trouvé would help the Tissandiers, who in turn would do a great deal to promote Trouvé. As Trouvé's name spread, he was approached by a wide variety of people.

One of the fields in which Trouvé's skills with electricity could be used was muscular stimulation. In 1835, Guillaume Duchenne, a neurologist from Boulogne, had revived Galvani's research and begun to experiment with therapeutic "*électropuncture*," whereby electric shock was administered beneath the skin with sharp electrodes to stimulate the muscles. In 1855, Duchenne had formalized the diagnostic principles of electrophysiology and introduced electrotherapy in a textbook titled *De l'électrisation localisée et de son application à la physiologie, à la pathologie et à la thérapeutique (Localized electrification and its application to physiology, pathology and therapeutics).*[10]

Among those inspired by Duchenne was his contemporary, Louis-Denis Jules Gavarret, a 55-year-old professor of medical physics at the Faculty of Medicine in Paris, and a renowned expert on the application of electricity in his profession. He had been writing papers and books on the subject for over 20 years. When Trouvé presented his Lilliputian battery to the world, Gavarret immediately saw its usefulness to medical instruments. He declared it "the true electrophysiological," element saying, "It ought to serve as the standard in all laboratories." Professor Gavarret then commissioned the young watchmaker, so far known for his electric jewels, to build a device for locating and extracting bullets from wounded soldiers.

Some seven years before, on 29 August 1862, the famous surgeon Auguste Nélaton had used a small, rough porcelain ball on the end of a metal stylus to search for a bullet received in his foot by the Italian patriot Giuseppe Garibaldi. Nélaton had introduced the probe into the wound in the approximate direction of the bullet, and rubbed the little ball with care against the obstacles that it encountered. He managed to make contact with the bullet, and when he retracted it, the roughness of the little sphere had detached very tiny pieces of metal, which had blackened it. After some trial and error, the surgeon had enough information to carry out his operation and extract the projectile from the wounded Italian. But given the progress in weaponry, Nélaton's process was no longer precise enough.

It took Trouvé only three weeks to assemble his electric explorer-extractor. It was composed of one of his mini batteries, an exploratory probe and a revealer equipped with supple or rigid styluses. When the revealer vibrated, it indicated that the metal body had been located. In fact, this was the world's first metal detector.

As he later explained,

> When a metal body, a projectile, for example, has entered our flesh, certain circumstances enable recognition by ordinary means: touching, tapping, friction, and chemical. But most often these resources become insufficient

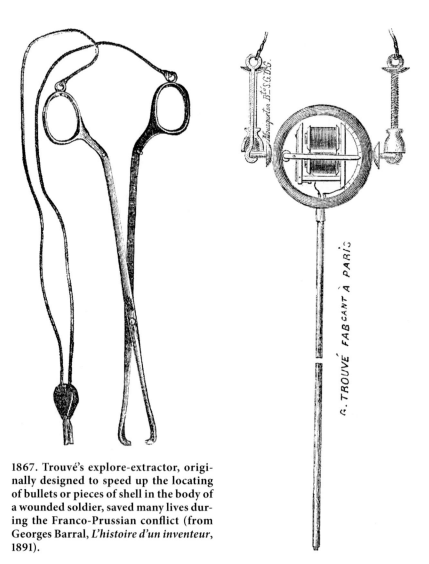

1867. Trouvé's explore-extractor, originally designed to speed up the locating of bullets or pieces of shell in the body of a wounded soldier, saved many lives during the Franco-Prussian conflict (from Georges Barral, *L'histoire d'un inventeur*, 1891).

and even impossible, when—as often happens—the ball is, to use a quite medical expression, encysted or, rather, covered with a mucous membrane, serous, or even a piece of clothing worn by the injured.

The challenge is to indicate, for certain, the presence in the tissues of any body, metal or not; its nature lead, iron, copper, stone or wood—and the direction it has followed; its depth, whether the wound is open or closed, whether the body is covered or not with a membrane or a piece of clothing and produce extraction so that any mistake is impossible.

When it was no longer a question of metal, but of wood, stones, or splinters, to get to them Trouvé ingeniously removed the stylus of the exploratory cannula and replaced it with his small auger. As this turned, it detached a few fragments, which became trapped in the thread. By placing these under a microscope, it could then be immediately ascertained whether the foreign body was of plant or animal cells.

While Gavarret presented this instrument to the Academy of Medicine in July 1869, it was a certain Edmond Becquerel who presented it to the Academy of Sciences. In 1839, at age 19, experimenting in his father's laboratory, Becquerel had created the world's first photovoltaic cell. In this experiment, silver chloride was placed in an acidic solution and illuminated while connected to platinum electrodes, generating voltage and current. His two-volume treatise, *La lumière, ses causes et ses effets (Light, Its Causes and Effects)*, had become a standard text. Trouvé must have read and admired Becquerel and may even have reflected on how he might put the photovoltaic cell to good use for his own batteries and instruments. Still encouraged by Gavarret, Trouvé also made a sanitizing discharger or exciter for the larynx, and a cystometric electrode or vesicular contractometer.

Almost exactly one year later, on 19 July 1870, France's Second Empire declared war on Prussia. For the next ten months, thousands of soldiers were wounded from gunfire and canon blast, the horrors culminating in the bloody Paris Commune of spring 1871. Trouvé's explorer-extractors were in constant use by army surgeons during this conflict, and also during the Russo-Turkish War of 1877 to 1879. It became an indispensable part of doctors' kit bags in both the army and navy.

A humorous article about Trouvé's explorer-extractor was published in the scientific column of the French journal *Le XIXe Siècle*:

> A sorcerer.—I went to see a sorcerer. My God! Yes, a real sorcerer, in the flesh, and this is what I saw him do. Often, in war or otherwise, a projectile, penetrating deep into one of the joints of the skeleton, still remains there and causes the most serious accidents. The surgeon examines the wound and feels a hard body that resists his stylus. Is a bone exposed? Is this the projectile? It is an undecided issue whose solution has more than once pre-

vented more than one surgeon from sleeping. If it is a bone, you do not dare snatch with force; if it's a projectile, you must, on the contrary, more often, go straight and bluntly to the point.

Nothing replaces, indeed, the tact and experience of the surgeon; but often experience is silent, and teachers are reluctant themselves. The stylus of Nélaton did wonders in the hands of Nélaton. But it can only be used to reveal the presence of lead.

Some time ago, a young man was shot in the face with a pistol. He did not die. The bullet was lodged somewhere, a few millimeters from his brain at the base of his skull. The danger was urgent: it had to be extracted. The surgeon of the hospital, an experienced practitioner, was consumed with anxiety. We did not know if the shot was a lead bullet or iron ingot. The time passed, the danger was increasing.

That's when my sorcerer intervened. From his pocket, he drew a small box that contained two instruments, both of them no bigger than a pen holder. One such instrument was a probe. He handed it to the surgeon, who carried it in the presumed direction of the projectile. A simple maneuver, the injured did not even feel, replaced by a special probe rod. Immediately a small acute buzzing, comparable to the murmur of a cricket in a good humor, was heard. My sorcerer claimed that it was the ball. He went further: he oscillated the probe and loudly declared, typical of such sorcerers, that, contrary to the information of the victim, it was lead shot. A clamp was engaged in the probe and in a jiffy, the projectile was withdrawn from the bottom of the wound. It was indeed a lead bullet. My sorcerer is called Trouvé: three centuries ago he would have been burned. Today he appreciated as the most learned inventor, the smartest electrician we have.[11]

In volume 12 of his *New Dictionary of Medicine and Practical Surgery*, Dr. Sigismond Jaccoud included an illustration of Trouvé's instruments.

Despite warfare, Trouvé worked on a flying machine. It took the form of an ornithopter, made of bamboo and feathers and covered in thick silk. Its engine was a compressed-air steam cylinder. Trouvé tested it in the experimental gallery of the Imperial Conservatoire des Arts et Métiers, assisted by 24-year-old Gustave Tresca. It crashed. He built another one, with a system of parachutes. It flew and was for many years known as one of a select handful of successful heavier-than-air flying machine models.

There were others: In 1857, some 13 years before, Félix du Temple, a naval officer, and his brother Louis enabled the first-ever motorized scale aircraft to take off. Weighing 700 grams (1 lb.) and with fixed wings, its propeller (inspired by ships) was first driven by clockwork, then by a steam engine. After an initial test flight in Toulon, the prototype was patented under the title "Aerial Locomotion by Imitation of Bird Flight."

In November 1870, Prussian shells were raining down on Paris, and the blockade had brought the great city to its knees. The Athenaeum in

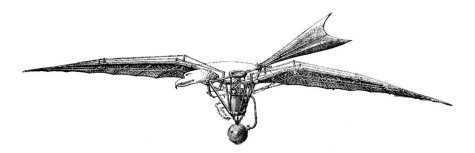

1870. Trouvé's first mechanical bird, built of bamboo, feathers and a thick silk. Its cylindrical motor worked by compressed air. Trouvé tested his machine in the experimental gallery of the Imperial Conservatoire des Arts et Métiers, with the collaboration of Gustave Tresca (from Georges Barral, *L'histoire d'un inventeur*, 1891).

the rue Auber, Paris, had been turned into a hospital, a powder mill and weapon repair workshops. Despite this, one winter's night Trouvé was invited by Dr. Jean-Baptiste Mallez to present his inventions to a gathering of soldiers. This is melodramatically narrated by Barral:

> Having shown his explorer-extractor, and his ornithopter, he explained his portable military electric telegraph. A soldier carried the receiving device, complete with battery and 1000 meters [1700 yards] of cable as a back pack. After the cable had been paid out, the officer then used a calibrated dial with 25 commands—as many letters as there are in the alphabet, to transmit his dispatch to the soldier: "attack," "reinforcements," "artillery," etc.
>
> Trouvé called for someone in the audience to help demonstrate his electric telegraph. A soldier from the Auvergne region volunteered and lifted the coil-backpack onto his shoulders. He went to the doorway of the hall. Trouvé began to transmit the messages. The soldier responded, calling out "Artillery! Cavalry! Infantry! Enemy!"
>
> Laughter was followed by enthusiastic applause. Trouvé was lifted onto the shoulders of the soldiers who insisted that his invention be presented to high command. The following day, Trouvé demonstrated his portable military telegraph to General Charles Frébault, artillery commander of the 2nd Army during the siege of the city. The combination of snap hooks and cables on spools allowed soldiers to establish relay lines as long as three kilometers over land and streams in just half an hour.[12]

The result: Trouvé received an order to build 120 machines. Unfortunately the raw material was faulty, and despite Trouvé's efforts, only 25 were built. Sadly, the days passed by, and by January 1871 Paris had fallen.

Meanwhile, Gaston Tissandier had used his balloon *Le Céleste* to take mail out of Paris, landing at Dreux. The following month, his brother Albert, in the balloon *Jean Bart I*, took 400 kg (882 lbs.) of mail from Paris to Tours. From 1870 to 1871, the Tissandier brothers were responsible for technical operations for aerial observation available to the armies of the Loire. In 1873, Gaston founded *La Nature*, a weekly scientific review. During the next 15 years, he would publish many articles about Trouvé's inventions.

Unknown to nearly all Parisians, this was the year in which a Belgian electrical engineer called Zénobe Gramme decided to install permanent voltaic arc lamps in a factory to replace 25 gas burners. Its smoother current came from the dynamo he had just developed with colleague Hippolyte Fontaine.

Trouvé was soon exhibiting outside France. From 1 May to 31 October 1873, a *Weltausstellung* (international exhibition) was held in Prater, near Vienna, Austria. A total of 35 countries took part, 53,000 exhibitors, with seven million visitors. Trouvé was presented with the Emperor's Progress Medal for his latest innovation: the polyscope, a device for lighting the inspection of vital human organs.

He was, of course, not the first to conceive of such a device. In 1806, Philippe Bozzini, a doctor from Frankfurt, had succeeded in looking into various body cavities by means of his "*Lichtleiter*" (light conductor). This apparatus, whose source of illumination was a candle, was successfully tested in the illustrious Medizinisch-Chirurgisch Josephs-Akademie (founded in 1785), for implementation in rectoscopy and colposcopy, initially on corpses and, subsequently, on living persons. Even a particularly fine cannula was intended for insertion into the bladder via the urethra.

Regrettably, Bozzini's early death interrupted the promising experiments, and his pioneer work in this field sank into oblivion. Half a century elapsed before the French physician Antonin J. Desormeaux resurrected Bozzini's invention and developed the *Lichtleiter* further, replacing the candle with a much brighter-burning gas flame. His instrument rapidly became established in the medical profession, and it was manufactured from 1853 in quite large numbers. As a consequence of its success, Desormeaux has gone down in medical history as the "father of endoscopy." Indeed, he created the word "endoscope." It was in 1869 that Trouvé took up the challenge, patenting his liquid fuel powered pantoscope, which could be adapted for laryngoscopy, rhinoscopy, otoscopy, uteroscopy, and urethroscopy. But of course, he preferred electricity.

Again, the use of electricity to power medical inspection instruments was not new. It had already been used for cauterization by G.S. Crusell in 1839, by John Marschall in 1850 and above all by Middeldorf in 1852 for galvanocautery, enabling the removal of polyps with a wire loop. The use of electrified incandescent platinum wire had been tested out by Grove

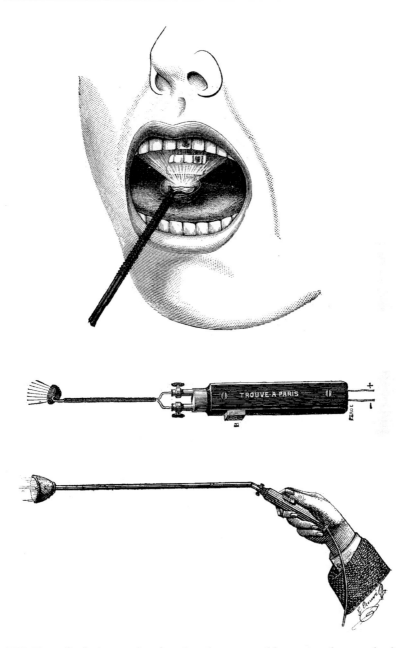

1873. Trouvé's platinum-wire electric polyscope could examine the mouth, the larynx and the nostrils. Versions of it could also examine the speculum, and other easily accessible cavities such as the vagina or the rectum (from Georges Barral, *L'histoire d'un inventeur*, 1891).

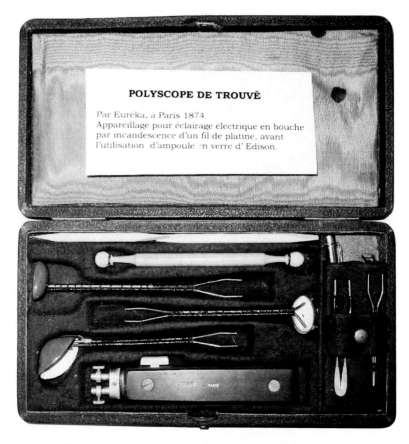

POLYSCOPE DE TROUVÉ

Par Eureka, à Paris 1874.
Appareillage pour éclairage électrique en bouche
par incandescence d'un fil de platine, avant
l'utilisation d'ampoule en verre d' Edison.

1877. One of the rare examples of Trouvé's polyscope to have survived (collection Fauchard du musée de l'APHP Assistance Publique des Hôpitaux de Paris/ ASPAD).

in 1840 and by the Viennese Moritz Heider in 1845, and had been demonstrated by Dr. Millot at a scientific congress in Paris in 1867.

In the summer of 1873, Trouvé's friend and colleague Gaston Planté had fitted his secondary battery to a device for cauterizing the lachrymal gland of patents. The operation could be carried out eight times before the device needed to be recharged. Following this work, Trouvé reported, "Inspired by the works of M. Bruck and Doctors Millot and Lazarevie, I was able to make the type of instrument that I called an electric polyscope."[13] Although Trouvé had already perfected his own batteries, he preferred to adapt Planté's battery into his polyscope, adding a rheostat of platinum wire so as to graduate the intensity of the light, depending on the length of wire used. Instead of platinum spirals, Trouvé used little

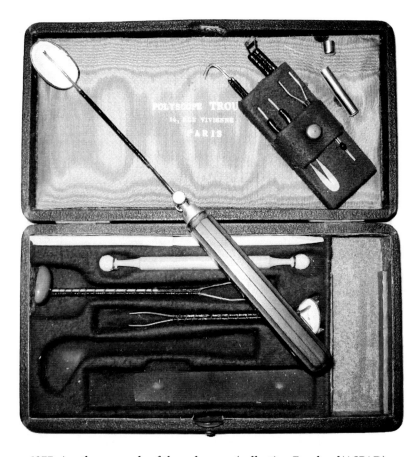

1877. Another example of the polyscope (collection Fauchard/ASPAD).

wires, flattened in the middle to form a small incandescent disc. This reduced the heat, making it bearable by the patient whose organ was being inspected.

Despite this, people were concerned that his polyscope might burn the areas being inspected—ear, mouth, uterus. So Trouvé conceived a demonstration. It involved placing his polyscope inside the stomach of a fish—pike, bream, perch, whatever. In total darkness, the fish began to glow, and all of its innards became visible. The fish was not in the slightest bit put out, either by the heat or by the light. This demonstration was publicly given in such places at the Sorbonne and the Academy of Medicine. It became known as his "luminous fish" experiment.

By 1877, as published in *Les Mondes*, ingeniously thinking about its potential, Trouvé had constructed a whole range of polyscopes:

Finely shaped for cauterizing of eyelashes.

Beak-shaped, enabling dentists to open up abscesses.

Mouth reflector for dentists, making teeth completely transparent.

Reflector with mirror for rhinolaryngeal examinations.

Reflector for lighting up natural cavities: the mouth, the throat, the back of the throat, the vagina and the rectum.

By a succession of small modifications, Trouvé's polyscope had been transformed into the urethroscope, the ophthalmoscope and the otoscope.

These instruments soon came into regular diagnostic use in physiological laboratories and dentists' surgeries, for gynecology, and in Paris hospitals such as the Necker, Saint-Louis and Lariboisière. At the Necker hospital, Professor Guyon used his polyscope to show his students the bladder and rectal mucosa. Professor U. Trélat very often used the rhinoscope. Trouvé assisted doctors Gallard and Amussat to explore the vagina and cervix. Gallard even asked Trouvé to fix a light source on the speculum. Professor Collin d'Alfort used it to enter the stomach of a bull; it was a voluntary fistula, but the vision was perfect.

At Lariboisière Hospital, the surgeon Le Dentu and Dr. Maurice Raynaud were able to confirm the present of a syphilitic stenosis of the lower esophagus. Jules Péan, "the prince of surgery," used a Trouvé polyscope to observe the contents of some large abdominal tumors on which he performed an ablation then unheard-of among surgeons.

In April 1879, Trouvé patented an improved version of his polyscope (N° 130235). By this time he had added reflective and magnifying prisms enabling a doctor to see the parts he was lighting at right angles, and thus to thoroughly explore a cavity such as the bladder.

At the Vienna Exhibition, alongside those curiously inspecting Trouvé's range of polyscopes was a Dresden physician, Maximilian Nitze, who presented his novel *"Blasenspiegel"* (bladder mirror), i.e., cystoscope, constructed in cooperation with the Viennese instrument maker Josef Leiter.

Later on, when Leiter of Germany and American instruments makers claimed that *they* had invented the polyscope, Trouvé modestly pointed to his Viennese Progress Medal of 1873. Two years later, he was awarded the Prix Barbier by the French Faculty of Medicine. He wrote:

What's more one can judge their usefulness by this true fact, even if incredible, that there is not a year which goes by without one and even several Germans and Americans claiming to have invented the electric polyscope, an instrument that we have made since 1869 and that has often been described several times by a slew of French and foreign journals—the main German and American scientific journals are proof of this—has featured in many exhibitions where it has systematically obtained the highest awards. In 1873, it was honored in Vienna with the Progress Medal.

The most incredible of all these supposed inventions, proclaimed as new, is that they give place to the most amusing claims to priority. Only a few months ago, the *New York Medical Journal* recorded one of these claims entered into between an American doctor and a Teutonic doctor! The priority remained, it appears with the American! Glory be to him. Please excuse this little digression, but our readers will soon notice that it is a never-ending topicality.[14]

By this time, Trouvé's inventions were being reported on at home and abroad, in the Austro-Hungarian Empire in such publications as the *Frankfurter Zeitung*, as well as in the *Medical Gazette* in Algeria.

In the spring of 1874, the fashionable photographer Félix Nadar who, some six years before, had photographed the helicopter model Trouvé had built for Ponton d'Amécourt, made available his former glasshouse-style studio at 35 Boulevard des Capucines for an art exhibition that was to change the course of history. It featured 165 unconventional paintings by a group of 30 struggling Parisian artists. Among them were Claude Monet, Edgar Degas, Pierre-Auguste Renoir, Camille Pissarro and Berthe Morisot; they called themselves the Anonymous Society of Painters, Sculptors, and Engravers. But then Louis Leroy, a critic for *Le Charivari*, titled his nasty, satirical review "Exhibition of Impressionists," which was inspired by Claude Monet's painting *Impression: Sunrise*, 1873. Leroy meant to discredit their work. Instead, he invented their identity. We do not know whether Trouvé, whose workshop was a few minutes' walk away, visited this exhibition, but several years later he would come into close contact with one or two of these unorthodox "Impressionists."

The years 1860 and 1870 saw an ever-increasing number of balloon ascents, the century being obsessed by the conquest of the sky. On 15 April 1875, the *Zénith* balloon made a new attempt on the altitude record. Following the advice of physiologist Dr. Paul Bert, the three aeronauts took oxygen bottles up with them. The *Zénith* reached 7,300 meters (24,000 feet) in altitude, but the crew lost consciousness due to hypoxia, unable to grab the oxygen tubes just a few feet away from them. Théodore Sivel and Joseph Croce-Spinelli died. Only Tissandier managed to survive.

In 1860, Benoît Rouquayrol had created a regulator for the circulation of compressed gases "for a safety device designed for miners caught in toxic gas." Four years later, working with Lieutenant Auguste Denayrouze, Rouquayrol developed the first autonomous diving suit. It received a gold medal at the Universal Exposition of 1867. This suit must have been seen by the 28-year-old Trouvé, for on 21 April 1875 he sent the following letter to the Société Française de la Navigation Aérienne (French Aeronautical Society):

Mr. President,

The ascensions to great altitude which have preceded the *Zénith* have established the evidence that the progressive rarefaction of the upper layers of the atmosphere hinder breathing and make life impossible; this was a main cause of their expiry. M. Paul Bert, by an admirable experiment to overcome a part of this difficulty, has made a minor step towards the answer to the problem. In averting all danger of asphyxia through the inhalation of oxygen, the aeronaut would from now on be able to rise to heights hitherto forbidden. The last ascension has shown us that there still remains much to do for the definitive solution of the problem of life ... caused by pulmonary apoplexy which was recently the case of the unfortunate aeronauts of the *Zénith*.

The system that we would adopt is simple and must come to the mind of everyone and it is as follows: we equip the nacelle with a tank of compressed air calculated in such a way to be able to sustain the life of a man without suffering for several hours. The cubic meters of compressed air at several atmospheres would be enough and the total weight of the gas and of the metal envelop would only add a moderate overload to the balloon.

When the balloon reaches an altitude of about 6,000 meters [19,700 feet] and the pilot begins to feel some difficulty in breathing, he puts on a type of thick rubber diving suit that encloses him from head to foot. The diving suit is linked to the tank of compressed air via a sealed tap, and all you need do is to turn on this tap and air from the reserve enters the diving suit. The pressure that supports the human body is from now on constant, since it is worked for the level of air which has just intervened between the body and the envelope.

On the other hand, the breaking takes place with perfect regularity, as the operator hold two little pipes between his teeth fixed to the mask and communicating with the reservoir; the other with the air outside. Whenever he breathes in, a valve opens. This is the valve to the reservoir of air and it allows the quantity of air sufficient for breathing out to escape; when breathing in, another valve opens in turn; it's the valve that communicates with the air outside and that closes as soon the carbonic acid has escaped. Another pressure gauge placed on the reservoir tells the aeronaut the exact quantity of air that it contains and the time that he can remain in the higher layers of the atmosphere.

Arrived at the maximum height of his journey, the aeronaut could still draw from the air at one or two kilometers [1 mile] above the balloon by means of a small tethered balloon of about 180 to 200 cubic meters' [6360 to 7100 cubic feet] capacity. This little balloon is full of pure hydrogen, which makes it extremely light, it carries in the shape of a nacelle an aspirator or recipient which one has previously emptied, and this recipient communicates with the main balloon via an electrically-conducting cable like my military telegraph, which only weights 6 to 8 kilos per kilogram-meter.... As soon as the little balloon has reached the desired height, an electro-magnet sets off a mechanism that opens a tap on the recipient, which fills it with air, the electro-magnet closes the tap, and one thus has a certain quantity of air taken from several kilometers above the balloon. A pressure gauge and a thermometer can also be placed in the little balloon.

The system has no other aim than to avoid from now on the repetition of accidents similar to the one that cost the lives of the unfortunate aeronauts of the *Zénith* and will enable a pilot at any height to calmly follow the program traced out without the terrible effects produced by rarefaction.

We even think that we could arrive at making available a reservoir of compressed air, by filling the conditions of the nacelle, capable of sustaining the life of several people during a voyage that would be relatively short, at altitudes from 6,000 meters [20,000 feet] to 8,000 meters [26,000 feet] and higher....

This is, Mr. President, the idea which presented itself to our mind immediately after the terrible accident to the *Zénith*. We say again that this idea must have occurred to all persons who interest themselves in the study.
Signed G. Trouvé, 6 rue Thérèse, Paris.

On 25 April, *Le Petit Moniteur* published Trouvé's suggestion and then added, "The inventor of this ingenious device will be submitted, in a few days, to experiments in the iron chamber of the Sorbonne, which one can empty with the help of a pneumatic machine. It claims that he will be able to support with impunity, with the aid of his device, barometric depressions indicating a minimum height of 15,000 meters [49,000 feet]."

To check the result of this brave experiment, in 2010, the author contacted Mme Isabelle Diry, the Sorbonne archivist, and received the following reply:

When your request for information was passed to me, already some time ago, I checked out the cataloguing of a series of postcards showing the premises of the Sorbonne and the teaching personnel of the faculties of Letters and of Science of Paris at the start of the twentieth century. During this work, I finally came across several views of physics laboratories, an electricity room, a "heat room," "the electric oven of Monsieur Moisson," but no "iron chamber."[15]

As he was the first to admit, Trouvé was not alone in his suggestion. Elsewhere the idea had been developed by Henry Fleuss for Siebe Gorman and Co., Ltd., of England for land-based breathing apparatus. It proved itself in a series of mine rescue operations in England, beginning in the 1880s. A similar application was suggested for protecting firemen from the smoke and flames. But Trouvé was the first to suggest the use of such a system by aeronauts.

It was not until 1913 that Georges Lagagneux, France's "*champion du vol en altitude*" (flight altitude champion), used an oxygen breathing system to fly an experimental Nieuport biplane to an altitude of over 6,000 meters (20,000 feet). The same year, Igor Sikorsky, a Russian, equipped his aircraft, called *The Grand,* with an enclosed cabin for both pilot and passengers.

Finally, in the 1960s, almost a century after Trouvé's suggestion, American astronauts on Project Mercury wore pressure space suits to pilot a spacecraft around Earth. They have been doing so ever since.

Trouvé's innovation was unbounded. During 1875, he submitted other inventions, such as Patent N° 109,170, which he placed at the French and Foreign Patents Office, 13 boulevard Saint-Martin, Paris, through the intermediary of a certain Desnos, an engineer, and a former student at the Central School:

> My invention consists in establishing a connection between a pendulum, or a clock, and one or several almanacs or calendars, placed at a distance from this clock in an apartment, in offices, for example. To this end, I am placing, on the pendulum, or clock, an electric contact that is made just at midnight, every day, and whose current is transmitted by two wires, to an electromagnet placed in the almanac or calendar, and that has as its function to make pass or advance $\frac{1}{365}$ of the strip, or disc, or paper, or other material, on which the days of the month are written, and as need be the lunar and astronomical tables, feast days and other ordinary indications of almanacs.
>
> It is understood that the battery will be placed somewhere in the electric circuit, either in the body of the almanac, or below in the apartment, and that I reserve all rights as to the making of the almanac or calendar, so called.
>
> I create, thus, a new type of days of the month indicator which I have called **electric almanacs and calendars**, for which I intend to claim entire and exclusive property.
>
> By proxy for M. Trouvé Paris, 10 August 1875.[16]

In another part of his workshop, Trouvé developed a hand-cranked, belt-driven dynamo, for use in physics laboratories, medical cabinets and classrooms (Patent N° 108,210). A development of the magneto developed for galvanic depots by Zénobe Gramme five years before, it needed the effort of one man turning its handles to produce "half a steam-power." Its light weight of 10 kg (22 lbs.) was partially achieved by the use of a many fine metal discs ($\frac{2}{10}$ mm/$\frac{1}{64}$ in. thick) sandwiched between paper washers.

The day Trouvé presented this to the Physics Society, the machine was severely criticized by another young inventor, Jacques Arsène d'Arsonval. But then Theodore Achille Louis, Viscount du Moncel, spoke out in its favor in his famous treatise *General Applications of Electricity* (1875). That year Trouvé was awarded the gold medal of the National Academy.

Apart from the Barral biography, there is precious little to give us a glimpse of Trouvé's activities, so the following letter, sent on 6 June 1877, is quite revealing:

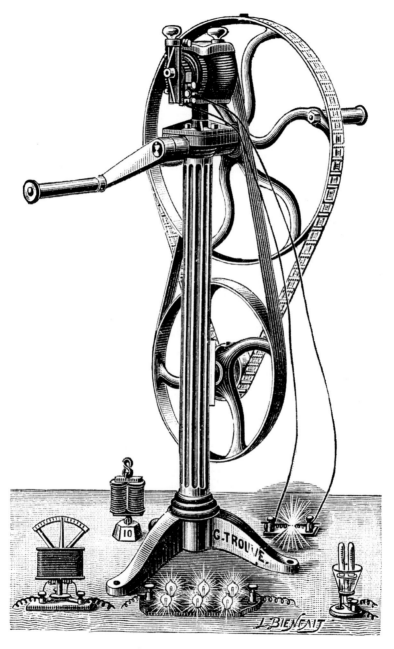

From 1875, Trouvé's portable hand-cranked dynamo electric machine was used for demonstrating electricity in lecture rooms and laboratories in Paris (from Georges Barral, *L'histoire d'un inventeur*, 1891).

Visit made by M. Hureau de Villeneuve on 8 June

Monsieur, I have heard it said that the Aerostatic Society, of which you are president, have the intention to bring together in the Exhibition of 1878,[17] all the various devices concerning aerostation in a public exhibition. Although already having a space at this exhibition, I think that it would be agreeable to amuse them by bringing together in your exhibition, certain devices, particularly relevant to the aeronautical art. Thus I have the honor to tell you that I could hand over to you three flying machines, of which two are birds, and some plans and drawings.

G. Trouvé.

Trouvé continued to contribute to the progress in the use of electricity in medical therapy, and was sought out by those who respected his ability. One of these was Ernest Nicolas Joseph Onimus, who for over a decade had been exclusively occupied with electro-therapeutical research. In 1877, he published his *Practical Guide to Electrotherapy*. Wishing to appreciate the influence of both slow and rapid irregularities of the heart and of muscular contraction, Onimus approached Trouvé, two years his senior, to build him some machines.

Struck by the considerable effects that a weak electric current produced on his muscles, Trouvé thought that here must reside one of the principal receivers of electromotive force. He therefore constructed an artificial muscle, replacing the active molecules of the muscle with little

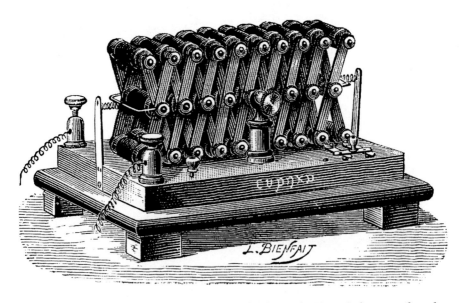

1877. By designing and building this artificial muscle, Trouvé also contributed to robotics research (from Georges Barral, *L'histoire d'un inventeur*, 1891).

electromagnets. Recalling the children's game of paper-chains, he built a machine that was made up of a chain of electro-magnets. His machine was aimed at giving students an idea of muscular contraction. But it is also an element of present-day robotics.

For heart palpitations, Trouvé built a large induction machine with a clockwork movement switch (like today's time switch), and then a smaller one, which Gavarret presented to the Academy of Medicine on 6 June 1877, stating, "This new induction device is, by its price and its size, aimed at medical practice. Trouvé has achieved considerable perfection. It is of the greatest importance for therapeutic applications."

During the next two decades, Onimus would commission Trouvé to build a succession of electro-therapy machines. On Trouvé's death, Onimus still owed him money.

From one day to the next, Trouvé could switch from a medical breakthrough to an amusing gizmo, or work on them in parallel. Always challenged by the miniature, alongside his luminous electric jewels, in 1878, Trouvé constructed a mobile electrical paperweight. Originating from Venetian and Bohemian glass foundries, Baccarat glass millefiori paperweights had become all the rage in Paris, with their delicate but static flowers.

For Trouvé, his paperweight must move. He conceived of mounting a tiny bird, insect, or butterfly, natural or artificial, onto the paperweight, which he covered over with a convex lens. By placing the paperweight onto its plinth, which contained a simple battery, an electric current gave life to the selected creature, which flapped its wings. Take the paperweight off its plinth and the wings stopped beating.

Then there was the telephone. In 1876, Alexander Graham Bell had presented the world with his method of, and apparatus for, transmitting vocal or other sounds telegraphically—the telephone. Only two years later, Trouvé presented the Academy of Sciences with his improvements for the telephone, with multiple vibrating membranes to reinforce the intensity of the transmitted currents.

Again in contrast, he developed his *électromégaloscope* for the examination of canons and of the interior of projectiles. Such an examination was done at the St. Thomas d'Aquin artillery works in Paris by Captain Henry Manceron with the aid of an adapted polyscope.

This was the year when thousands of Parisians, including Trouvé, were being entranced by a new and brighter form of street lighting, developed by a former engineer officer of the tsar of Russia, Pavel Yablochkov. His system, developed a few years before, used arc lamps, initially the "electric candle" or "Yablochkov candle." This was a carbon arc lamp employing

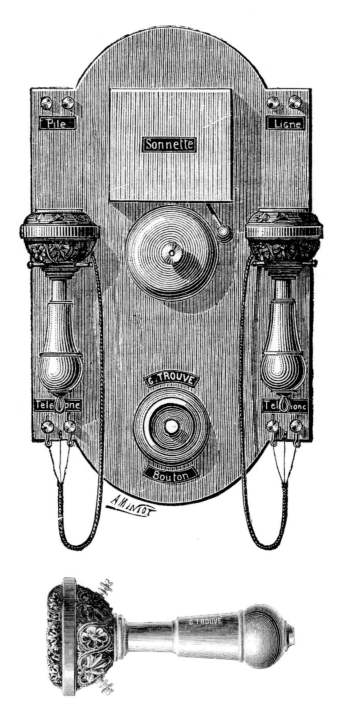

1878. Trouvé also modified the telephones recently invented by Alexander Graham Bell of America (from Georges Barral, *L'histoire d'un inventeur*, 1891).

alternating current, which ensured that both electrodes were consumed at equal rates and had the advantage of no longer requiring manual adjustment. Yablochkov candles were first used to light the Marango Hall of Les Galeries du Louvre, a department store in Paris. Eventually 80 candles were installed in the same department store. In his novel *Au Bonheur des Dames (Ladies Paradise)*, French writer Émile Zola writes, "Into the distant depths of the departments penetrated a white brightness of a blinding fixity.... There was nothing now but this blinding white light."[18]

Paris's Third Universal Exposition, held throughout 1878 at the Palais du Trocadéro, presented Yablochkov with the unique opportunity to make a spectacular demonstration to a world audience. Through the promotional efforts of his collaborator Zénobe Gramme, he was successful in having 62 of his arc lights installed along the half-mile length of Avenue de l'Opéra, Place du Théâtre Français and around the Place de l'Opéra. Thus Paris earned its nickname "City of Lights."

It was only two years later when American Charles F. Brush of Cleveland equipped the Wabash, Indiana, courthouse with four of his electric lights, and that town proudly claimed to be the "First Electrically Lighted City in the World."

This Paris Exhibition celebrated France's recovery from the bloody 1870 war. The Palais de l'Exposition, also called the Iron Palace, housed the exhibits of all the nations and could be compared to a long patchwork greenhouse. The Work Gallery exhibited all the riches of human know-how and even enabled visitors to watch workers at their tasks. The World of Toys presented clever toys, little steam engines, clockwork trains, building games and even animated dolls. Among the endless exhibits, there was the telephone of Canadian Alexander Graham Bell and the megaphone and the phonograph of Thomas Alva Edison, over from Menlo Park, New Jersey. Then there was the latest full-scale steam-engine flying machine of Félix du Temple. Its longerons were in rolled sheet aluminum, and the wingspan was 12 meters (40 feet) for a weight of 80 kilograms (176 lbs.). The landing gear was retractable. Du Temple's first test flight in 1874 with a young sailor at the helm was the first attempt at powered flight in the history of aviation.

Elsewhere, the inventor Henri Giffard had built a tethered balloon of 25,000 cubic meters (8,829 cubic feet), for the exhibition. It was capable of carrying aloft 40 to 50 passengers. It was said that this balloon, located in the Tuileries, had given flights in just two months to as many people as had gone aloft since the start of flying, about in about a century. A dozen ascensions per day took passengers up to more than 500 meters (1,640 feet). It was one of the star attractions of the exhibition where

35,000 people had enjoyed flights in the ingenious Giffard's gondola. Without doubt, Trouvé joined the queue for the Giffard balloon experience, perhaps several times.

At the same exposition, in the section marked Medicine, Hygiene and Public Assistance, Trouvé himself was exhibiting a range of some 70 instruments at Showcase N° 161. They were grouped into a square of no more than 1.7 m (5.6 feet). Alongside each instrument there was a card giving a reference to material published about it in magazines. Abbé Moigno wrote,

> It's true that M. Trouvé is essentially the man of little wonders.... For us the masterpiece of his masterpieces is the electro-medical device reduced to a minimum of volume and elements in really extraordinary energy conditions. It's really hard to believe that an induction machine which, with its battery, its coil and the accessories necessary for electro-therapy, is contained in a kit as big as a wallet, and just fitting into a trouser or waistcoat pocket, can give muscular contractions energetic enough to reach the limit of the strength of a vigorously built man. M. Trouvé's exhibit is a strong crowd puller and one leaves it with regret, delighted by the miracles of his charming and fertile industriousness.[19]

Trouvé was awarded the exhibition gold medal.

THREE

From a Workshop in the Rue Vivienne

On 1 July 1878, Trouvé moved to new premises—14 rue Vivienne, in the second arrondissement (district) of Paris. His landlord was the Comte de Caumels and d'Espiès.

In residing in the rue Vivienne, Gustave had chosen a very central part of the city. It is just behind the National Library. The nearby Galérie Vivienne was an arcade housing fashionable shops including prestigious clockmakers; jewelers; engravers; and piano, harmonium and music box makers. Most of those visiting the arcade knew little of the inventor down the road.

Trouvé took rooms in a five-story building. Its apartments were rented by businesses, dressmakers, jewelers, a metal engraver, a chemist, an artificial flower maker, an ornament maker, and a carpet dealer. The trade of the tenants was not always indicated.

Trouvé's living quarters and workshops were on the first floor, overlooking the courtyard. They included to the right an antechamber, shop, dining room, and kitchen, and to the left a second workshop. In the corridor to the right were cabinets and toilets. For a rental of 3,000 francs, for the next 25 years, Trouvé, a confirmed bachelor, would be renewing his lease here to live, invent and construct his machines for the rest of his life.

Unfortunately it has not been possible to find any information about the size of his team. It was most certainly limited to no more than a dozen people, like other growing electrical businesses. Instruments made were either one-offs or part of a limited series. Only a handful of these would grow to a larger size such as that of Christophle (electroplating; 1,000-person workforce), that of Breguet (250-person workforce), and that of Leclanché (battery manufacture; 50-person workforce).

43

1877. Trouvé moved into new lodgings at 14 rue Vivienne, in the 2nd arrondissement of Paris. For the next 25 years, this would be his home and the workshop from where his succession of inventions would go out and change the world (photograph Holfeltz).

As a sign of recognition for the arrival of an industry, 15 April 1879 saw publication of the first issue of France's very first electric journal, entitled *La Lumière électrique (The Electric Light)*, sponsored by Count Théodose du Moncel. In the first article, headlined "Our Program," the editor stated, "We plan to bring together the individual efforts of well-intentioned people and to accompany them towards a better-defined situation of electrical data."

In June 1879, the Ecole Centrale des Arts et Métiers celebrated their fiftieth anniversary at the Hotel Continental, Paris:

Some of the guests are wearing Trouvé's charming electric jewels: a death's head tie-pin; a rabbit drummer tie-pin. Suppose you are carrying one of these jewels below your chin. Whenever someone takes a look at it, you discreetly slip your hand into the pocket of your waistcoat, tip the tiny battery to horizontal and immediately the death's head rolls its glittering eyes and grinds its teeth. The rabbit starts working like the timpanist at the opera.

The key piece, a bird, was a rich, animated set of diamonds, belonging to Princess Pauline de Metternich, the famous Vienna and Paris socialite and close friend of the Empress Eugénie.

The princess was a passionate patron of music and a real leader of society fashions. Be it in Paris or Vienna, she always wore the latest trends in society costume. She taught French and Czech aristocrats to skate, and women to smoke cigars without their fearing for their reputation. She was known in particular for having met many composers and writers. Carrying it in her hair, the princess could at will make the wings of her diamond bird flap.

Another feature of this evening's party is the "luminous fish" demonstration of Trouvé's remarkable polyscope: "Nothing more interesting than to see by transparency the interior of the fish which did not besides appear otherwise put out by its transformation into a new type of Venetian lantern."[1]

The report in *La Nature* was taken up by *Scientific American*: "Among the specialties for which the French are noted there is nothing more curious than the electric jewelry."[2]

That summer Trouvé devised a way to improve the telephone ringing system. He created a domestic room-to-room telephone system. Having developed microphones capable of picking up the weakest, clipped sounds, he assembled a microphone-telephone set with two cords and a double battery. The switching operated automatically simply by hanging up the telephones or by taking them off with the hand.

1879. Electro-mobile jewels of M. Gustave Trouvé: rabbit, bird, death's head. Princess Pauline Metternich amused her circle of friends whenever she used the little hidden battery to make the wings flap on this diamond-studded bird, which she was wearing in her hair—courtesy Trouvé (from Georges Barral, *L'histoire d'un inventeur*, 1891).

That October 1879, Trouvé exhibited his polyscopes and other medical equipment at the sixth Amsterdam International Congress of Medical Science and received a unique reward. Joseph Lister of Edinburgh, who had pioneered antiseptic surgery, was also a delegate at this congress.

Although in France labor organization was considered illegal, this was the year in which Hippolyte Fontaine, administrator of the Gramme Magneto-Electric Machines Company, set up an Electrician's Trade Union to protect the interests of the new trade. Trouvé became one of the 21 founding members. Other members included Antoine Breguet, Jules Armengaud (telephone engineer), J. Carpentier (inventor of the electric melophone), P. Lemonnier, F. Chrétien (Paris electric railway pioneer), and P. Jablochkoff. The statutes of the chamber defined it as "a meeting place for businessmen and merchants who are occupied with the development and the applications of industry."

France's current union, the Syndical Chamber of contractors for electric bells, voice-carriers, megaphones and lightning conductors, was set up two years later. It was not until 1889 that the Electrical Trades Union was formed in Great Britain, while the following year, the Electrical Wiremen and Linemen's Union No. 5221 was founded in St. Louis, Missouri. By 1891, after sufficient interest was shown in a national union, a convention was held on 21 November 1891 in St. Louis. Out of this grew the International Brotherhood of Electrical Workers (IBEW).

Over in Germany, Werner von Siemens of Berlin had recently developed his revolutionary electromechanical dynamic coil into a battery-powered motor. In 1878, examining the Siemens coil engine, French electrician Marcel Deprez improved the motor by placing the coil between the branches of a U-shaped magnet. But his motor still had a neutral moment.

Trouvé thought up a way to eliminate this weakness. He substituted an electromagnet between the poles where the Siemens coil was placed. The current circulated in the wire of the electromagnet and then passed, via the brushes of the switch, into the wire of the coil. In this way neutral was avoided. As Trouvé explained to the Academy of Sciences,

> When we track the dynamic diagram of a Siemens coil, making it carry out a complete revolution between the two magnetic poles which react on it, we see that the work is almost zero for two fairly large periods of rotation. These two periods correspond to the time during which the cylindrical poles of the coil, having reached the poles of the magnet, pass before them; during these two fractions of the revolution, which are each approximately 30 degrees, the magnetic surfaces to react one the other, remain at the same distance; so the coil is not required to turn. This results in a significant loss of work. I have deleted these periods of indifference and increased the effec-

1880. Two-coil electric motor. With this more efficient and more compact motor, linked to a rechargeable lead-acid battery invented by his friend and admirer Gaston Planté, Trouvé knew he had a unit with universal possibilities, from medical instruments to transport (from Georges Barral, *L'histoire d'un inventeur*, 1891).

tiveness of the machine by so modifying the coil: the pole faces, instead of portions of a cylinder whose axis coincides with that of the system are shaped like a cochlea so that in turning, they gradually approach their rotating surfaces with those of the magnet. The action of repulsion starts, so neutral is practically avoided.[3]

The little motor built by Trouvé was only 20 cm (8 inches) long and weighed in at only 3.3 kg (7 lbs., 4 oz.). Simply by adding more coils in the magnetic field, Trouvé stepped up the power. His motor could run up to 18,000 revolutions per minute. In addition, as with all electric motors in general, it was

1880. Electric motor (Musée EDF Electropolis, Mulhouse).

reversible, so it could be used as a generator of electricity instead of as a generator of power. With such a compact motor coupled to Planté's rechargeable battery, Trouvé envisioned its use in many fields: powering dental drills, clocks, Holtz machines, Carré machines, air conditioners, amateur lathes, chromatropes, turning-mirror devices—even lightweight boats. As for Marcel Deprez, instead of scaling down the electric motor to miniature instruments, he went on to devote himself to the transmission of electricity over longer distances.

Elsewhere in the world, in October 1880, Thomas A. Edison started to sell his light bulbs from his factory at Menlo Park, New Jersey. His British rival, Joseph Swan, opened his own factory in Newcastle, early in 1881. A Siemens AC alternator driven by a watermill was being used to power electric street lighting in the town of Godalming, United Kingdom.

Trouvé's batteries were coming to be used for all sorts of applications. Antoine Breguet, son of Louis Breguet, was working on the standardization of time in the big towns, using electricity. Writing in Le Génie Civil, Breguet stated:

> In the new transmitter, the contacts are three in number and operate in parallel. It is therefore one third of the main current which passes through each of them, and thus the oxidizing effect is greatly reduced. The battery works twelve hours out of twenty-four, which is considerable, and which was a new challenge to overcome, most batteries unable to withstand such a prolonged work without requiring a careful and frequent maintenance. After some research, it was the wet stack copper sulfate one chose, and the results that could be obtained were quite unexpected. This battery, invented by Mr. Trouvé, is a particular form of the Daniell; but instead of containing completely liquid dissolutions of copper sulfates and zinc, it contains them in the pores of washers made of blotting paper. Transport caused by the secondary electrolysis is therefore prevented and what follows is an almost absolute regularity of current.[4]

Trouvé became a welcome guest at many a soirée. One evening in February 1881, Admiral Amédée Mouchez, the director of the Paris Observatory, invited him to demonstrate his inventions to rather a select gathering. Among the politicians were Sadi Carnot, soon to become president of the French Republic; Gambetta, president of the Chamber of Deputies; Freycinet, former minister of foreign affairs; Magnin, finance minister; and Ferdinand de Lesseps, diplomat behind the Suez Canal success and currently planning a sea-level Panama Canal. Among the scientists were Becquerel, noted physicist; Dumas, 81 years old, noted chemist; Daubrée, geologist and president of the Academy of Sciences; and Camille Flammarion, famous astronomer and balloonist. Among the artists were Garnier, well-known architect; Meissonier, famous painter; and Carrier-

Belleuse, sculptor and painter, the tutor of Rodin. An article in *Le Voltaire* reported on the event:

> What more ingenious devices than those of M. Trouvé. How not to marvel at them! It seems to us that our ministers of state took a particular interest in them. Here are unquestionably the most interesting applications of electricity that have ever been made. M. Trouvé's device for searching out a bullet in the depth of a wound and withdrawing it scientifically: material force has launched it: the mind removes it with a marvelous elegance. However, the knowledgeable inventor showed me an aerial propeller, which could indeed, in its application to aerial navigation, one day lead to the abolition of frontiers and militarism.[5]

In his *Memoirs of an Astronomer*, Flammarion tells how every Wednesday evening he received the Moignos, and that meeting at his home were also Jules Grévy (president of the Republic), Victorien Sardou (playwright), Gustave Doré (engraver-illustrator), Charles Garnier (architect), Charles Cross or "Willy" Gauthier-Villars (musical critic), Figuier, the Tissandiers, Fonvielle, and Charles Tellier (inventor of the chemical refrigerator). Flammarion wrote, "On one evening Trouvé explained his instruments and demonstrated the luminous fish."

Trouvé was also invited to demonstrate his little instruments to a bourgeois public desperately seeking novelty. These demonstrations were held at the Sorbonne University, the Conservatoire des Arts et Metiers, and private theaters, organized by the Abbé Moigno, the Polytechnic Association, the Philotechnical Association, the League for Teaching, or the Library of the Friends of Instruction. For example, the regular Sunday conference-visits to the Conservatoire des Arts et Métiers allowed more than 3,000 Parisians to see in operation electromagnetic machines, accumulators, electric lighting, and a whole series of experiments. Instrument makers and inventors, such as Gaston Planté and Gustave Trouvé, explained the principles of their instruments to those present. It was thus a large public, from the popular to the managing classes, who became familiar with both electricity and its applications through experiments and the apparatus built for them.

By now Trouvé, considering how his little engine might be used for motive power, thought that perhaps the most lightweight and stable vehicle to test it out on would be a pedal tricycle.

Since the mid–1870s, James Starley of the Sewing Machine Co. of Coventry, England, had been building and improving tricycles—the Coventry Rotary and the Coventry Lever—for a world enamored with "wheeling." In the summer of 1881, Starley proudly delivered two of his stable "Salvo tricycles" to Osborne House on the Isle of Wight, for possible

PLAYER'S CIGARETTES

COVENTRY ROTARY TRICYCLE

1881. A British-built Coventry Rotary Tricycle was the unit chosen by Trouvé to electrify and to test along the rue Valois, central Paris, that April (cigarette card, author's collection).

use by Her Royal Highness Queen Victoria and her daughters. The Salvo was renamed the "Royal Salvo," and before long there was not a crowned head who did not have a fleet of tricycles, both within and outside Europe. A firm called P. Rousset and Ingold became the general agents for France.

For Trouvé, the Salvo seemed the ideal mount. On 16 April 1881 he reported his trials along a straight road near his workshop in the Tissandiers' magazine *La Nature*:

> On a heavily built English tricycle, I fitted two of my little electric motors and six electric accumulators like the one in my polyscope. One of my friends climbed onto the tricycle, switched it on and accelerated it several times along the rue de Valois, certainly as rapidly as a good hackney cab. The experiment lasted an hour and a half. A speed of 12 km/h [7.4 mph] was recorded.
>
> The weight of the vehicle and of my friend amounted to 160 kg [352 lbs.] and the force of the engines corresponded to 7 kilogrammètres [1.1 hp].
>
> Encouraged by these results, I immediately began to build a motor which was alone more powerful than the two others, even up to 10 kilogrammeters, so as to get each greater speeds, that is from 20 to 30 km/h [12 to 18 mph].[6]

There were eye-witnesses: "One of Trouvé's friends has tried the new velocipede on the bitumen of the rue de Valois. He went up and down the road several times at the speed of a good carriage."[7] The loyal Abbé Moigno was also there:

> I had just cross the Palais Royal and arrived on the Rue de Valois, when my attention was drawn by a man who was on a tricycle and was arriving at

1881. This artist's impression of "Trouvé on his electric tricycle" was published in *Physique et chimie populaires*, volume 2, by Alexis Clerc, 1881–1883. Although it is the only contemporary image of arguably the world's first electric vehicle, reports state that the bearded Trouvé did not himself ride his invention, preferring to act as an observer (Musée EDF Electropolis, Mulhouse).

full speed. I would have left immediately if, upon the approach of the tricycle, I had not heard a few exclamations uttered by passers-by who said, "Of course it is steam or electricity which propels it!" Upon hearing the word "electricity," I paid closer attention to the vehicle which was going by me at that precise moment and it was easy for me to notice that the "soul" of the movement was indeed electricity, because I immediately recognized the small motor which had been presented and demonstrated by its inventor during a social gathering given by Vice-Admiral Mouchez in the Paris Observatory. However, I did not recognize M. Gustave Trouvé, the famous electrical engineer, as being the person who was on the tricycle, but I soon heard he was standing apart and that from a window in the Hotel de Hollande, he had followed all phases of the experiment. Let me tell you about it.

The tricycle had two steering wheels and a simple, large propelling wheel, the latter being, I believe, of English manufacture, and appearing quite heavy. Placed beneath the axle joining the two small wheels were two small, Trouvé motors, each the size of a fist. These motors were communicating movement by means of two link chains, each of which engaged its respective sprocket gear on either side of the big propelling wheel.

Behind the seat and sitting on the axle, a rough, newly fashioned wooden box contained six secondary batteries. These accumulators were quite similar to those of Mr. Gaston Planté and actuated the motors. To the left of the seat was a brake lever easily reached by the driver. On the lever was an electrical switch by which the driver could easily stop or start immediately.[8]

Writing some 14 years later, journalist Georges Dary explained:

It's true to say that its success at first did not respond to the attempts, even perfected, which took place in this order of ideas…. We are unable to believe that the pleasure of eating-up a kilometer without fatigue could ever completely satisfy the recordmen: they always prefer to peal their lightweight machines rather than adapt an instrument which would transform their beloved sport into an invalid's outing.[9]

Usually, Trouvé took out patents on his latest inventions, but not for his electric tricycle. At present, no documentary explanation has been found for this. But there is perhaps one possible explanation. Since 1869, Louis-Guillaume Perreaux, also of Paris, had been developing his steam velocipede, often modifying his original French patent, N° 83691. This was to address the well-known drawbacks of ordinary bicycles and hopefully to make a machine capable of seriously competing with the horse.

Perreaux coupled one of his smaller steam engines, a single cylinder with a weight of 62 kg (136 lbs.) onto an iron velocipede manufactured by Pierre Michaux. Perreaux exhibited this at the Exposition Universelle of 1878, but he never met with commercial success. This may have been because it took too long to build up steam pressure, while climbing onto and pedaling a simple velocipede remained so much easier.

For Trouvé, the answer was quite simply his electric motor, less heavy and quicker in response. But Perreaux's detailed patent may have prevented Trouvé from taking out his own patent. After all, the Perreaux patent covered any form of motor installed in a velocipede, including electricity.

During the following years, Trouvé left others to develop electric land vehicles. For example, on 29 April 1899, Camille Jenatzy of Belgium drove his electric car *La Jamais Contente* at faster than 100 km/h on the Achères road. Two engines were placed between the rear wheels with a maximum power of 50 kW with 80 batteries, given the car a total weight of 1.5 tons.

In 1993, when Ernest H. Wakefield, PhD, of Warrendale, Pennsylvania, produced his 540-page *History of the Electric Automobile*, he stated: "This book is dedicated to Gustave Trouvé, who in 1881 first assembled an electric vehicle."[10]

As for the irrepressible Trouvé, he very swiftly reoriented his genius towards another challenge he had been developing in parallel. Within one month of the electric tricycle trial, he was ready to test a prototype electric boat on the River Seine. The date was 26 May 1881 and the reporter was Georges Dary:

> Crowds of passers-by stop on the bridges to gaze with astonishment, for among the many *bateaux-mouches* and *hirondelles* [passenger ferries] which are running up and down the Seine in Paris, a lightweight vessel is heading up river without any visible engine, nor steam machinery, nor telltale funnel. It stops, continues or slows down without any movement from its "patron," who without moving steers from the stern. This boat at such a strange pace seems alive, as intelligent as a horse which obeys the slightest sign, under the simple pressure from the knees of its horseman.
>
> It did not take long to learn that here was a new advance in electricity realized by the friendly constructor whom all Paris already knows: Gustave Trouvé, who is always on the trail of innovations considered impossible.[11]

This time Trouvé was able to make his own report to the august Académie des Sciences, long time situated at the quai de Conti, just across the Pont Neuf of the River Seine from his workshop:

> A motor of 5kg [11 lbs.] powered by six Planté secondary elements, producing an effective work of 7 kg per second, was placed, on 8 April, in a tricycle whose weight, including the rider and the batteries, amounted to 160 kg [352 lbs.], and took it at a speed of 12 km/h [7.4 mph].
>
> The same motor, installed on the 26 May on a boat of 5.50 m [18.5 feet] long and 1.20 m [4 feet] wide, containing three people, recorded a speed of 2.50 m/sec on going down the Seine to the Pont-Royal [bridge] and 1.50 m/sec on going back upstream. The motor was powered by two pile batteries of potassium dichromate each of six elements, and the propellant was a three-bladed propeller.
>
> On the 26 June 1881, I repeated this experiment on the calm waters of the upper lake of the Bois de Boulogne, with a four-bladed propeller 28 cm in diameter and 12 électrique of Ruhmkorff-type Bunsen plates, charged with one part hydrochloric acid, one part nitric acid and two parts water in the porous vase so as to lessen the emission of nitrous fumes.
>
> The speed at the start, measured by an ordinary log, reached 150 meters [164 yards] in 48 seconds—or little more than 3 meters [3 yards] per second; but after three hours of functioning, this had fallen to 150 meters [164 yards] in 55 seconds and after five hours, this had further fallen to 150 meters [164 yards] in 65 seconds.
>
> One bichromate battery, enclosed in a 50 cm [20 inch] long case, will give a constant current of 7 to 8 hours; this is a great saving of fuel and cleanliness.[12]

On June 23, *La Science Populaire*, a weekly illustrated journal, reported on the first of Trouvé's experiments:

1881. Dressed for the occasion, Trouvé tests his electric boat along the Seine, only weeks after he had tested his tricycle; he named it *Le Téléphone* in homage to Alexander Graham Bell (from Georges Barral, *L'histoire d'un inventeur*, 1891).

Several newspapers have already spoken of the amazing solution provided by Trouvé to the problem of electric traction applied to boats. We had the good fortune to attend, on the Tourist dock at Pont-Royal, one of the experiments by the inventor. An elegant skiff for two rowers, christened *La Téléphone*, equipped for a pair of oars, was moored alongside the pontoon. Between the helmsman's bench and the first bench for rowing, there was a potassium dichromate battery composed of 12 couples of zinc and carbon, grouped into two batteries mounted in tension, each element having approximately 4 square decimeters surface and affecting the layout devised, if we are not mistaken, by M. Grenet, that is to say, the zincs and carbons connected by a rod that simultaneously ensures the contacts and can be lifted via a crank to emerge from the tanks.

It was then that M. Trouvé, a charming man by the way, very amiable and remarkably intelligent, arrived with the rudder of the boat under his arm. This rudder is all the mystery: Imagine the standard tiller supporting a mahogany frame that is certainly not more than 25 centimeters [9 inches] long by 15 cm [5 inches] wide and 5 or 6 cm [roughly 2 inches] thick. This frame encloses the electric motor on which we do not have to give lengthy details, but we were struck by its small size compared to its power and how it seems to make excellent use of electricity. The rudder itself, metallic and hollow at its center, receives a single helix of 25 or 30 centimeters [9 or 11 inches] in diameter, which is transmitted by a gear movement of the electric motor. The latter receives its power through the metal cables covered with an insulator and connected by terminals to the batteries.

With three people, including the inventor, sitting in the skiff, the zinc and carbon were immersed as a mechanic might open the drawer of a steam engine, and the mariners pushed off, putting on a show, following the meanderings of the shore, crowded with boats, promenades and bathhouses.

And indeed, as we remarked to Trouvé, the skiff was moving beautifully. On various occasions methods have been sought to place the propeller behind the rudder, in large vessels, so that, by escaping the reactions produced by its rotation of this, it should retain its maximum effectiveness.

It may well be that at this point of view, the issue was fully resolved, if the application becomes electro-motive, as we hope, useful for large vessels: the thruster body was placed in the rudder and moving with it when it was steered by the cables, the direction of the driving force is to make a more or less acute angle, the keel of the boat, and its action, acting sideways on the stern, forcing the back of the boat to drift and the boat itself to turn, if desired, on its own length more easily than I could do pulling with two oars on one side and releasing the other. Many collisions could perhaps be avoided by this ease of development.

But unfortunately, the installation that we were shown has a weak point: it is the very source of electricity we have described. There is nothing new about this problem, namely, the impossibility of transporting a liquid cell. In addition, the dichromate battery, if it is very strong, is very expensive and runs out quickly and is especially suitable for short and intermittent action, as in the electric igniter. A dry battery would be preferable, but we do not know whether it has enough energy. Is there not a test to try with the Planté secondary battery, or better, with the Faure cells, currently being tested out on a tram car?

We submit this idea to the inventor, if we have the honor of being read by him. Moreover, this was probably not the given problem he had to solve. In terms of transforming the electricity into work, this is a remarkable achievement and a provision of a rare happiness. We are far from imitating the trembling fish tail of which we had thought a few years ago. It is hoped that the attention of the Administration of the Navy wants to focus on the good experiment we have described and which will not be, hopefully, the last.   L.D.

In his patent (N° 136,560), which he would revise several times from 1880 to late 1881, learning from similar trials, Trouvé eventually came up with a "rudder containing the propeller and its motor, the whole of which is removable and easily lifted off the stern of the boat." With this invention, Trouvé can lay undisputable claim to the world's first marine outboard engine.

He was not, however, the first to exploit electricity to propel a boat. More than 40 years before, in 1838, one year before Trouvé's birth, Professor Moritz von Jacobi, financed by Tsar Nicholas of Russia, built the

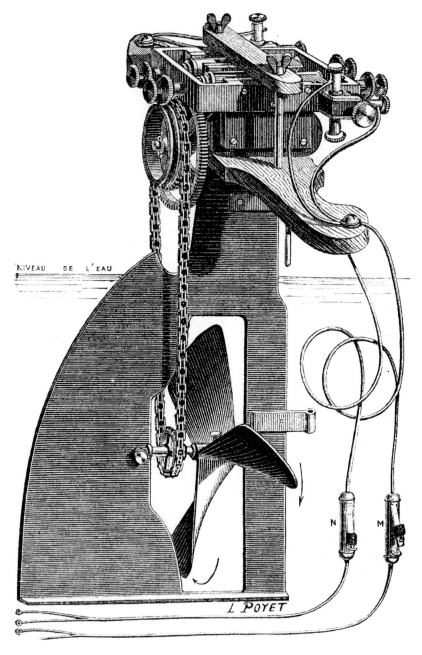

NIVEAU DE L'EAU

N M

L POYET

1881. Close-up of Trouvé's detachable marine electric motor as published in his patent. The world's first outboard engine (from Georges Barral, *L'histoire d'un inventeur*, 1891).

Eleketrokhod, an electric paddleboat. Nine meters long, powered by a 220-watt electromagnetic motor, this boat transported 14 passengers at a speed of 2.5 km/h (1.5 mph) against the current of the River Neva. Jacobi's non-rechargeable battery used zinc and platinum, very expensive. But the motor gave out nitrous fumes in as big a quantity as smoke from a steam train. Jacobi and his volunteer passengers, choked and asphyxiated by these sickening and suffocating fumes, were obliged to temporarily halt their observations.

In 1848, William Grove, a young British electrical machinery inventor, visited Penllergaer in Wales to see the experiments of John Llewelyn Dillwyn on a boat propelled by an electric motor. At the same time, Robert Anderson of Aberdeen, in Scotland, built the first rudimentary electric car. However, these three vehicles had encountered the same problems: bulky machinery, and limited autonomy caused by a weak battery, in contrast to Trouvé's compact solution.

Since Gustave Trouvé had left his native region to go and work in Paris, the capital had been receiving a radical face-lift. Commissioned by Emperor Napoleon III, Georges-Eugène Haussmann, prefect of the Seine, had been carrying out a massive program of new boulevards, parks and public works. In 1881, the main boulevards were equipped with electric street lighting.

As the electrical industry began to grow, there was an increasing need for parts. A significant breakthrough was made that would eventually lead to the industrial manufacture of lead-acid batteries. A Paris-based chemical engineer called Camille Alphonse Faure had taken out a patent that significantly improved the design of Gaston Planté's lead-acid battery. He had found a way to coat lead plates with a paste of lead oxides, sulphuric acid and water, which was then cured by being gently warmed in a humid atmosphere. The curing process caused the paste to change to a mixture of lead sulphates, which adhered to the lead plate. During charging the cured paste was converted into electrochemically active material (the "active mass") and gave a substantial increase in capacity compared with Planté's battery.

Alongside this, Trouvé had devised a method of making powerful magnets:

> My straight magnets can carry up to 14 times their weight. And if the magnet is bent round in horse-shoe form, the load can be quadrupled, that is, from 45 to 56 times its weight. Magnets in these conditions, equipped with coils having 120 meters [130 yards] of wire N° 36, with a resistance of 240 ohms, make up, placed in an envelope of hardened wood, sensitive and powerful Bell telephones.[13]

In the autumn of 1881, Paris decided to organize an international electrical exhibition to display the advances in electrical technology since the small electrical display at the Universal Exposition only three years before. Georges Berger was the commissioner general. Aside from the provision by the French government of the building, the Palais de l'Industrie, in the Champs-Élysées, the exhibition was privately financed. The organizers planned to donate profits to scientific works in the public interest. A total of 1,786 exhibitors came from the United Kingdom, the United States of America, Germany, Italy and Holland, as well as from France. It caused a great stir.

Many of the 880,000 visitors had their first-ever experience of an electric tram. The tram ran from the Place de la Concorde to the galleries of the Palais de l'Industrie (Industry Palace), where they were able to discover and marvel at a new branch of science: electrical engineering.

The first thing that hit them in the center of the nave of the Palais was "The Lighthouse of Progress," a full-scale electric lighthouse of the Ministry of Public Works, which projected alternating beams of red and white light in every direction. At its foot was an artificial clover-leaf-shaped pond. Circulating around the pond was Trouvé's electric skiff, enabling visitors to enjoy seeing "its little evolutions on the clement waters of this tranquil ocean of Lilliput."

The boat's very first trip was witnessed by the commissioner of the Exposition, by a representative of the *Revue Scientifique*,[14] and by a representative of the Russian navy. Contrary to accounts published much later, Trouvé did not exhibit his electric tricycle.

There were other crowd-pulling features. There was Monsieur Clément Ader's *theâtrophone*. This was a suite of four telephone rooms where every evening, between eight and eleven o'clock, you could listen to singing and orchestral music transmitted via microphones from the Grand Opera.

Then, floating under the roof of the gallery was the oblong aerostat of the Tissandier brothers. It measured 3.5 meters (11 ft.) long, 1.30 meters (4.27 ft.) diameter at the middle. It had a volume of 2 cubic meters (71 cubic feet) and 200 grams (7 oz.). Filled with pure hydrogen, it had a lifting force of 2 kg (4 lbs.). The lower part of the nacelle of the little balloon was equipped with a minuscule electric motor, built by Trouvé and weighing just 220 grams (7.7 oz.). What made the motor unique was that to make it lightweight, parts of it had been machined in the then-revolutionary aluminum.

The shaft of this little machine was connected to a two-bladed propeller, made of wood and textile, and turning at six and a half revolutions per second. Energy came from two small, secondary lead-acid batteries

1881. The International Electricity Exhibition at the Industry Palace, Paris. At the foot of the electric Progress Lighthouse, one notes Trouvé's electric launch. Among those who enjoyed a ride was Alexander Graham Bell, inventor of the telephone, especially over from America to meet Trouvé (Musée EDF Electropolis, Mulhouse).

supplied by the Tissandiers and Trouvé's friend, Gaston Planté. The motor and the batteries had a weight inferior to the lifting force of the balloon and would be raised by this when it was filled with hydrogen.

Before arriving at the exhibition, the team had tested out the aerostat in the rooms of the Conservatoire des Arts et Métiers, with the enthusiastic approval of its director, Hervé Mangon. Further experiments were then made in the workshops of M. Lachambre, in the rue de Vaugirard.

For the exhibition, in full view of the public, the little aerostat was tethered to a guide rope, which towed it to and fro like a circus horse. It had a stern rudder to enable it to move right or left. Throughout the exhibition, demonstrations of the aerostat were given twice a week—on Thurs-

days at 4:30 p.m. and on Saturdays at 9 p.m. Tissandier now calculated that with Trouvé's motor, a scaled-up aerostat, in calm weather, could reach between 20 and 25 km/h (12 mph and 15 mph).

Back on the ground, Trouvé, at Stand 551, was again exhibiting his instruments for medical electricity: "M. Trouvé is an

Top: 1881. This rare close-up is the first photograph ever taken of an electric boat. Note the size of the batteries, not accounting for the fumes they must have emitted! (collection Musée de l'Air et de l'Espace–Le Bourget). *Bottom:* 1881. Tissandier's Aéronef with a Trouvé motor at the Paris International Electricity Exhibition (Musée EDF Electropolis, Mulhouse).

ingenious researcher and a skilled constructor and he brought interesting devices to the Exhibition."[15] These included the Trouvé-Onimus interrupter, the polyscope and an updated explorer-extractor with an electric bell that tinkled the moment the foreign body (such as a bullet) was located.

Elsewhere in the exhibition was a *pianista* of the type invented some 18 years before by Henri Fourneaux of Paris. This was the first pneumatic piano player with mechanical fingers; it had punched folding cards for the tune sheets. The system was based on technology developed for card-operated looms. Many such pianistas had been manufactured at one of Jérome Thibouville's four factories. But this one was included in the exhibition because it was driven by an electric motor, "very similar to that of Trouvé," encased in a box measuring only 19 centimeters (7 inches) long by 12 cm (4 inches) wide by 9 cm (3 inches) thick. It had two Siemens

1881. The Tissandier airship at this exhibition was powered by a special version of Trouvé's electric motor, made lighter by his having built certain parts in aluminum (Musée EDF Electropolis, Mulhouse).

coils slightly off-center, turning between the poles of a three-branched electromagnet. The electric pianista worked perfectly, to the great satisfaction of the curious who each day gathered around it. It was thus one of the first electrically powered music players in the world, and could be considered the remote ancestor of modern digital audio players.[16]

Also present at the exhibition, a Monsieur Journeaux had adapted a sewing machine. Instead of a hand or treadle-mechanism, a Trouvé motor was hidden under the table. A single, light movement of the foot was enough whenever Madame wished to start it, to stop it, to slow it down, or to accelerate it. Eight years later the New Jersey–based Singer Manufacturing Co. introduced its first mass-produced electric sewing machines.

Finally, among the toys, Monsieur G. Parent was exhibiting toy trains and boats, again powered by Trouvé's miniature motor.

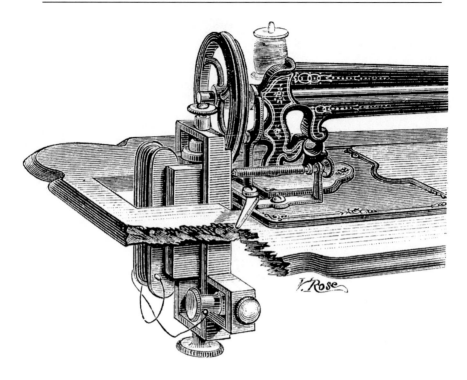

1881. Trouvé was the first to electrify the sewing machine, even if Singer of America was the first to manufacture one, some eight years later (Musée EDF Electropolis, Mulhouse).

Among those visiting the exhibition was Professor Alexander Graham Bell, 34 year-old Scottish-born inventor of the telephone and the photophone, having travelled over from Boston, USA.

On 11 December 1878, Bell had delivered a paper to the American Academy of Arts and Sciences, Boston, entitled "Trouvé's laboratory." The proceedings state only that "Professor Bell gave a description of various ingenious appliances of M. Trouvé of Paris."

On 2 July 1881, President James A. Garfield, accompanied by his sons, was walking through downtown Washington when he was shot by a man called Charles J. Guiteau. Once he had been rushed to the White House, the main concern was for the bullet that had entered his back. Where was it? Could it be found in time?

Professor Bell had already been considering how he might combine Trouvé's explorer-extractor with his telephonic receiver. Indeed, he had made a sketch for this on 25 June 1881. With the president at death's door, he now had an urgent reason to build a working prototype.

In a letter written on 8 July by Mrs. Mabel Bell to a relative, she states,

I cannot possibly persuade him to sit, just these days as he is hard at work day and night trying to arrange Trouvé's idea for the President's benefit. He does not believe that Trouvé ever went beyond the mere idea, at all events there is no instrument here, and no one knows anything about it so he is trying to carry it out himself. His great difficulty is the necessity of having a very bright light without heat, and he has not solved it yet. When he has, he is going to have physicians experiment with it and if successful will take the instrument to Washington. Whether the doctors there will accept it is of course another thing, but they all say that by and by the President's life will hang on their finding the position at all events of the abscess they expect will form over the bullet.[17]

Alexander Graham Bell and his wife came over to Paris, where Bell met Trouvé, who took him for a little ride in the exhibition electric launch (Alexander Graham Bell National Historic Site, Parks Canada).

Soon after, Bell took his "bullet probe," his version of the explorer-extractor, to the White House. The ends of the primary coil were connected to a battery and those of the secondary coil were fastened to posts of the telephone. When a piece of metal was placed by the circuit breaker, a hum could be heard in the telephone receiver. When tried on the president's left side, it did not locate. The device's signal was thought to have been distorted by the metal bed springs. Later the detector was found to work perfectly and would have found the bullet had the chief doctor, Willard Bliss, allowed Bell to use the device on Garfield's right side as well. After a steady deterioration in his health, Garfield died on 11 September 1881.

Weeks later, Bell decided to voyage across the Atlantic to visit the Paris Electrical Exposition and in particular to meet up with Trouvé:

Mr. A.G. Bell arrived in London 20 October at 6 o'clock from Leeds. I joined him and we started for Paris at 8 o'clock pm, arriving in Paris this morning and went to the Continental Hotel.... In the evening we went with Henck to the Electrical Exhibition. We saw M. Trouvé in his electrical boat and Mr. Bell took a ride in the boat with him. M. Trouvé then took us to see his private exhibit. We then returned to the hotel.[18]

As Barral recounts in his biography, Bell explained to Trouvé: "I wanted to surprise you among your works that I so much admire. In addition, I want to take a complete collection of all your inventions back to America, because for me they make up the highest expression of the perfection and the ingenuity of the electric science in France."[19] Bell also informed Trouvé that had he been based in America, he would be a very wealthy man. Trouvé smiled modestly.[20]

This great exhibition did not escape certain electrical faults and breakdowns. A Lane-Fox lamp set fire to several elements of the decor, and several other electrical faults caused flames here and there. Seeing one of these, Baron Rothschild announced that he would remain faithful to the more reliable gas. The highly popular Siemens tram killed a man on the Cours de la Reine. Although this was not due to an electrical fault, the fact that the tram was electric did not help the cause, as gas production companies were quick to point out.

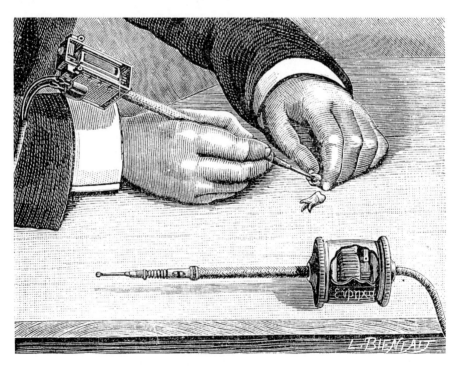

Trouvé adapted his little motor to power one of the first dental drills (from Georges Barral, *L'histoire d'un inventeur*, 1891).

The exhibition over, the International Jury awarded specially struck gold, silver and bronze medals to virtually every exhibitor, including over a dozen to U.S. exhibitors such telephone rivals Elisha Gray of the Western Electric Company and Alexander Graham Bell's collaborator Sumner Tainter. Trouvé was awarded a silver medal.

Trouvé continued to seek out applications for his inventions. By modifying the design of his miniature motor that had been installed in the model airship of the Tissandier brothers, he next constructed a device for Doctor Laillier, at the Saint-Louis Hospital. Lallier wished to use it to treat the lupus in skin diseases. The instrument, weighing no more than 150 g (5.3 oz.), could be easily held in the hand and moved around like a pencil. Trouvé called this instrument an "electric drill." It was later abandoned because the softness of the skin tissues did not support the use of the drill. But the efficient and reasonably priced motor was soon attracting the dental profession.

Trouvé was not the first to electrify a dental drill. Dr. George F. Green, a mechanic at the S.S. White Company of Philadelphia, is credited with developing an "electric burring machine" in 1872. Twelve years later, a Professor Griscome added a flexible tube between the storage battery and the dental engine. S.S. White bought this and added a modified sewing machine motor. But the American model was neither so compact nor so lightweight as Trouvé's.

For several years, the drawings Trouvé made of his succession of instruments, and the photos taken of them, would be converted into fine engravings by the Poyet brothers, Louis and Jérôme, based at N° 67, rue de la Victoire. Many of these first appeared in the Tissandier brothers' journal *La Nature*.

By this time Gaston Tissandier had taken out his patent called "Application of Electricity to Aerial Navigation" and was forming a company with the intention of scaling-up his aerostat to man-carrying dimensions.

The Legion of Honor, or in full the National Order of the Legion of Honour (French: Ordre national de la Légion d'honneur) remains the highest decoration in France. On 29 December 1881 the legion declared: "Trouvé, Gustave Pierre, Constructor in Paris, has been named Chevalier de la Légion d'honneur by decree, on the 29 December 1881, based on the report from the Ministry of Posts and Telegraphs."[21] On 3 March 1882, Trouvé submitted the required papers:

> Monsieur the Grand Chancellor of the Légion of d'honneur. I have the honor of sending you enclosed the documents relative to my nomination into the Order of the Légion d'honneur. I have chosen as sponsor Monsieur Gaston Planté to whom you can hand over the insignia and the powers

necessary for my reception. Please accept, Monsieur Le Grand Chancellor, the homage of my profound respect and my distinguished sentiments.

G. Trouvé[22]

Raymond Gaston Planté lived at N° 56, rue de Tournelles, in Paris. Five years Trouvé's senior, he was known for his modesty, considering himself primarily a geologist, but he was also the inventor of the lead acid cell, the first rechargeable battery. It was Planté whose batteries had supplied energy to his friend's polyscope, tricycle, boat and the Tissandier model airship.

Planté, already a Chevalier de la Légion d'honneur, was made a commander the same year, with, as his sponsor, Georges Berger, general commissioner of the International Exhibition of Electricity. But he would not be decorated until five years later, on 21 January 1886. Trouvé wrote: "Gaston Planté, of whom we are forever honored to have been his friend, was modesty itself. He never looked for honors that had been so due to his fine works and to his noble life full of work, these honors that have so belatedly come for him, of which he only saw the dawn, and about which impartial posterity surrounds his memory more and more."[23]

From his workshop in the heart of Paris, Trouvé continued to innovate. He adapted his little motor to power an electric razor. In 1928, 46

years later, the first electric razor was patented in 1928 by the American manufacturer Col. Jacob Schick. The Remington Rand Corporation developed the electric razor further, first producing the Remington brand of razor in 1937.

With the Seine just down the road from his workshop, Trouvé continued to improve his electric boat. On 8 October 1882, to show the speed with which an electric boat could go around a race course, a "Trouvé" was launched onto the River Aube, near Troyes, five minutes before the starting gun. At gun-

1880. It was Gaston Planté who proposed that Trouvé be awarded the coveted Légion d'Honneur. Planté, who was revered worldwide as one of the major pioneers of lead-acid batteries, was a great friend and supporter of Trouvé (Musée EDF Electropolis, Mulhouse).

fire it accelerated away and covered over 3,200 meters (3,500 yards) in 17 minutes, making four turns around the buoys, for a speed of 11 km/h (6.8 mph). This boat was also demonstrated on the Seine at Rouen.

Electric technology was now making ever bolder steps around the world. Over in England, inventor Joseph Swan's house in Gateshead became the first in the world to be lit by light bulbs, and the world's first electric-light illumination in a public building was for a lecture Swan gave in 1880.

In the United States, the Edison Company established the first investor-owned electric utility in 1882 on Pearl Street, New York City. It was on September 4, 1882, that Tom Edison switched on his Pearl Street generating station's electrical power distribution system, which provided 110 volts direct current (DC) to 59 customers in lower Manhattan.

Still in New York, three months later, at his home in New York City, Edward H. Johnson, vice-president of the Edison Electric Company, proudly displayed his Christmas tree, with its 80 red, white and blue electric light bulbs the size of walnuts. This was the first time a Christmas tree had been lit by electric lights. Previously candles had been glued with melted wax to tree branches. As Johnson lived in one of the first areas of New York City to be wired for electric service, this innovation was possible.

Those who regularly subscribed to *Scientific American* magazine would have discovered a full-page article about Gustave Trouvé in the 9 December 1882 Supplement. It was translated from an article by Georges Dary in the French magazine *Electricité*. This was the first time that Trouvé's works were presented in detail to the American public, including Edison. But by this time, his inventions were being reported around Europe by *The Electrician* (London), *La Electricidad* (Madrid), *Electrotechnisher Anzeiger* (Vienna), and *L'Elettricità* (Italy).

On 25 November 1882 Edison's and Swan's light bulbs were used for a very dramatic event. This was the opening night of the brand new Savoy Theatre in the heart of London, the first to be lit entirely by electricity. This was provided by a 120 hp steam-powered generator placed just outside the theater. The audience, used to gas-lit theaters, was a little anxious. To set their minds at rest, the manager, Richard d'Oyly Carte, made one of his rare on-stage appearances. He was carrying a light globe. He wrapped it in muslin and then smashed it with a hammer. The audience gasped. This extinguished the light, but then Carte held up the muslin to demonstrate that it was not even singed. He was given a standing ovation.

Then the electric lights were dimmed and the première of Gilbert and Sullivan's fairy opera *Iolanthe* began. In the last scene, the fairy queen and her three chief attendants tripped onto the stage, each wearing an electric star in their hair, while carrying a discreetly hidden battery. The effect of this brilliant spark of electricity was wonderful. The audience applauded with delight.

A program announced, "The entire Theatre, Stage and Auditorium, is lighted by Electricity. The arrangements for this lighting, and for the Electric Stars on the Fairies' heads, are carried out by Siemens Bros. & Co. (Limited), the lamps used being Swan's Incandescent Lamps." The lamps were supplied by the Edison and Swan United Electric Light Company, better known as Ediswan.

Iolanthe ran for 398 performances. In February 1883 a very special matinee performance was given to which London's entire theater community was invited. On this occasion, "a still wider application of electricity than had previously been ventured upon was adopted. Electric sparks glittered on the heads of all the fairies instead of being limited as before to the leading members of the band, and the effect thus produced was charming in the extreme. Of course this arrangement involves the carrying of a small battery by each electrically lit fairy; but the details are all so admirably managed that no inconvenience seems to be experienced."[24]

Over in New York, on 26 March 1883, Alva Vanderbilt, the highly competitive wife of millionaire William K. Vanderbilt, threw a masquerade ball at her French-style chateau at 1 West 57th Street, at the corner of 5th Avenue, the largest private residence ever to be built in an American city.

Among the hundreds invited were the highest members of New York society wearing some breathtaking costumes. But it was Alva's own sister-in-law, Alice, wife of Cornelius Vanderbilt, who upstaged every one when she showed up as "Electric Light." Her stunning gown, made of white satin and trimmed with diamonds, was created by Charles Frederick and Jean-Phillippe Worth, of the House of Worth, based both in New York and Paris, world-famous as much for opera and theater costumes as for high fashion. What made Alice's costume really sparkle was the torch she held above her head, powered by batteries hidden in her bustle, reminiscent, some thought, of the Statue of Liberty then under construction and three years away from completion. Alice Vanderbilt told her admirers that it was in honor of Thomas Edison's new Pearl Street power station. But those New Yorkers and Londoners who had visited Paris, knew full well that this special stage effect was also being marveled at thanks to the skillful engineer Trouvé.

FOUR

A Point of Light

Today, many millions of mass-produced, battery-powered headlamps are in regular use for a wide range of tasks including disaster rescue work, subaquatic activities, mining, speleology or quite simply popular outdoor activities such as hiking. Although head-mounted lighting likely started with candles, problems with exposed flame and hot dripping wax motivated the development of better alternatives.

The first battery-powered unit, and then the first batch of them, were made by Trouvé in answer to a request from a 38-year-old surgeon working in the town of Rouen, 70 miles from Paris and the historic capital of the northwest region of Upper Normandy. Doctor Paul Hélot, consultant surgeon at Rouen Maternity Hospital, had already experimented with use of electricity to provoke contractions in pregnant women. At the beginning of 1883, Hélot had an idea that he believed only Gustave Trouvé could help him to realize: a lamp that a doctor could wear on his forehead to better see the area he was inspecting or operating on. Trouvé devised a light bulb enclosed in a metal cylinder whose bases were taken up by a reflector and a convergent lens. It was adjustable in every direction and was mounted on a forehead patch held by a strap and buckle onto the physician's forehead, passing behind his head to lead to a Trouvé battery.

From February to October, Trouvé and Hélot were to correspond over the technical challenges, manufacture, promotion and copycatting of their "photophore." These hand-written letters, conserved over 130 years by the Hélot family, give a priceless insight into how the inventor developed one of his innovative instruments:

20 February 1883
Tomorrow I will send you the polyscope and everything that lends itself to it. I have made a photophore, which is being nickel-plated. There are great difficulties in obtaining a regular circle of light with two lenses because the

69

light bulb does not present one point of light, but with this closed, a single lens is better than two. I have attempted to make a lamp with one luminous point in the center, which will overcome this difficulty....
All to you. G. Trouvé.

At 3:40 p.m., 30 March 1883, Trouvé applied for the principal patent for the photophore:

Up to now for certain operations—surgical or for medical investigations of the larynx, the genitals, etc., doctors have used a sort of reflector instrument, adapted to the forehead and sending rays through a luminous focus onto the parts to examine. This system presents the following capital disadvantage: each time the patient makes a movement, one is obliged to move the luminous focus.... My invention consists essentially in the arrangement of a frontal instrument, carrying its light focus by being able to move around in all directions around a fixed articulation point. The instrument, once adapted to the forehead can be directed at will and follow the movements of the patient, without paralyzing the use of the doctor's hands.[1]

5 April 1883
I have put 24 photophores into production.... The lenses are being supplied by the Société des Lunetiers....[2] I am not partisan to embossing your name on the instrument and here is my reason. Doctors and mainly specialists will never agree to acquire the instrument, claiming that they cannot show their patients the name of a colleague as inventor of an instrument they are using. No doctor in Paris wanted to buy my clockwork inductor if I made the name of Dr. Onimus feature on it.

As for explanatory notes supplied with the instrument, your name will always be there as well as in all the publications. Whenever I will be able to put in on the instrument without inconvenience, I will

Gustave Trouvé. This rare portrait of Trouvé is archived at the BNF in Paris (BNF).

1883. Doctor Paul Hélot, chief surgeon at the hospitals of Rouen, contacted Trouvé and asked him to design and construct a battery-powered lamp that could be worn on the forehead, so leaving the wearer's hands free to operate (Fonds Hélot).

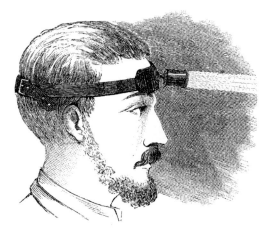

1883. Trouvé had constructed the first photophore within weeks of Dr. Paul Hélot's request (from Georges Barral, *L'histoire d'un inventeur*, 1891).

always do so because foreigners will have no objection. I will even put it on all of them if you so wish, but sales will be reduced.

On 16 April, the Hélot-Trouvé photophore was presented in Paris to the Academy of Sciences at the Institute de France by M. Boulay and to the Academy of Medicine the following day by Profess Georges Dujardin-Beaumetz of the Cochin Hospital. Trouvé to Hélot: "The two official presentations have taken place successfully."

6 May 1883

I am still waiting for you to tell me about the medical journal articles— as I've only received one. I have nevertheless seen:

> *Le Progrès Médical*
> *Gazette des Hôpitaux*
> *Revue Médicale Française et Étranger*
> *La France Médicale*

Les Mondes should have published it in today's number that I have not yet received. *L'Electricité* has already published it. I do not know why *La Nature* has not published it. Probably because they would have had to indicate it as a first. With so much publicity, don't you think?

I have only received one order and it's from Gaiffe.

A little mystification. Several of our colleagues have come to see me in good faith and asked to look at the instrument of Doctor Poyet, the pupil of Doctor Fauvel. It's so funny![3]

---

12 May 9:30 pm

Dear Mr. Hélot,

I received your two dispatches; the second above all gave me pleasure. On reflecting a little, I have not been surprised, indeed on the contrary I knew that it could not have been otherwise in your hands. The photophores are progressing, yet nothing but badly. I have been obliged to alter all those which had been made (some thirty in number). The half-bowl lens was not outside enough … on the light as you must have noticed on the little one I sent you. I believe I have surpassed myself in what it was possible imagine, the most simple; you know, all conceit put aside, it's certainly wonderful.

1882. Trouvé's letterheaded paper certainly did not miss a punch! (author's collection).

Left: **1883. One of the several batteries constructed at the rue Vivienne workshop for universal use (from Georges Barral, *L'histoire d'un inventeur*, 1891). *Right:* 1883. This is perhaps the best surviving example of the photophore Hélot-Trouvé. It is conserved at the Science Museum, London, UK (Science & Society Picture Library).**

One should already think about having the plates made for your brochure so as to have the plates a little better than those of the photophore, which left a lot to be desired. They are even poorly done. One must finally take away the name of Poyet, which has been made too prominent and has caused among one quarter of the doctors the somewhat amusing surprise that I already told you about. The proves once again that we do not read in France and that we are a little carried away by nature and not by our education to judge a little superficially or glance at a title and the figurine where one reads Poyet, and here you have an instrument by Doctor Poyet, the laryngologist, student of Fauvel!

Your brother has asked me for the second—his wish is my command. You will show him the maneuver these holidays....

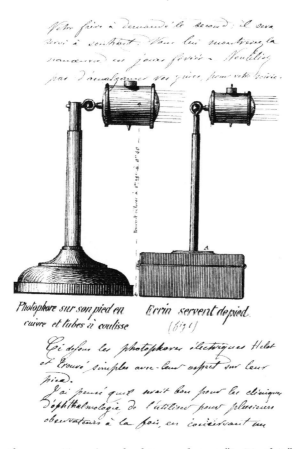

1883. Over the years, Trouvé, under his pseudonym "L. Bienfait," did many preparatory drawings of his wide range of instruments for the engravings by Poyet. Among the rare cache of letters he wrote to Dr. Hélot, in this one he draws out an idea for the multiple use of the photophore. Notice also his style of handwriting (Fonds Hélot).

Above are the simple Hélot-Trouvé photophores with their angle on the base. I have thought that it would be good for ophthalmic clinics to use for several observations at a time, by considering a unique light mounted on a stand. This device could give service by enabling 2, 3, 4, etc., observers to do ophthalmology simultaneously without increasing the expense. The light as such used in all directions would again be more than sufficient for the ophthalmoscope. If I do not make it immediately, one must at least define it and speak about it in the brochure so as to cut the grass from under the feet of those who will not miss out in walking on our tracks. We have already incurred enough costs in order for us not to stop so short. So do the editing or the text for the brochure already. As I have sent my brochure about electric lighting to all architects and to all engineers, I will also send it to doctors, but only with yours. In this way, they will present themselves reciprocally, the one with the other. One must hurry because, with the publicity made about this instrument, we have aroused the curiosity even of those previously disinterested.

As my intention is to put our two names on the little plate that will figure on the sliding tubes of the photophore, one must order a punch to be made by Poyet.

All to you, G. Trouvé

He adds:

This photophore will be placed in the middle of a round or square table around which four ophthalmologists and four patients would position themselves. Thus the ophthalmologists could, by the play of lenses, give themselves the desired light—converging, diverging or parallel—at will, without following the other observers. In a word, the device with a unique focus would supply lighting effects to each independent observer. Just as separate devices would do. Laryngologists could even use it by increasing the lighting power and lengthening the focus of the lenses, which is very easy to do. It should be noted that the light intensity does not change for each focus—whether it has one, two or four. For the rest I have already noticed, concerning the reflector, that in this case because of the sphericity of the globe, which gives out the light, it becomes completely useless. (I made the light with flat and more or less parallel sides without increasing the intensity very much, which is nevertheless good to report.)

So, as of today, the *photophore électrique Hélot-Trouvé*, simple or composed, is ready for a beam for two, three, etc. That of two and four can answer all needs, and then, it will enable a second message to the Academy, which will recall the first, which should not be ignored. I am stopping, because it's time to go and dine.

All to you a second time, G Trouvé.

---

15 May 1883

I saw Gaston Tissandier on Sunday and he will carry an article in his journal, probably in the next number. Your letter pleased him and he will reply to you.[4]

Due to his work on the photophore, Trouvé found little time to contribute to his other interests, such as flight. On 24 May 1883 he wrote to Dr. Hureau de Villeneuve, permanent secretary-general of the Aerial Navigation Society (Société de Navigation Aérienne) regarding an aeronautical exhibition at the Palais du Trocadéro:

> I am very grateful to you for having wanted to tell me about the interesting exhibition that you are preparing at the Trocadéro. I would have been very flattered to have been able to feature a large number of my instruments concerning aerostation, but the time is really short to prepare such an exhibit to my satisfaction. Nevertheless if you really would like to give me, via one of the secretaries, the information necessary to the agreement that is incumbent to the exhibitor, I could perhaps take an immediate determination and make time to do something acceptable.

A week later he again wrote to de Villeneuve: "It was scarcely my intention to exhibit at the Trocadéro, but since you are employing me in a very special way, I am going to be agreeable to you. I would have few things, my bird being partly destroyed. I have a little glass showcase 2.30 m [7.5 feet] long and 1.90 m [6.2 feet] wide."

Trouvé needed a holiday like anyone else who worked as hard as he did. On 13 July he wrote to Hélot: "I am leaving this evening for Courseuil, where I will stay until Monday evening by the seaside to take a little rest. Perhaps it's not very patriotic but it will be healthy for me."[5]

Courseulles (Calvados) was the main supplier of oysters to Paris. These were transported in wagons called *les Comètes*, named after the passing of a comet back in 1819. But for the previous eight years, there had been a railway connection to Courseulles. Trouvé most probably stayed at the Hôtel des Etrangers (established 1827), run by Monsieur Leboeuf, with a set menu in the gardens. It was also called the Normandy Hotel. There was also an oyster restaurant run by a Mme Chedeville, not to mention boatyards, lace-making establishments, oyster farms and a sugar-refinery.

While on holiday he must have been reflecting on the possible applications of the photophore, for on 25 July he wrote:

> Dear Mr. Hélot,
>
> We did not understand your dispatch very well. We thought that the words, additions and corrections were related to the bills that you have asked for, while they were related to my previous letter.
>
> Here are the applications outside the medical applications about which I have been thinking:
>
> (1) On the helmets of firemen for moving through the darkness while leaving their two hands free.
> (2) For musicians—mainly for military music, enabling reading the music in the darkness, so doing away with smoking torches or any light capable of causing accidents.

(3) For gas workers, enabling them to look for leaks without fear of accident and at the same time to carry out repairs immediately.

(4) For miners or workers called to go down in the cages.

(5) For aeronauts (I have delivered one to Count de Dion for his nocturnal accessories).

(6) For sailors, who could then read the indications of their instruments in the night without any danger.

(7) I have already fitted it to several small pleasureboats as a projector. It enables picking out any obstacle or other boat from one hundred meters with which one might have a collision.[6]

(8) Finally, any situation where it is necessary to have light and to have both hands free.

For each of these cases, we could develop the applications as much as you like and indeed others are so simple that they think themselves up.

All to you G. Trouvé

Trouvé added a note:

I am at present applying it with success in a theater play by replacing the ordinary lenses with pieces of every color cut into facets so as to imitate precious stones. The effect is amazing! I will have the pearl of Brazil and the diamonds of the Cape approaching the effects that M. Trouvé is busy obtaining.

I have written these things to you a little in a hurry, you have understood them sufficiently to carry out their development if it takes place.

Among Dr. Hélot's hobbies was graphology, linking handwriting with personality. A simply glance at Trouvé's handwriting reveals that here was a man in a hurry.

On 4 August 1883, Trouvé made the following addition to his original photophore patent:

I quote its application to hairstyles, clothes, theatre accessories or ornaments, taking as an example, diadems, bracelets and necklaces … a completely new effect, I set these stones, real or fake, white or colored, in a socket designed to carry my luminous focus, powered by a strong source of suitable electricity.

In the next two decades, *"la femme à l'étoile,"* a woman carrying a radiating star or diadem on her forehead, became the pin-up for electricity. She would inspire novelists, painters and choreographers and also feature at exhibitions. Another description of her is *"la fée électricité"* – "the Electricity Fairy."

On 3 September 1883, an adaptation of a novel by the highly popular Jules Verne, *Kéraban-le-Tetu*, was presented at the Gaîté Théâtre, in Paris. It was a play in 5 acts, with 20 scenes. In the critiques of the play, more attention was given to the special effect of the luminous electric diamond, supplied by Trouvé, than to the play itself. Verne, feeling he had been

When in 1883, Trouvé fitted his frontal headlamp to his electric boat as a projector, to pick out any obstacle or other boat from 100 meters with which one might have a collision, it was the first time an electric headlamp had been used on any vehicle, land or water (from Georges Barral, *L'histoire d'un inventeur*, 1891).

eclipsed, literally, forbade its use in the subsequent performances. After only 49 performances, the play closed, perhaps because the light had gone out of it.

Verne was of course most interested in electric propulsion. In his book *Twenty Thousand Leagues Under the Sea* (1869/70), Verne remained silent about the way in which Captain Nemo uses electricity for his submarine *Nautilus*. In *Mathias Sandorf* (1885) there are some vessels called "Electrics," while an electric airship features in *"Robur-le-Conquérant"* (1886). It is strange that Verne never mentioned Trouvé.

A growing number of ophthalmologists were rapidly adopting the Hélot-Trouvé *"photophore frontal,"* with its travelling case provided. They used it for the removal of fibroids, laparotomies, tracheotomies, cataracts, and other procedures. Louis de Wecker, a highly respected Parisian ophthalmologist, wrote in the *Revue clinique d'oculistique* (10 October 1883):

> The instruments of M. Trouvé, mainly the photophore, which he has built
> with the collaboration of Dr. Hélot (of Rouen) are known by everyone; but
> something strange, those who have the greatest interest in possessing a pow-

erful source of light, the ophthalmologists, have until now paid no attention to it; the reason is doubtless that, overburdened with an ever bigger and more expensive set of tools, they do not want to be cluttered even more by the batteries necessary for electric lighting.

De Wecker went on to describe the *photophore frontal* and reported having carried out a cataract operation while wearing it.

Another ophthalmologist who adopted the photophore was Xavier Galezowski (1832–1907). This Polish émigré had established an important ophthalmologic clinic in Paris, training many prominent ophthalmologists and treating numerous patients. Three years later, Galezowski introduced the use of "plaquettes" to cover the corneal surface. These were gelatin squares that had been soaked in mercury chloride and were designed to reduce the possibility of infection after cataract surgery. This might be considered as the first use of a therapeutic contact lens.

Another Polish researcher based in Paris who paid a visit to Trouvé's workshop was Dr. Julian Ochorowicz. Ochorowicz was a pioneer of empirical research in psychology and conducted studies in occultism, spiritualism, hypnosis and telepathy. It was for his experiments in hypnosis that he asked Trouvé to make him a small, inwardly magnetized tube, which the hypnotized patient would wear on their index finger for a matter of minutes. The ring was then removed and the patient asked to describe their feelings: from tingling to acute pain. In Trouvé tradition, the device was called a hypnoscope.

Like Trouvé, Ochorowicz was a versatile researcher. In 1877 back in Poland, he had elaborated the theory for a monochromatic television, to be constructed as a screen comprising bulbs that would convert transmitted images into groups of light points. While in Paris, in 1885, on several occasions, he demonstrated his own improved telephone by connecting the building of the Ministry of Posts and Telegraph with the Paris Opera, four kilometers away.

Trouvé, in collaboration with Paul Hélot, continued to innovate with his usual speed: from a photophore mounted on a rod and a stand; to another version mounted on a foot sleeve; then a micrographic photophore, enabling the lamp to slide along the stand and take horizontal, vertical or oblique positions.

M. Henri van Heurck, director of the botanical gardens at Anvers in Belgium and an expert on the tiny siliceous-shelled plants called diatoms, was the first to replace paraffin lighting with electric lighting, when he used the Trouvé-Hélot electric photophore to take some superb microphotographs of his specimens.

One of the very first installations of electric lighting at home was planned and carried out by Trouvé at a Monsieur Schlesinger's home in Paris. Schlesinger was already very pleased with his electric skiff, assembled by Trouvé, for cruising up and down the Seine. His sitting room, office, dining room, bedroom and kitchen were lit individually or at the same time. Among Trouvé's other clients for domestic electric lighting were a Doctor Pietkiewicz, and a Monsieur Bartholini for his greenhouses on reception days.

Trouvé also put together lamp stands and candelabra where the user could choose either downward-pointing electric lights or upward-pointing traditional candles. This was ingenious given that the supply of electricity was not always reliable. He patented these in France, England, Italy and Belgium.

Up to this point, Trouvé had patented and sold nothing in the United States.

On 25 September 1883, Trouvé wrote to Hélot,

It's indeed the excess of my occupations that has prevented me from replying to you but also the little annoyances over setting up the manufacture of the portable battery. This manufacturing is progressing, but there is still a slight problem concerning the lamp. The lights that I deliver now work perfectly with the large batteries, but they consume too much for the small batteries. So I shall not deliver until I have arrived at a light com-

1883. In supplying electric lighting to domestic homes, Trouvé ingeniously came up with hybrid lamps, which could work either using a candle or an electric light (from Georges Barral, *L'histoire d'un inventeur*, 1891).

pletely suitable for the little battery, otherwise I would be obliged to install two lights with the photophore.

I'll take care to finish your little dynamometric machine next week.

All the best to you, G. Trouvé

p.s. Completely overwhelmed at the moment with a light. *The contract with America is signed.* Everything is going well. Dr. Bellencontre has not only bought a photophore but another light installation. It's a serious competitor from this side only. I have, however, sent a brochure with prices to Dr. Osborn. I'm going to send him another.

One continues to pay us compliments from all sides, because the photophore is working wonderfully and its applications are expanding every day.

Trouvé had been setting up a deal with some U.S. investors:

A syndicate of American speculators was set up to exploit all the inventions of the new French Edison. He agreed on condition that he was paid a retainer of 700 dollars per week until the firm had assembled its capital; this income was paid for quite some time, but nothing ever came of the project, since the president of the syndicate committed suicide, having been ruined on the New York Stock Exchange.[7]

The same year, 1883, a 27-year-old Croatian engineer called Nikola Tesla, living in Paris and working for the Edison subsidiary, was unable to find a backer, either in the capital or in Strasbourg, for his two-phase induction motor. He left Europe to go and work for Edison in the United States. Thereafter, Tesla would take out patent after patent for electric motors and equipment, particularly the asynchronous motor, backed by American businessmen such as George Westinghouse. There is no record of Tesla ever having met Trouvé, but both electrical geniuses must have known if not admired the other.

On 4 October 1883, Trouvé wrote to Hélot:

I have not forgotten the portable battery; on the contrary, I am putting it forward with those of my jewels. Nevertheless, there is always a little gap to fill; the obligation to use two lights with different consumption corresponding to one big and one little battery.

By using finer filaments with equal light intensity, they are more exposed. However, I must choose one way or another. Compliments from all sides continue to be paid to us, because the photophore works wonderfully and its applications widen every day.

I am sending you by post the article of M. de Wecker from which I have taken an extract that I am sending with your brochure. It has made a great impact, as well; almost all the oculists of Paris are now working like that. I have improved the defect that resulted from the leaking of the liquid on a carpet or parquet. I do not deliver batteries without delivering with a big bowl in which the battery is placed. I have also paid careful attention to the manufacture of the bowls, a series of which were found defective. They will from now on be in pure rubber. I am not content with this; for eight months I have tried to have them in glass but am still not satisfied.

As I have patented the photophore, let me know about the imitators who you believed have come close to it. Commercial honesty no longer exists in this fine country of France, as abroad. I really believe that scientific honesty will also disappear.

In the next few days, I am going to send you the four lamps, the three bowls, together with two big bowls so that you are safe.

My regards to Madame Hélot and to all your family and a warm handshake to you.

There was, however, one day when Trouvé took some time off from his relentless photophore development to support and encourage his friends and article publishers, the Tissandier brothers, Gaston and Albert. They had been building the full-scale version of the tethered Trouvé-engined aerostat they had demonstrated at the Electrical Exposition two years before.

On 8 October 1883, at Auteuil, southwest Paris, the 28-meter (92-foot) airship rose up into the sky with the intrepid brothers on board. It was equipped with a D4 long-coil motor specially built in their workshops by Siemens Frères and weighing just 54 kg (119 lbs.). It was mounted on a wooden chassis with special transmission. Energy came from heavy duty dichromate-of-potash batteries. The two-bladed, canvas and bamboo pusher propeller turned at 180 rpm and could be warped by pulling on steel wires.

This was the first time an electric airship had taken to the skies. Thousands of Parisians, including Trouvé, looked upwards with awe and wonder. The airship flew at a gentle speed of 10 kilometers per hour (6 mph), passing over the Bois de Boulogne. It held its head against the wind, but the rudder had little effect and the Tissandiers had to land 20 minutes later, at Croissy-sur-Seine.

Back at the rue Vivienne workshops, Trouvé continued to make additional applications to his photophore patent: "for all toiletry accessories in general, and notably tie pins, hairpins, walking stick heads, to increase the effect or project a light."

As the year drew to a close, he scored a great theatrical success. On 14 December 1883, Théodore Dubois's pretty ballet *La Farandole* was presented by the Paris Opera at the Palais Garnier. In act 2, the spectator was presented with the grandiose amphitheater at Arles. It is the midnight hour. The infidel souls appear among the ruins, and they dance *la farandole* by the light of the moon.

The *Gazette de France* wrote, "It is unnecessary to say that the wandering souls of the dancers are skin and bone, dressed in white muslin,

1883. Nacelle of the Tissandier brother's electric airship, just before lift-off.
Directly below the nacelle is a bearded man wearing a straw boater, who has a
close resemblance to the few portrait engravings of our inventor (collection
Musée de l'Air et de l'Espace–Le Bourget).

1883. The Tissandiers' first electric airship was uncontrollable, due a weak rudder system (Musée EDF Electropolis, Mulhouse).

hair falling behind their heads. They are all wearing diadems on their foreheads, and when they throw themselves into graceful *rondeaux*, in the middle of rocks and old walls, you at once see a light shoot out from their diadems like a will-o'-the-wisp."

As scenic director, Trouvé had ingeniously and tastefully combined his *bijoux électriques* with the principle of the *photophore frontale*, with one remarkable addition: a miniature silver chloride battery developed by a Russian called Grigori Scrivanov, and discreetly concealed in the belts around the dancers' waists.

The *Gazette* continued: "The idea of the star of true fire, which suddenly lights up their foreheads, is charming and very novel, at least in Paris. These young ladies have a belt with a little electric wire attached to a glass globe. A simple gesture and there is light. It's modern progress put to the service of ancient dreams."[8] *La Patrie* exclaimed, "Each dancer has in her belt two little batteries. At a given moment, she presses a button, the star lights up. And the public is totally astonished to see the world overwhelmed: women who light up!"[9]

ACADÉMIE NATIONALE DE MUSIQUE : **La Farandole**
Ballet en trois actes, de MM. Philippe Gille, Arnold Mortier et L. Mérante ; musique de M. Théodore Dubois (1er, 2e et 3e actes).
Dessins de Henri MEYER. — Voir l'article *Théâtres*.

1883. In the ballet *La Farandole*, put on at the Paris Opera, Trouvé demonstrated the multiple effect of his *bijoux électriques* when a troupe of ballerinas danced around a recreation of the amphitheater at Arles (BNF).

Trouvé was not the first to contribute electric lighting effects to the theater. In 1849, electricity had been used for the first time in the Salle le Peletier at the new Paris Opera to spotlight the skating scene in act 3 of Giacomo Meyerbeer's opera *The Prophet*. This special effect of sunshine had required 360 Bunsen cells set up in a large room on the ground floor of the Opera. The ice skaters used a recent invention: roller skates. During 1850, this opera was presented throughout Germany, as well as in Vienna, Lisbon, Antwerp, New Orleans, Budapest, Brussels, Prague and Basel.

In 1849 the Paris Opera started using arc lights as special effects; the arc light was created by passing a strong current between a pair of carbon electrodes to create blindingly white light. Jean-Danie Colladon duplicated his light-guiding trick as a special effect in a ballet called *Elias and Mysis*. Then for Gounod's *Faust* in 1853, light from an arc lamp focused along a red-glass tube filled with water in a scene where the Devil (Mephistopheles) makes a stream of fire flash from a wine barrel.

In March 1884, the Trouvé-Hélot frontal headlamp was used for the first time in a disaster zone. At 8 a.m. on the 18th, Mme. Vendel, owner of an old house in the rue Saint-Denis, went down into her cellar with a candle in her hand. An explosion took place and the poor woman, engulfed in flames, was badly burned. That afternoon several police officers and two firemen entered the neighboring cellars to investigate. One policeman was holding a candle. There was a second explosion. Two officers were killed and the others seriously injured. One of the neighbors was an oil lamp manufacturer and the fumes from his oil tank must have drifted into the other cellars. The explosion could have been avoided if a naked flame had not been taken into those cellars.

The population of Paris was deeply disturbed by this terrible catastrophe, and the main newspapers devoted a lot of column inches to it. One paper stated that since the end of the previous year, the Paris Gas Company *has been using Trouvé's forehead photophore* to check gas counters and pipe work and that if such equipment had been used at Saint-Denis, the disaster might never have happened.

But the show must go on, this time at *Les Folies-Bergère* at 32 rue Richer in the ninth arrondissement. In contrast to the Paris Opera, their business was light entertainment, including operettas, comic opera, popular songs, and gymnastics. In 1882, the artist Édouard Manet had painted his now well-known *A Bar at the Folies-Bergère*, which depicts a bar-girl, one of the demimondaines, standing before a mirror. Now, in the spring of 1884, it was Trouvé's turn with *Le Ballet de Fleurs,* with music by Louis César Désormes, orchestral director at the Folies-Bergère, choreography by Gradelue and costumes by H. Gray. The audience was delighted when

20 pretty dancers, each one representing a different flower, came on stage wearing diadems in their hair that lit up, just like the chosen flowers in their bosoms.

Almost at the same time, across the English Channel, Trouvé was also highly appreciated at the Empire Theatre, Leicester Square, London, for *Chilpéric: Grand Music Spectacle, in Three Acts and Seven Tableaux.* The libretto was by Harry Farnie, the music was by Hervé Ronger, the designer was by Bruce Smith, the armor and jewels were by Hirsch of Paris and Genty of London, and the electric effects were by Trouvé of Paris.

In act 3, scene 6, a ballet of 50 Amazon women appeared on stage. They had been divided into four corps. Mlle Sismondi commanded the Diamond Corps, Mlle Aguzzi the Ruby Corps, Mlle Louie the Emerald Corps, and Mlle Matthews the Topax Corps. Each of the 50 girls was wearing a helmet, a shield and carrying a spear. After performing various evolutions with precision and grace, suddenly their armor lit up: four jewels on the helmet, five on the shield and one on the spear. Diamonds, rubies, emeralds and topaz all glittered and glowed.

Trouvé had been ingeniously working with Hirsch of Paris and Genty of London so that for the first time, three electric lamps were carried and manipulated by one person. This marvelous and gorgeous spectacle, never before seen on any stage, caused wild applause. Among those there to approve was a 30-year-old up-and-coming Irish playwright, recently married, called Oscar Wilde.

By the following week, every newspaper and magazine in the capital had written glowing reviews and the name "'Trouvé' is on the lips of many a Londoner"[10]:

> The last word in scenic magnificence was achieved in the third act, at the moment when an army of Amazons, carrying armor plated with silver, spears and shields, suddenly appeared in the light projected by more than four hundred electric incandescent lamps.... The instrument used for this occasion, and for the first time in a theatrical scene is the patented invention of M. Trouvé, of Paris. The movements of the Amazons so lit up by the electric light produced a wonderful effect, and they were only withdrawn from the scene to make way for new surprises.[11]

> This wonderful spectacle never before exhibited on any stage, evolved a hurricane of applause, which gathered fresh strength when the Amazons performed various evolutions and arranged themselves in successive tableaux.[12]

> And one incomparable effect, when the electric light is brought into play, and suddenly from spear, and shield and helmet of fifty Amazons, flashes

1884. One of the 50 Amazons adorned with luminous electric jewelry built by
"Trouvé of Paris" for the ballet *Chilpéric* at the Empire Theatre in London (from
Georges Barral, *L'histoire d'un inventeur*, 1891).

through many-colored glasses. The stage can but be compared to a perpetual kaleidoscope of color.[13]

~

The employment of the electric light in the forms of stars etc. on the dresses of the ballet has an extremely beautiful effect; and altogether the performance is among the most brilliant we have ever witnessed.[14]

~

Fifty beautiful ladies arranged in armor of exquisite design, after performing various brilliant evolutions with a precision and grace worthy of the utmost commendation, halted, and suddenly from their shields, their helmets, their glittering breastplates, even from their spears there was soon a dazzling electrical illumination of the most enchanting kind it is possible to imagine. The colors were varied and intensely brilliant; and the effect, contrasted as it was with the shadowy foliage of the distant forest was absolutely startling in its novelty and splendor. All London will talk of it when all London has seen it. Nothing to compare with it of its kind has been witnessed on the modern stage.[15]

Chilpéric ran for several months. Its designer, Bruce "Sensation" Smith, from working with Trouvé, went on producing such spectacular effects at London's Drury Lane Theatre, providing an inspiration for the infant silent cinema.

On 26 April 1884, the *New York Times* published an article entitled "Electric Girls":

The introduction of illuminated ballet girls has greatly added to the attractions of the spectacular stage. Girls with electric lights on their foreheads and batteries concealed in the recesses of their clothing first made their appearance a year ago. The Electric Girl Lighting Company, located in Gold Street, New York proposes to supply girls of fifty candle-power each in quantity to suit householders ... for everyday use from dusk till midnight—or as much later as may be desired, to illuminate a dinner, to help the troubled by the flicker of his gas light student in his studies. The girls are to be fed and clothed by the company, and customers will, of course, be permitted to select at the company's warehouse whatever style of girl may please their fancy.[16]

Once back in Paris, realizing that the weight of his batteries were restricting the dancers and artistes to wearing a limited number of luminous jewels, that summer of '84, Trouvé came up with and applied for a patent for the ingenious idea of combining his luminous "*foyers*" with reflecting mirrors, so giving the illusion of a much larger number of jewels. Thus a belt, necklace and bracelet of lights could, surrounded by just 5 mirrors, give the illusion of 15. The mirrors could be mounted in various ways depending on their use and could be flat, concave or convex. The system could be applied to all theater accessories—belts, bracelets, diadems, hair, helmets, shields, armor and sandals, as well as to decorative devices used in the town, or as a lamp or chandelier. His patent, N° 160901, was granted.

At the end of 1884, Trouvé was once again creator of special effects at the Théâtre des Nouveautés Parisiennes in the Boulevard des Italiens for the operetta *Le Château Tire-Larigot* by Ernest Blum with music by Gaston Serpette: "One suddenly saw magnificent luminous decorations appear on the clothing of the characters in the Château ... composed of a central headlight equipped with reflector and featuring a big diamond, surrounded by precious stones."

In the same play, Brasseur and Berthelier played cards; on the hat of each of these two actors, the public could see the cards of the opponent, brightly lit. At the same time, Alexandre Coquelin Junior, the master of the monologue, wore an electric pince-nez, built by Trouvé, for his play *The Hypnotiser* at the Théâtre de la Porte Saint-Martin. He was also behind the scenes at the Châtelet Theatre in Paris and the Victoria Theater in Berlin for *La Poule aux oeufs d'or (Hen with the golden eggs)*: "It's the palace of lights with its great ballet which has so much contributed to the success of the play. A human chandelier of women wearing some sixty light bulbs!"[17]

Another venue was the Éden-Concert at 17, boulevard de Sébastopol. Known through the capital as "la Comédie-Française des cafés-concerts," it was here for several evenings that the popular singer Maria Rivière and her composer husband Bruet performed *Les Amours d'une paire de candélabres* (*The loves of a pair of candelabras*), each of them holding twinkling staffs and wearing glittering jewels, as supplied by Trouvé.

Signora Francesca Zanfretta, a 23-year-old Milan-born dancer, was much admired for her Italian-style mime dancing. Among her acclaimed and sparkling performances, sometimes incorporating Trouvé's electric tiara, were those at London's Covent Garden, the Empire and the Prince of Wales theaters.

Alongside theatrical special effects, the applied electrician was continuing to investigate ways he could be of service in more serious matters. Concerned by the frequent and terrible fires that resulted from the accidental upsetting of paraffin or oil lamps, he conceived and patented an ingeniously simple device to stop such lamps from falling over. He fit a circular rod around the lamp from which a series of iron rods hung freely from hinges. Should the lamp start to fall over, either from its poor design or through the clumsiness of the user, two of these rods would swing outwards and stop its path. His patent, N° 162673, was granted.

He continued to keep his client in Rouen, Doctor Hélot, regularly informed. Using a simple delivery note and not his usual letter-headed paper, on June 11, 1884, Trouvé wrote to Hélot:

> I have received your esteemed letter and I immediately began to construct the latest model of my device for the firemen which will, I hope, be adopted by the city of Paris but not with the photophore because there is always someone in the Commissariat who wishes to give the impression of having made something. Nevertheless I will show it with the photophore. Tell me the deadline, because if I the new model is not ready, I will send you the old one.

In the margin, he added,

> I have something at this moment which is admirable; I have never made anything so ingenious for gaining money. I will launch it in one or two months.

On 14 July 1884, the Abbé Moigno, the first journalist to report on and to praise Trouvé, died at Saint-Denis, a suburb of Paris. A lunar crater of about 23 miles' diameter would be named in his honor.

The Tissandiers had been improving their electric airship or aerostat. On the afternoon of Friday, 26 September 1884, it took to the skies again, the brothers on board. Its rudder had been improved, and it flew for two hours, but it was unable to go against a strong headwind and landed at Marolles-en-Brie. During the flight, Gaston Tissandier was splashed with acid, but without harm.

Some weeks before, *La France*, the bigger and more powerful airship of French army engineers Colonel Rénard and Captain Krebs, made a perfectly controlled circuit flight from Chalais-Meudon. Its puller-propeller gave it greater steerability. Making another four such circuits during the next year, *La France* has since come to be considered *le dirigéable*. The Tissandier-Trouvé experiments were soon but a memory, eventually forgotten.

On 31 October 1884, employees of the Edison Electric Lighting Company went on a presidential campaign parade in New York. Every one of them wore an electric headlamp, but not battery-powered. The marchers were surrounded by a horse-drawn, electricity-generating plant dynamo made up of a steam engine, boiler and water tanks, and the electricity was conveyed to the bulbs on their heads by wires up their sleeves. Except for one stretch when mud clogged the water pipes and stopped the steam engine, it was "one of the most unique and attractive displays ever seen in a torchlight procession.... The lights flooding every nook and cranny of the streets passed through" and clearly showed "the perfection to which electric lighting machinery has been brought."[18]

FIVE

Lamps Without Danger

Moved by the catastrophe of the rue Saint-Denis and adapting his device used for the electric diadems in theatrical spectacles in Paris, London and Berlin, after only several months' research and development, Trouvé came up with a portable, automatic, adjustable, universal safety lamp. Using one of his dichromate-of-potash batteries for power, he enclosed the light bulb in a double envelope of crystal, itself protected by a metal cage and a copper grill to take any shocks.

The first type, an industrial version, switched on the moment the user fastened his belt, allowing him to have his hands free. With a Planté battery, with a weight of 840 grams (30 oz.), it gave a luminous intensity for 10 hours, and with a weight of 1,260 grams (44 oz.), the same lighting for 15 hours.

It was designed for firemen, gas workers and miners, in fact for all those who were obliged to enter dangerous places filled with explosive or inflammable material, including sewer men, and distillers; and workers in powder magazines, cartridge factories, and the navy.

During the next few years, this lamp came to be used in the state powder magazines of Sevran-Livry and le Ripault; in the schools of artillery application and engineering at Versailles, Toulon, Verdun, Epinal and Belfort; and by the Paris Gas Company, the Paris Fire Service and the Italian navy.

The second type of lamp was for use in the home. It switched on automatically the moment the user took hold of its handle and switched off the moment it was put down. Trouvé wrote to the Academy of Sciences, "For the rest, it would be superfluous to insist, in front of an assembly of men as competent as those who have indeed wanted me to retain their attention until now, of the usefulness, the advantages or the simple amenities which can result from the use of electric lighting for the aid of practical

Left: 1885. The universal electric safety lamp, designed and built by Trouvé following a fatal fire in an oil storage cellar in Paris. This was perhaps the biggest step forwards in such instruments since Davy designed his safety lamp back in 1815 (from Georges Barral, *L'histoire d'un inventeur,* 1891). *Right:* 1885. This is perhaps the best surviving example of Trouvé's universal battery-electric safety lamp, currently exhibited at Teylers Museum in the Netherlands (Teylers Museum, Haarlem, the Netherlands).

means which I have just had the honor of showing you."[1] By May 1885, the news vendors of the political review *Le Soir* were parading along the streets, attracting passers-by with their Trouvé lamps.

Among Paris's many attractions from this period was a waxworks museum, le Musée Grévin, open for two years and a formidable success, to the great pleasure of journalist Arthur Meyer and financier Gabriel Thomas. Alfred Grévin, the sculptor in wax, was also the costumer for Judic and Théo and other fairylike dancers who wore Trouvé's luminous jewels in their costumes.

On 22 December 1884, the minutes of the administrative council meeting of the museum declared, "Electric jewels, Trouvé system, will be adapted to the Golden Fly exhibit."

In the descriptive catalogue of the 1885 35th Edition of the Musée Grévin catalogue, one learns:

> The Winter Garden which the visitor enters first of all, has been constructed in the style of Louis XV; the décor, made up of palm trees, of

1885. "La Mouche d'Or, Phantasie Aérienne" by Alfred Grévin created a sensation in the third year of the waxwork museum's existence. The light on the waxwork's crown was supplied and installed by Trouvé (collection archives Grévin).

1884. Electric light jewelry: (1) hairpin; (2) and (3) tie pins; (4) walking stick handle; (5) and (6) large diamond tiara mounted to form a necklace (from Georges Barral, *L'histoire d'un inventeur*, 1891).

chimeras and of rockeries, has been scrupulously copied from models of the period. One should notice the luminous ceiling with its foliage, its bull's eyes and its chandeliers, the light from which, filtered by glass of every color, produces the greatest effect. In the middle, the GOLDEN FLY, aerial fantasy by A. Grévin, adorned by the ingenious electric jewels of M. Trouvé, 14, rue Vivienne.

As the reader has been able to understand by the pictures used in the text; Trouvé luminous electric jewels can undergo all sorts of transformations desirable for theatres, concerts, soirées, etc. It is the same for the luminous flowers which, in the most varying shapes, bouquets, baskets, clumps, wreaths, garlands, etc., serve as decorative embellishment, and have also been applied on a great scale to theatres, concerts, evenings, receptions, banquets, reunions, etc., etc.

For all G. Trouvé instruments applied to medicine, to surgery, to domestic lighting, to electric safety lamps, to electric boats, to electric tricycles, etc., anyone interested can obtain the brochures and leaflets relative to each instrument at the inventor's himself, 14, rue Vivienne.[2]

Also at the Musée Grévin, a young magician and illusionist calling himself "Le Docteur Mélius" (real name: George Méliès) was drawing the crowds with his skillful prestidigitation. He also gave demonstrations in the elegant shopping arcade called La Galerie Vivienne, N° 6 rue Vivienne, a very short walk from Trouvé's workshops at N° 14. Several years later, Méliès would become very well-known as one of the world's first pioneer cinematographers. One wonders whether the two creators of enchanting visual effects ever met.

For any interested customer, Trouvé had produced his own brochure, printed in 1885 by A.L. Guillot, Printers, 7 rue des Canettes, Paris:

ELECTRICITY IN THE THEATRE
ELECTRO-MOBILE JEWELS
NEW LUMINOUS ELECTRIC JEWELRY
By G. Trouvé
Qualified Engineer-Constructor
Chevalier de la Légion d'honneur
14, rue Vivienne

For all the Instruments of G. Trouvé
Demand the trademark εὑρηκα

Outline of Prices
Luminous Electric Jewels
Trouvé Sole qualified inventor
in France and abroad

Rosette and luminous diamonds	15 fr.
Tie pins	20
Hairpins	20
Great variety of pins in jewelry: stars, birds, butterflies, insects, etc., etc.,	50 to 60
Shawl pin (owl's head)	45
Headlight tiara for theaters	25
Headlight tiara; Great variety of jewelry tiaras in stars, crescent, etc.	
Daisy brooch with headlamp and reflector mirrors	30
Jewelry brooches with reflector mirrors (for theater effects)	35
Luminous Electric Flowers	
Bobble rosette	15
Bodice bouquet	20
Luminous electric walking sticks	25
Trouvé pocket battery to power all the jewels set out above	15

1885
Price outline for an everyday installation of the
TROUVÉ DOMESTIC ELECTRIC LIGHTING SYSTEM

Patented in France and Abroad
Ask for the brochure: "Practical Solution of Domestic Electric Lighting"

Two Trouvé batteries with glass plates	280 fr.
With plates in hardened rubber (M. Trouvé's battery is the most simple and the most lively of known batteries)	300

Four lights to choice, of 15 candlepower each, with little reflectors and wires to hang them	40
Special conductors for the light; with vitrified string for installation, about 25	
Two special basins with ground taps, acid-proof, with bowl, stool, etc. (with these basins, no matter which servant makes very properly the solution for battery maintenance)	55
A four-switch circuit-breaker, enabling switching on or off from the hall, or of only keeping the desired number of lights in the apartment switched on.	25
One can replace this unique circuit-breaker with 4 separate ones, at 3 fr. 50 each	
TOTAL	445 fr.

Maintenance Expense for the Batteries
2 kg (41 lbs.) of dichromate of potash, 3–7 kg [60–150 lbs.] of
  sulphuric acid
Wear and tear of the zincs and amalgam
Products bought in bulk: Total 4 fr. 20
Products bought in detail: Total 5 fr. 55

Cost price of the Trouvé domestic electric lighting system compared to that of gas…. These results come from information supplied by *more than 500 installations made by M. Trouvé.*

Taking an average of 32 hours, in rounded numbers a lamp costs 0.13 fr. or 0.17 fr. per hour, depending on the way of acquiring the raw materials. According to the evaluations of competent men, published in scientific reviews, the price of gas, by 9 candlepower burners and by hour, would have been found equal to 0.08 fr. in the great warehouses of the Louvre. A gas burner of 15 candlepower would therefore cost 0.13 fr. It would result from this, that with equal intensity, the electric light from the Trouvé system would be the same price as gas by buying the products firsthand. Few people find themselves in these conditions; one must also take account of the last figure, 0.17 fr. In these conditions, maintenance costs would be about ⅓ higher than gas. This is, in fact, what takes places in practice, although the Trouvé system is the most economical of all for small installations.

We are emphasizing these figures so as not to allow an often-spread-around error to gain currency: that electricity costs nothing, or almost nothing.

One specific use of Trouvé's electric lamp took place in Egypt. In June 1885, news arrived in Paris that a dredger had sunk in the Suez Canal, Egypt, and was holding up navigation for several days. It cluttered up the passage so much that Ferdinand de Lesseps, who had developed the canal, gave an order to blow it up. The first attempts failed because of the difficulty in properly positioning the dynamite fuses. At first, they had to put up with demolishing part of the dredger so as to open up a wide channel of about 20 meters, sufficient for the basic needs.

1885. The navy uses electrical lamps on the Trouvé system for underwater repairs in ports and in the Suez Canal (from Georges Barral, *L'histoire d'un inventeur*, 1891).

Having asked in Paris for a luminous device able to light up the divers to a depth of 8 meters, the canal engineers were advised that the Navy Ministry was using Trouvé electric lamps for its *undersea* works in ports. These hermetically sealed lamps were connected to the surface by an electric cable.

Elsewhere, Professor Henri de Lacaze-Duthiers, the eminent 64-year-old naturalist, chair of Comparative Anatomy and Zoology at the Sorbonne University, had established two laboratories devoted to marine biology: one at Roscoff in Brittany, northwest France, in 1876 and one at Arago Laboratory at Banyuls-sur-Mer beside the Mediterranean in 1882. Trouvé created a crystal glass cylindrical vase with a mirror as its base as an observation instrument for the professor. The vase was covered by a silvered reflecting lid with a parabolic surface. It was filled with seawater and marine life. Between the lid and the base there was an electric light that enabled a more meticulous study, particularly with a magnifying glass. "The electric light produced by the simple devices of M. Trouvé will help us a lot in the observation of delicate and transparent animals which float on the surface of the sea and that we gather in our pelagic nets."[3]

In 1885, Trouvé, always concerned about safety, developed a new

Electric lighting devices by G. Trouvé in the Roscoff Laboratory (from Georges Barral, *L'histoire d'un inventeur*, 1891).

switch for very powerful, high-voltage currents. The central electricity factory of Tours, near his hometown, had no less than 300 such switches installed.

In July, 20 years after developing his electric rifle, Trouvé announced his firearm for nocturnal use, including a luminous electric front sight and a powerful electric projector. The front sight used a fine platinum wire placed in a little glass tube, itself in a metal tube. It was activated by the miniature battery so that whenever the gun was raised to the horizontal, the battery functioned and the light enabled the marksman to take aim. The projector was another adaptation of the Hélot-Trouvé photophore. It was a metal tube enclosing a little light bulb in front of which he had placed a convex lens, which concentrated the light rays that the bulb projected. In the same way as the electric front sight, the projector could be adapted to the extreme end of the weapon, alongside the barrels, with the aid of two rubber bracelets. Trouvé wrote:

> It would be superfluous to elaborate in front of you, Messieurs, the advantages that can result, in diverse circumstances, from the use of these fixtures. I would however cite their convenience in hunting from a hide, and their usefulness for sentries on night duty, by which they will avoid any suspicion by providing them with a new security, in the same way for lookouts on warships, who would find themselves armed individually to signal the presence of destroyers and repulse attacks which their very suddenness make disastrous.[4]

La Lumière Electrique commented, "At the Academy of Sciences, in the Salle des Pas-Perdus [Concourse Hall], one can actually see the Trouvé gun, the sight of which lights up by electric incandescence, which can be used at night to shoot at an enemy whom one lights up while remaining in obscurity."[5] Another added,

> The new instrument will be of great utility for artillery and especially naval artillery. We already know the light sighting and above the projector of his electric rifle. Now it will no longer be necessary set the spark to naval guns; detonation will take place automatically when the ship to bombard passes in front of the reticle of the telescope. It therefore seems to us that the latest invention of Mr. Gustave Trouvé is a combination and development of his reticle illumination system for telescopes, his headlight and his electrical guns.[6]

On 9 October 1885, Trouvé wrote to Hélot, "While waiting, I am sending you the latest application which I have made of [the photophore] for the microscope and micro-photography of which you have already read some reports either in *La Nature* or in other journals. I have been in bed for eleven days with bronchitis, but now I have recovered and have resumed my usual occupations." Trouvé supplied the adapted photophore, which he called the microspectroscope, to a client called Yvon.

At this time, Tom Edison of Menlo Park was busy setting up the American Graphophone Company to sell his latest invention, the wax phonograph disc. His European agent was a Colonel George Gouraud. During the American Civil War, Gouraud had received the Medal of Honor for bravery as a captain with the Third New York Cavalry Regiment on 30 November 1864. Although living in Beulah Hill in south London in a house called "Little Menlo," Colonel Gouraud's French origins often took him over to Paris. Curious about all electric novelties, Gouraud could not have missed the electrical innovations of French engineers such as Trouvé. Indeed Gouraud had electric lighting and gadgets in his home, as well as an electric tricycle, and an electric boat on the Thames. Inspired by the 1881 Paris Exhibition, he had a direct telephone connection to the Crystal Palace, and so was able to listen to live concerts in the comfort of his home.

Impressed by Trouvé's use of electric light effects in the Parisian the- aters, and certainly having watched the electric Amazons at the Empire Theatre, Leicester Square, Gouraud suggested an idea to the very popular London actor Sir Henry Irving for a play the latter was preparing at the Lyceum Theatre. The play was Goethe's *Faust*, in which in act 3 there was a swordfight between Faust and Valentine. Gouraud suggested an electric- light swordfight. The actors had to stand on iron plates screwed into the stage, with the 90-watt current passing through the right boot via a wire to a steel grip in their India rubber gloves and up through the backs of the swords. Whenever the swords crossed, sparks would fly. The effect required a very careful arrangement so as to ensure accuracy at each rep- etition and at the same time be free from the possibility of danger. When- ever Faust was getting the worst of the duel with Valentine, the demonic Mephistopheles, played by Irving, intervened, and as his sword broke those of the others, further sparks flew. Occasionally when, via their moist hands, the actors received electric shocks, Irving yelped with loud sardonic laughter to mask their cries of pain.

The first run of *Faust* lasted from 19 December 1885 to 31 July 1886; it was resumed with the re-opening of the Lyceum on 11 September, from which date *Faust* was played continuously until 22 April 1887. On the last date, the 375th performance took place, a record in the great productions of the Lyceum that stands absolutely alone. Allowing for the vacation of six weeks during the summer of 1886, this meant a continuous perform- ance, and to crowded houses, for 16 solid months! It was played in America on the tour of 1887.

Over in Paris, Trouvé decided to create a *safer,* lightweight electric swordfight. A sword and a breastplate became the polar opposites of a portable dichromate-of-potash battery worn by the combatant. The sword had been rubbed to create iron filings. Whenever a sword touched the breastplate of the other combatant, this produced sparks, and a powerful light came on so long as the sword was touching the shield. When both swords touched both breastplates at the same time, the effect was spectacular. The Trouvé electric swordfight effect was used first at the Théâtre Déjazat in *La Grenouille,* and then at Les Nouveautés in a review.

While there is no evidence that Colonel George Gouraud created other special effects for the London theater, Trouvé's *bijoux lumineux,* adaptations of the Hélot-Trouvé photophore, were also internationally admired at the Grand Concert Parisien (*Venez me voir*); the aforementioned *Mouche d'or* (golden fly) at the Musée Grévin; La Scala music-hall in Paris (*Dans la mille*); Niblo's Garden Theatre and Opera of Broadway, close to Houston Street, New York (the final performance at Niblo's was given on 23 March 1895); the Victoria Theater, Berlin; and the vaudeville theater of the Casino Saint-Hubert in the Galleries Saint-Hubert, Brussels, Belgium.

1884. This electric swordfight, set up by Trouvé, was admired for the first time at the Déjazat theater in *La Grenouille* (*The Frog*), and then at a review in the "Nouveautés" (from Georges Barral, *L'histoire d'un inventeur,* 1891).

With his workshop so near the River Seine, Trouvé continued to seek out ways of improving marine technology. In July 1886, he presented his newly patented method of constructing marine propellers to the Academy of Sciences. He explained that with his electric boats, the power of his electric motor enabled his propellers to spin at up to an unprecedented 2,400 rpm. This was considerably faster than those attached to less powerful steam engines. But this propeller speed set up entirely new problems of water resistance, such as air bubbles at the back of the boat (later known as cavitation). Determined to maintain this speed, Trouvé decided to test out a great many different propellers of variable shape and pitch in order to arrive at the greatest efficiency.

1884. "Mondaine adorned with a lighthouse and a luminous electric corsage" (from Georges Barral, *L'histoire d'un inventeur*, 1891).

At first he had these made for him. Finding only an elite group of mechanics who were charging exorbitant sums of money for their propellers, Trouvé was led to thinking up a far simpler way of constructing them. His device was basically a cylinder equipped with nuts and furrowed with grooves and welded rods for the shaping of a spiral of given pitch. For a different pitch, a different cylinder was used.

Trouvé's system enabled any worker to make a model of a propeller and at very little cost. It could even be used to make variable-pitch propellers. And as it was in metal, a material that holds its shape well, it would remain as standard to compare either the products from the casting, or the propellers that, having already worked, would have been distorted.

With the right propeller, Trouvé succeeded in making his electric boats reach an unprecedented speed of over 15 km/h (10 mph).

To control this propulsion system, Trouvé constructed a very simple switch both to start and stop the boat and to make it go forwards or astern as swiftly as possible. This switch was made up of six metal brackets, arranged in pairs on a base of insulating material; the middle two supported

1884. Ballet dancer adorned with luminous electric jewelry by Trouvé (from Georges Barral, *L'histoire d'un inventeur*, 1891).

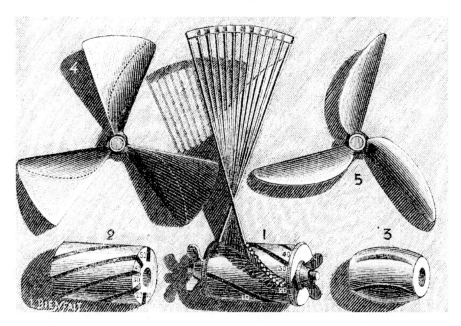

1886. Disappointed by the expense of subcontracting, Trouvé soon devised his own method of designing and building marine propellers, leading to faster electric boats (from Georges Barral, *L'histoire d'un inventeur*, 1891).

the operating lever, while the other four were connected to the terminals of the motor and the generator.

Another challenge at this time was to transmit electricity over long distances. In the United States, a major battle was being waged between Tom Edison, advocating direct current, and George Westinghouse with his inventor Nikola Tesla, advocating alternating current.

In 1886, after ten years of development, French engineer Marcel Deprez became the first electrical engineer in the world to transmit 100 horsepower of electricity over a distance of 15 kilometers (10 miles) from Creil to Paris. He used direct current. That same year, AC power at 2 kV, transmitted 30 km (19 miles), was installed at Cerchi, Italy.

Trouvé, however, remained interested in very local, almost playful, electric instruments. That autumn, a regatta was held at Chatou on the Seine, some 14 km (9 miles) downstream from the center of Paris:

> The great presentation of this week was given at Chatou. There was a nautical spectacle day and night in several acts and many tableaux, presented on a scene unique in the world. It was an immense success. Authors, actors, and actresses have been acclaimed, encored and even embraced. The greatest lamplighter of our epoch and others, was charged with the lighting: the so-

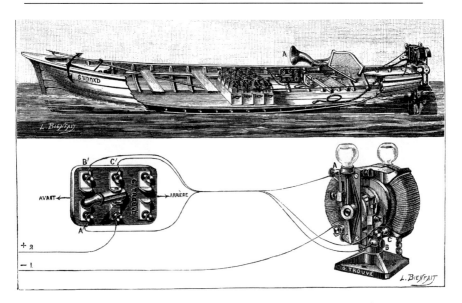

1886. The electric boats fitted out by Trouvé were quite sophisticated for their day. Here is a cross-section of one of his boats with electric devices, plus the plan and view of its engine, its electric switch and various communications, including its horn. This was the first time on any vehicle anywhere that an electric horn had been fitted (from Georges Barral, *L'histoire d'un inventeur*, 1891).

named Sun merited all the praises. It's in a ravishing decor that the presentation took place between the two bridges of Chatou.

The first part was made up of masculine and feminine regattas, of duck-punt racing and lance jousting. The female regatta was a charming innovation. All young and for the most part pretty, these rowing women struggled with a determination and an energy that it was a pleasure to see. One single criticism: The costumes that they had chosen for rowing are neither gracious nor practical; one can certainly find better. All the races, perfectly organized, have been very interesting. Jewels were presented as a prize for ladies, and objets d'art for the gentlemen.

The duck punt races and jousting having been directed by M. Fournaise, town councilor of Chatou, it would be superfluous to say that they were admirably successful.

Next followed an interval during which a joyous dinner of several hundreds of dishes has been admirably served by the three maids of the hotel. Immediately after dinner, the two sides of the river were illuminated and the Venetian fête began. It was simply dazzling. As one pen, no more authorized than ours, could alone could depict it for you, we must content ourselves with trying to describe to you the strangest and the most remarkable boats.

The most curious was certainly that of M. Trouvé, the well-known electrician. It represented a floating island.... The *île Fleurie*, said an illuminated sign.... At the simple pushing of an electric button, thousands of flowers and fruits of all colors were piercing and glittering in all the bushes and were instantly changing color. The effect was stunning.[7]

During this period, Alphonse Fournaise, boatbuilder, was attracting people out of the city to this little community. Impressionist painters such as Pierre-Auguste Renoir, Claude Monet,[8] Camille Pissarro, and Alfred Sisley would come to lunch, to paint and to go canoeing. Writers such as Guy de Maupassant came to write such novels as *Bel Ami*.

Rowing and sailing brought together a very varied population who frequented the island of the Impressionists (at the time île Fleurie). The Monot brothers, close to Paul Poiret, lived in Chatou and worked on fashion items. Cardeilhac, a renowned goldsmith (creator of the French Cup among others), also resided at Chatou. So this select band of creators would have known Gustave Trouvé, 47 years old, celebrated for his electric jewels, theatrical effects, boats and scientific wonders.

Renoir wrote to a friend, "I have returned to Chatou because of my painting. It would be really nice of you to come to lunch. You will not regret your journey; it's the prettiest place in the surroundings of Paris." Among Renoir's better-known paintings is *Le Déjeuner des Canotiers* (*Canoeists' Lunch*).

Trouvé, concerned with the accidents created by his silent electric boats—others simply could not hear their approach—designed and built an electric siren for his fellow *canotiers*. It was like his device already in use in doctor's surgeries. An electrically driven, four-bladed fan blew air through a series of holes "starting with a raucous vibration, then rapidly passing up all the notes of the musical scale to a sharp, strident note which it is impossible to confuse with any of the other signals in use." Trouvé patented his electric siren that year, had a four-page pamphlet printed ("*Signal Avertisseur Universel Trouvé, à l'usage des canotiers*") and even patented a child's toy version of it. (In his Declaration of Transfer by death, he would leave "personal furniture at Chatou." It has been impossible to ascertain whether this was his electric boat.)

One Trouvé electric boat was even called *La Sirène*. Belonging to Paul-Bernard Carrère de Nabat, of the Cercle de la Voile de Paris (Paris Sailing Club), it was 9 meters (30 feet) long. It could either be propeller-driven or paddle-driven. The paddles were conical, based on an invention by a Monsieur Dupassieux. They behaved differently from ordinary paddles regarding the entry and exit of the water, reducing resistance to virtually nothing, so improving performance. The increased propulsion was achieved by the water entering a larger opening in the paddle and leaving it by a smaller exit. This thrust was tangential to the radius of the wheel.

1887. The *Siren*, belonging to Monsieur de Nabat, was a hybrid with propulsion either by propeller or by paddles (from Georges Barral, *L'histoire d'un inventeur*, 1891).

De Nabat had been using *La Sirène* three times a week throughout the season. It travelled at a regular speed of 14 to 15 kilometers an hour (9–10 mph), its propeller turning at 1,200–1,800 revolutions per minute. Trouvé considered that for electric propulsion, the Dupassieux paddles were more efficient than a propeller. Madame Louise de Nabat took her husband's boat and had it temporarily converted into a Japanese junk, complete with a Chinese pagoda decorated with luminous electric flowers. This won Madame Nabat first prize in a benevolent regatta given on the Marne River in 1887. Another boat, belonging to Monsieur de Dampierre, travelled on the River Eure. It could carry six passengers, and its two paddle wheels enabled it to travel on rivers where water weed was abundant and could foul up a propeller.

Pleasure boating aside, Trouvé returned to Paris, where he remained of valuable service to the medical profession. On 23 August 1886, a patient was admitted to the La Pitié Hospital. He had swallowed a fork. Professor J.F.B. Polaillon was the consultant surgeon:

> I had recourse to Monsieur Trouvé who, with his readiness to oblige, had an esophageal probe constructed. This is based on the principle of his stiletto with electric ringing for revealing the presence of a metal foreign body in tissue.... At the moment when the end of this probe entered the stomach,

one of my housemen, Monsieur Trouvé, and I, heard the revealing noise of the electric battery for a fraction of a second.

In the presence of several doctors, housemen, externs, students, and Trouvé, Polaillon successfully operated on the chloroformed patient and removed the fork from his stomach. Polaillon's only reserve was that "Monsieur Trouvé should increase the power of his electro-magnets."

In 1886 Trouvé also adapted his ear-piercing, air-compressed siren to transmit from the handles of walking sticks and umbrellas as an alarm signal against prospective pickpockets or a distress signal for mountain walkers (Patent N° 176,745).

Trouvé had many grateful and appreciative clients. One of these, who had enjoyed owning a luminous electric brooch and walking stick, was Elie Ferrand of Segonzac in the Charente Region. Ferrand was renowned as a distiller of one of the finest cognacs in France. He had also assembled a rare collection of exotic birds and animals, including a grey crowned crane, flamingoes and a domestic toucan. In his appreciation of Trouvé's skill, Ferrand sent the inventor

> six bottles of my fine champagne cognac, harvested by my aged father in 1844. This is the most precious that I can offer you and witness to my gratitude.
>
> What characterizes fine champagne, is the aroma it gives off. Let me tell you how to appreciate it, if you do not already know. General rule: never taste it after a sweet dessert, but after cheese and nuts. Put two thirds into a little glass, heat it for five minutes between your hands and then instead of swallowing it, sip it drop by drop. When it is empty, continued to warm the glass and the perfume which it gives off is exquisite.[9]

At the start of 1887, Parisians began to see the laying of the foundations for an iron lattice-work tower that was to serve as the entrance arch for the World's Fair two years later. It was designed by two engineers, Maurice Koechlin and Emile Nouguier, led by a Monsieur Gustave Eiffel. During its construction, the Eiffel Tower would surpass the Washington Monument to assume the title of the tallest man-made structure in the world, a title it held for 41 years, until the Chrysler Building in New York City was built in 1930. While interested in the project, Trouvé remained more involved in the miniature world.

Although the French Revolution had put an end to a line of kings and queens, the French crown jewels, comprising the orb, scepters, diadems and jewels that symbolized royalty within the French aristocracy between 1752 and 1825, had been kept together. To put paid to those royalists who would have a return to a monarchy, the republican government decided that the crown jewels should be broken up, auctioned off and dis-

1887. In this illustration of the official photographing of the former French crown jewels, in the background we catch a rare portrait of Trouvé holding his smaller electric lamp (from Georges Barral, *L'histoire d'un inventeur*, 1891).

persed. In the words of one member of the National Assembly, "Without a crown, no need for a king."

But before this controversial decision was implemented, in February 1887 Albert Dauphin, the finance minister, called a group of experts together to inspect these jewels, worth a staggering 22 million francs, in the security of the cellars of the Palais du Louvre. As the collection was to be photographed, it had to be lit, so Gustave Trouvé "the eminent electrician" and his assistants were requested to come and fix the lighting in the cellar.

For Trouvé, master of *bijoux électriques*, to light such a collection of real jewels was the chance of a lifetime: thousands of diamonds including the legendary "Regent," rubies, amethysts, opals, pearls, turquoises, emeralds, pink topazes, sapphires and other diverse stones. He brought his batteries and his portable lamp, and set up the lighting. The photographs were taken. The jewels inspected were sold on May 17 that year, although *Le Régent* was bought by the state, which returned it to the Louvre. Others were sent to the museum of the Mining School and the others destroyed.

At the same time, Trouvé had been preparing a speech for the Paris Sailing Club at their clubhouse in Argenteuil. He had come up with a revolutionary new approach that would enable electric boats to make extended sea voyages by converting sea salt into the required energy. His generator was made up of a series of swift discharge batteries for winching; the number of these batteries would be greater or smaller depending on the power required. Each of these batteries was contained in an oak trough equipped with ebony vats and topped by a ratchet and latching winch of six elements of zinc and carbon, their voltage created by mobile contacts, of the exciter fluid, sulphuric acid and dichromate of potash in predetermined proportions.

According to his calculations, an electric ship of 100 meters (330 feet) long, towing a battery raft using large zinc and copper plates that were regularly plunged 4 meters (13 feet) into the seawater as the exciter liquid, could develop 5,120 horsepower and cruise for thousands of sea miles. Henri De Parville criticized Trouvé's proposed system, saying that the zinc and copper would wear out very quickly, questioning whether such a battery would continue to work as it became covered with algae and crustaceans. Nor did he think that this system could be set up along the riverbanks to produce electricity for local inhabitants.

By this time the Paris Sailing Club was holding regattas on the Seine at Argenteuil for up to 12 steam launches per race. Electric launches were not considered as competitive.

Since the 1881 Electric Exposition, Trouvé's enthusiasm for what he called "*télélectricité*" had not been shared by the majority of Parisians. Some electric lighting installations that had been fitted before any other cities in the world had even been removed. Isolated attempts to create small central power stations, as in Trouvé's very own neighborhood of the Palais-Royal, had failed due to a lack of a sufficient number of consumers and also by a reluctance to commit capital.

But then on 27 May 1887, a disastrous fire broke out at the Comic Opera's Favart Hall, where the first act of an opera *Mignon* was being performed. The fire, caused by defective gas lighting located above the stage, cost the lives of 84 people, including 4 dancers, 2 singers, 4 dressers and 4 ushers. As a result of this fire, electric lighting became mandatory in all theaters and concert cafés.

The need to introduce electricity in public places and especially the approach of the Universal Exhibition of 1889, which risked showing the world that the name "City of Light" was ill-merited, accelerated discussions at the city council to provide the capital with an electric supply service. By late 1887, a draft specification had been developed. Six private companies obtained the rights to install electricity in private homes: 16 km (10 miles) of electric cabling had been laid in Paris for the first 220 subscribers. There would be 72,000 by 1906, the date of the end of concessions.

Toulouse is a town some 680 km (423 miles) south of Paris, and it was here that the French Association for the Advancement of Sciences held its congress on 26 September 1887. In front of delegates, Trouvé, "engineer electrician in Paris," explained and demonstrated his clinical polyscopes, his safety lamp, the photophore, the instrument for lighting liquids in laboratories, the underwater lamp and a new light switch. But the great surprise came when they saw, projected on a screen, portraits of famous French scientists such as the centenarian chemist Michel Chevreuil and of the microbiologist Louis Pasteur, medals and coins, the movements of a clock and the flickering of a lighted candle. This was no longer a magic lantern whose light came from gas, mineral oil or arc lamps. It was Trouvé's latest innovation—the lightweight electric *auxanoscope*.

The origin of his auxanoscope was simple. Following the use of his photophore for micro-photography, his associate and friend, Doctor Paul Hélot of Rouen, asked Trouvé whether he could create an electric lampascope for opaque bodies. During a moment of respite, in a matter of just a few days, he conceived and built a working model of what he called the electric auxanoscope. As a lover of ancient Greek, he chose the word *auxanô* ("I increase"). He combined focal lenses with parabolic reflectors inside cylindrical tubes and installed a 70-watt light bulb, connecting the machine to a battery that gave it 3 hours' autonomy, with a projecting power of 4 meters (12 feet). He then developed it for combined projects. Then for continuous projections—a slide show—he devised two little rollers for subjects printed either on a band of ordinary paper, or subjects photographed on a band of transparent gelatin. One journal reported, "For all our teaching establishments, big or small, it will cost a minimum of 40 francs to 60 francs to buy either the simple or double auxanoscope. It will become a powerful aid in the hands of professors for the projection of minerals, dead or living insects, even enlarged natural or artificial anatomical parts, and without any alteration in the details or the colors."[10]

Elsewhere during the Toulouse Congress, Trouvé spoke about electric pleasure boating, successively describing the generators which he had used, his lightweight and powerful motors, his new way of constructing propellers, his system of switching on or off or controlling the speed of the boat, the alarm signal or electric siren as well as a powerful electric headlamp for avoiding collisions. Trouvé then predicted that in the near future, electric navigation would be used on a large scale. He presented conclusive figures on this subject. Everyone knew that steam did not enable easily covering a distance of 8,000 kilometers (5,000 miles); electricity, even at its beginnings, when the steam engine was at its peak, would easily lead to double that distance. Before the congress was over,

Trouvé fit his rudder-motor-propeller to a rowboat provided by the Society for the Encouragement of Nautical Sport (established in 1879) and took congress delegates in groups of three or four on short trips up and down the local River Garonne.

Trouvé also gave a demonstration of his 90-gram (3-oz.) Lilliputian electric motor, which, fitted with an aerial propeller then attached to one end of a scale, once electrified, lifted the scale arm up. Occupying less than a 3 cm (1³/₁₆ inch) cube, the motor could rise to a height of 22 meters (72 feet) in one second and would enable future experimentation with electric helicopters and aeroplanes.

Trouvé's presentation of his auxanoscope would soon convince the Ligue d'Enseignement (Teaching League) to adopt it for their itinerant teachers. Its lightweight compactness would enable them to take it from village school to village school and show pupils drawings, photo-

1887. In developing his auxanoscope, Trouvé replaced the heavier gas-lit magic lantern with a lighter, more compact projector that is the ancestor of electrical image projection, such as cinema and PowerPoint around the world today. This one was used by the itinerant teachers of the Education League (from Georges Barral, *L'histoire d'un inventeur*, 1891).

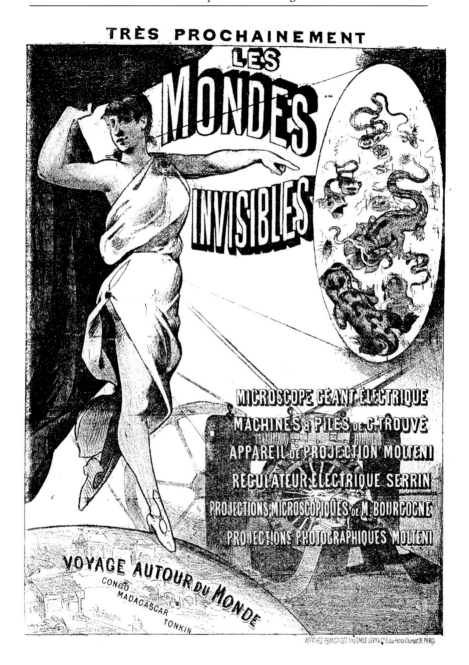

1887. Preceding the Lumière brothers' revolution by a few years, this slide show owed part of its success to Trouvé's lighting (from Georges Barral, *L'histoire d'un inventeur*, 1891).

graphs, insects (dead or alive), fruits, and plants. But it would also be useful for doctors, scientists, architects, painters and designers for projecting
their designs or specimens onto a screen. A travelling road show company
calling itself "Les Mondes Invisibles" used Trouvé's machine and battery
to project the "Voyage Around the World—Congo—Madagascar—
Tonkin" onto a screen measuring some 15 meters (50 feet) either side.
Trouvé priced his simple auxanoscope at 40 francs, while the double was
20 francs more.

From 1887 to 1890, Gaston Tissandier was writing his *History of Ballooning and Famous Aeronauts*.

In 1888, Trouvé, approaching his fiftieth year, continued to apply his
practical approach to medical matters. That spring, Monsieur Serres,
mechanics professor at the Paris Dental School, reported,

> M. Trouvé has constructed others, more suitable to dental applications;
> the little motor weighs 2.5 kg [5.5 lbs.] and gives 10 kilogrammeters [72 foot-
> pound force], enough for the drill. It costs 200 francs. The battery can work
> for an hour, at a cost of 0.40 fr. For this conference, Monsieur Trouvé has
> built a little instrument that appears to me to resolve in the most satisfying
> way the problem of turning the drill with electricity.... Monsieur Trouvé has
> called his instrument the *electro-drill*.[11]

Trouvé boats continued to be built for various purposes. In September 1888, a delegation from Imperial China arrived in Paris. The mission
was to find a boat that could fight against opium smuggling in the China
Sea. The boat commissioned was a 30-horsepower Trouvé electric launch.
It was steel-hulled, weighed 8 metric tons, and measured 15 meters (50
feet) long, with a bronze propeller of about 50 cm (20 in.). It was capable
of a speed of 18 km/h (11 mph). It also had an electric spotlight capable
of projecting a beam of light with a range of 6 kilometers (3 sea miles).
The Emperor Guangxu of the then-ruling Qing Dynasty, who since his
childhood had been fascinated by clocks and gadgetry, was so impressed
that he commanded a scale model for exhibition at his Palace Museum in
the Forbidden City in Peking.

Closer to home, in Switzerland, Baron Boucheporn, having recently
built a stately home at the side of Lake Geneva, decided that it would be
fine to have a large electric yacht to cruise up and down the lake. He asked
Augustin Normand of Le Havre to build the yacht based on a number of
conditions: that it could be transported by rail, that it had a draft of 2
meters (6 feet), that it was stable enough to take the storms of Lake
Geneva, and that it had a minimum speed of 16 to 17 km/h (9–10 mph).
It must be equipped with batteries functioning for about 20 hours at half-
speed without the need to change the liquid. Normand ambitiously

planned a 15-meter (50-foot) boat with twin 30-hp Trouvé electric motors. To date we do not know whether it was ever built.

Trouvé continued to keep Hélot informed about the progress of their photophore. On 6 March 1889, he wrote:

> I am sending you by post the issue of the *Illustrated Review of the Medical and Orthopaedic Surgical Polytechnique*, which has published a clinical photophore of Monsieur Pierre Boursier, which is which is none other than our photophore with insignificant variations. The lens, the reflector, even the sleeve in ebony are like those in the clinics of doctors de Wecker, Abadie, Galezowski and Gilet de Grammont. Nothing has been left out, as you can see. It is impossible that we let this article pass by unnoticed, without a claim. Should you be coming to Paris, we can write a protest letter. Awaiting your news.

Today, no speleologist would descend into any cave in the world without wearing their headlamp. Prior to the mid-nineteenth century, the scientific value of caves was considered only in its contribution to other branches of science, and cave studies were considered part of the larger disciplines of geography, geology or archaeology.

From 1888, Edouard-Alfred Martel, 24 years old, began to explore caves and grottoes and galleries around France. This was the beginning of what has since come to be known as speleology. In his book *Les Abimes* (*The Abysses*), Martel tells how at first he used the Trouvé battery, carbon and zinc, in dichromate of potassium, and that it gave a good light for 1 hour 30 minutes. He used this for his first campaign in the Grandes Causses in the Massif Central region. But he was also using another battery made by his own cousin, Marcel Gaupillat, which projected a light for 4 to 5 hours. This worked with chloro-chromic acid, delicate to use below ground. Martel is today respected worldwide as the founder of modern speleology.[12]

On 6 May 1889, six days after the official opening of the Universal Exposition, the Eiffel Tower was opened to the public. It proved an immediate success with the public, and nearly 30,000 visitors made the 1,710-step climb to the top using the stairs before the elevators entered service on 26 May. By the end of the exposition, there had been 1,896,987 visitors, among them, of course, Gustave Trouvé, who could look down and across at his workshop in the rue Vivienne and perhaps at one of his electric boats cruising up the Seine.

Among the displays at the exposition were plans and a model for a railway bridge across the English Channel, a project created by Henri Schneider, a weapons manufacturer with factories and electricity workshops at the facilities of Le Creusot and H. Hersent, a public works entrepreneur. Although not a businessman, Trouvé purchased 131 shares. The Minister of the Marine vetoed the project as it would impede shipping.

Tragedy struck when on May 21, Trouvé's friend and colleague Gaston Planté died of a cerebral hemorrhage at his laboratory in Bellevue, near Paris. He was only 55 years old. He had been suffering nervous disorders for some time and then recurrent eye pains. In his will, he left his property of Bellevue as a retirement home for impoverished scientists. He also set up a biannual prize of 3,000 francs for the author of a discovery in electricity.

Interest in electricity and electric vehicles went as far as North Africa. Despite his people living a daily life on camels and horseback, since 1873 the Sultan Moulay-Hassan of Morocco and his son Abel-El-Aziz had been passionate about European technology, but they played on European rivalries to maintain their independence.

In 1888, Moritz Immisch and his colleague Magnus Volk of England sent out a four-wheel, four-seater electric dogcart, two in front and two behind. The energy was supplied by 24 accumulators, weighing 358 kg, protected inside a box placed between the seats. With an overall weight of 550 kg (1,212 lbs.), the dogcart was capable of running for 5 hours at 16 km/h (10 mph). The sultan and his son derived great pleasure from driving it around the courtyards of Ksar el Batha, their large palace at Fez. They also had an electrical laboratory, powered by a steam generator.

In spring 1889, Jules Patenôtre, the new French minister in Tangiers, decided on the diplomatic gesture of taking some fine gifts for the Sultan Moulay-Hassan. Concerning this, on February 27, he wrote to the minister of foreign affairs, Paris:

Dear Minister,

If the rain season does not upset my projects, I am proposing to set off for Fez towards 29 March. I would desire that the four mares that the Government of the Republic must send to Moulay-Hassan would be shipped in sufficient time for them to arrive in Tangiers before our departure. I have already received one part of the other presents destined for the Sultan and I would like the complement to be sent to me as soon as possible.

Where *the electric-engined launch* is especially concerned, there will be room to get it accompanied by a foreman from the Trouvé firm who can assemble it on the spot and indicate its running to the Sultan's mechanics. The costs required to transport the foreman will not be very high. We will obtain, without doubt, from the Paquet Company, his free transportation from Marseilles to Tangiers: he will, during our voyage, have his expenses paid and I can, once he will have completed the assembly of the launch, send him back to France. So it only concerns paying him, beside the cost of his voyage, return ticket, 2nd class, from Paris to Marseilles.

A daily salary to negotiate with M. Trouvé and which will be, if Your

Excellency authorizes me, carried by the general expenses of the extraordinary Embassy. I would be grateful if you would let me know the decision that you take concerning this…. Patenôtre. Legation of the French Republic in Morocco [emphasis added].

The mares mentioned, four-year-old, white-socked bays, demi-thoroughbreds, came from the internationally renowned National Haras of Saint-Lô in Normandy, where no less than breeding 300 studs were looked after by some 80 blacksmiths. Their names were Mercedes, Heroïne, Hermosa and Hermine. They were purchased by Froidereaux, inspector-general of the Haras, who made the necessary arrangements for them to be sent, first to Port Vendre in Paris, then to Marseilles for 16 March, then shipped to Tangiers, and then taken to Fez, accompanied by the Haras blacksmiths. While they were considered the finest horses France could provide, the Trouvé launch, built of mahogany, represented the finest technology.

On 12 March, Paternôtre reported:

I am at present without news of the horses and the electric launch intended for the Sultan. I hope they are already en route so as to arrive here before the end of the month…. Has Monsieur Trouvé decided to supply you with a foreman to steer his boat? I have learned that the Italian Mission at Fez is at present busy servicing the electric machinery of the Sultan. It would be most regrettable should we be obliged to depend on them for the boat in question. They tell me that you have asked Monsieur de la Martineau, just about to return to Morocco, to study under the direction of M. Trouvé the reassembly and the functioning of his boat. I do not suppose that he would wish to assume responsibility….

Patenôtre.

On 14 March, the following telegraph was sent from the port of Marseilles to the Minister of Foreign Affairs, Paris: "We will be able to embark the packages making up the electric boat for Tangiers, but warn that the ship of the 22nd will be several days late."

In his *Memoirs*, Patenôtre later recalled,

We took an electric boat in mahogany, intended for taking the harem of His Cherifian Majesty, around the artificial lakes in the imperial gardens. This boat, which was not less than 20 meters long and could not be dismantled, had to be a big element of complication for the progress of our caravan. Having tried all ways of transporting it, we had to end up with a procedure renewed from Pharaonic times, and 40 blacks were charged with carrying for 12 days, on their heads or on their shoulders, this gigantic package which, by its shape, evoked the idea of some monstrous monolith.[13]

Paternôtre's 18-strong delegation included a young naval officer called Julien Viaud, later a famous novelist called "Pierre Loti." In his book *In Morocco* Loti would recall the event:

An extraordinary object, which has followed us from Tangiers and which we are also used to looking for, sometimes ahead of us, sometimes behind, in the far distance, is the electric launch (! ! ?), six meters long, that we are carrying as a present for His Majesty the Sultan; it is enclosed in a greyish case which gives it the aspect of a block of granite, and it progresses with difficulty, via the ravines, the mountains, carrying on the shoulders of about 40 Arabs. In the Egyptian bas-reliefs, one has already seen these enormous things moving past, carried, like this one, by a series of men in white robes, with naked legs.[14]

1890. Portrait of Pierre Loti, who accompanied the electric boat out to Morocco.

The caravan arrived in sight of the crenelated walls of Fez on the afternoon of 15 April, and the following day, the French made an entry into the holy city, welcomed by a crowd of 20,000 people who marveled at the strange packing case, still on the shoulders of the Arab porters.

Ironically, no mention was made, either by Patenôtre or by Loti, of the sultan's reaction to the boat and of its ultimate use by his harem. But Loti does mention other objects, obviously made by Trouvé:

It was about showing them how the presents work which we have brought for the intention of the ladies of the seraglio; pickets of electric flowers, electric jewels, stars and crescents, to put in the hair of these invisible beauties…. The batteries take a long time to prepare; they seem to bear us ill will.

And all these little toys of the XIXth century, which we have brought here, light up with difficulty, just managing to shine like glow-worms, in the great surrounding darkness.

No Trouvé batteries had ever travelled so far from Paris, some 1,800 km (1,000 miles), and one doubts whether they had been given a recharge either en route or upon arrival.

Not long after, on another French diplomatic mission, an electric toy yacht, its minuscule motor and battery installed by Trouvé, was shipped to Japan as a gift for the young Prince Yoshihito, later the 123rd Emperor of Japan, to play with on the pond at the Aoyama Detached Palace, Tokyo.

SIX

Luminous Fountains
and Mechanical Birds

Having chosen not to leave the relative comfort of his workshop in the rue Vivienne for the rigors of Morocco, that May Trouvé devised a system for mounting and dismantling large plates of glass, using split tubing and screws: "My system applies to the construction of windows of all shapes and sizes" (Patent N° 198,450). The mass production of glass had only recently been developed, in 1887, by a British firm of Ashley in Castleford, Yorkshire. It would enable big department stores to show their wares through large windows, which would in turn launch "window shopping."

That June, at the Paris Opera, there was a production of *La Tempête*, a fantastic ballet based on Shakespeare's play by Messieurs Jules Barbier and J. Hansen, with music by Ambroise Thomas, starring the Spanish ballerina Rosita Mauri. Usually, to create the effect of a hurricane with thunder and lightning, a broken line was cut through a backdrop, behind which a bright and instantaneous light was produced by the lighting of lycopodium powder. Trouvé recounted, "In this case it was not possible to have recourse to this means, and the substitution that I made of an electric process only gave a more complete illusion to the public." At the end of a long, flexible pole like a fishing rod, he mounted a little light bulb, whose focus was both very concentrated and powerful. A foot switch enabled making or breaking contact at a precise moment. With this arrangement, it was enough, at the desired moment, to agitate the rod in a zigzag from top to bottom, to imitate the lightning bolt. A cushion, if this were necessary, would soften the impact and prevent the bulb from breaking. Trouvé wrote, "I obtain the noise of hail by throwing heavy salt crystals against a wicker rack. The whistling of the wind which is reproduced by the play of my double siren completes the effect, and one believes one is witnessing a veritable hurricane!"[1]

During the Second International Electricity Congress in Paris, Trouvé presented his hand-cranked dynamo machine. It was at this congress that the watt and the joule were recognized as units of electrical energy. In December he exhibited at the First Congress of International Dentistry, promoting the advantages of the electric motor and his battery:

> The electric motor ... does not make a smell, it is very simple, does not have any friction, its rotary action is direct, it lends itself to all uses, and finally it is little subject to disturbance; only the stays are worn away. The generator, it is true, presents inconveniences, but when you have electricity everywhere, you will be able to do everything you wish and this will be the ideal; until then, one must have a battery, and only the dichromate battery supplies electric horsepower at 3 francs per hour; it is true that one must carry out maintenance every 15 days. My battery presents just ½ hp. The motor, though very small, is enough to develop up to 15 kilogram-meters, and it can be positioned on its axis or pointing upwards.
>
> This battery supplies light with the aid of a reflector and a lens, in galvanocautery for which one can graduate the heat at will: it also enables the use of a diversity of little instruments.
>
> Finally it enables transmitting electricity from 500 to 1,000 meters [546 to 1,000 yards] in the form of heat and of light.

In 1890, the Postal and Telegraphic Ministry published their very first list of subscribers to the telephone network of Paris. Although Trouvé had invented crucial improvements for the telephone, the name G. Trouvé does not appear. The only Trouvés in the telephone directory are two embroiderer-decorators, Edmond Trouvé and Siméon Trouvé. It may have been that as he was a tenant, Trouvé was using the instrument of the owner of 14, rue Vivienne, or it may have been be that his phone was subscription-free.

Trouvé continued to receive recognition for his medical instrumentation: La Société de Médecine Pratique de Montpellier (the Society of Practical Medicine of Montpellier), founded in 1799, nominated him as their secretary of the 15th section.

On 21 March 1890, at the Paris Opera, Palais Garnier, Camille Saint-Saëns, the well-known composer, presented his new work, *Ascanio*, based on a libretto by Louis Gallet. In Act 3, in the scene of the garden of Fontainebleau, dominated by the forest, there was a mythological ballet. Phoebus Apollo, played by Mademoiselle Torri, appeared among the nine Muses, holding the genie's torch in her hand. This torch, compact and elegant, had to be brilliantly lit for 12 to 15 minutes, for each performance. Only an incandescent bulb, cleverly hidden by red, yellow and white gemstones, had solved the problem. The challenge had been to power this bulb, but without a cable or external source of energy. So Messrs. Eugène Ritt and Pierre Gailhard, directors of the opera, called upon Monsieur Trouvé, whose skill was incomparable in the construction of luminous electric jewels.

Deciding to use the resources of the power station that supplied the opera, Trouvé ingeniously fitted six little portable Planté batteries inside the torch. With this, the torch could be switched on to last for 20 minutes, not only for one but for two performances. A little switch was placed just above the two wires so that with the slightest pressure, the bulb lit up; it went out as soon as the pressure was lifted. The effect was complete stage-craft, and the result obtained at the opera gave the greatest honor to Trouvé who conceived, designed and built this torch himself in less than three days. For the less important theaters, Trouvé made another torch. To switch it off, the bearer pointed it down. To switch it on, they pointed it upwards. These two types of torch were then exhibited at the physics exhibition in the capital.

1890. The battery-powered "Flambeau d'Ascanio," after the opera by Saint-Saëns of the same name, is held aloft by Mademoiselle Torri. Thanks to Trouvé, its flame-colored light lasted 20 minutes for each of the two daily performances at the Paris Opera before needing an overnight recharge (BNF).

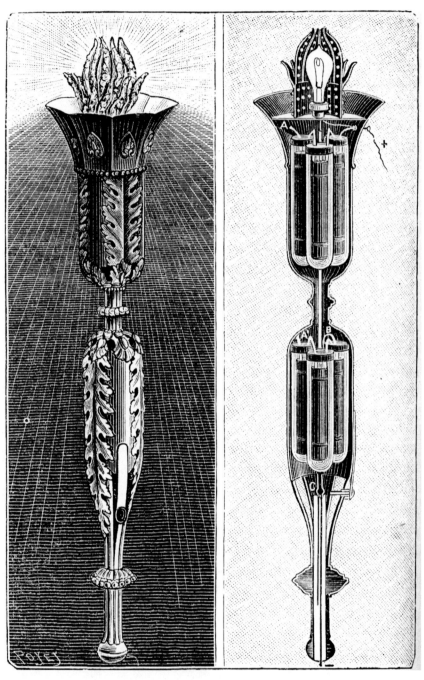

"Flambeau d'Ascanio" (Musée EDF Electropolis, Mulhouse).

During the same month, Trouvé decided to build a second model of his electric gyroscope, originally built for Léon Foucault some 25 years before to demonstrate the rotation of the Earth. As it would serve for the verification of marine compasses on board ships in all sea conditions, he made it more robust. It would enable the practical determination of the meridian line and the evaluation of the latitude at the place of observation. He also equipped it with astronomical glasses, stating, "My electric gyroscope would not only serve to rectify the compass, but to replace it favorably, since it could indicate perpetually and directly to the captain *his track angle.*"

Trouvé was not the only one to have invented an electric gyroscope. According to the firm of Messieurs Dumoulin-Froment and Doignan, the application of a gyroscope for the rectification of compasses was made by E. Dubois in 1878 with the help of a gyroscope built by Dumoulin-Froment. *Yet Trouvé's electrification of the Foucault gyroscope predates Dumoulin-Froment by 13 years.* But then in July 1889, Captain Arthur Krebs asks Dumoulin-Froment to build an electro-gyroscope for the *Gymnote* submarine of Monsieur Zedé; this was delivered in November of that year and was used several times underwater. One wonders whether there was any love lost between Krebs and Trouvé.

But then, Trouvé did not win everything. In April 1890, he was one of 16 engineers who took part in a competition for electrical energy counters. Trouvé's entry number was N° 15. Although he successfully constructed a dynamometric brake for industrial use, fully capable of direct reading of work and tachometric readings from a distance and on several points at once, he did not win the competition.

His explorer-extractor continued to be used in the Paris hospitals. In February 1890, a patient who had had a teaspoon stuck in his stomach for 18 days was successfully treated by Professor Périer of the Lariboisière Hospital, Paris:

> To make sure, I used the Collin resonating catheter; I immediately had the sensation of contact with a hard body, but it was impossible for me to avoid the shock of the instrument against the molar teeth, and my embarrassment remained the same. Then M. Trouvé brought me his electric explorer. Scarcely had the instrument penetrated the stomach than its ringing indicated contact with the metal, so the spoon was indeed in the stomach. I did not hesitate to extract it via the natural route using instruments introduced into the esophagus.[2]

In June 1890, a Portuguese steamship weighed anchor. Her destination: Portugal's colonies in East and West Africa, such as Mozambique. On board was Mariano Cirilo de Carvalho, a diplomat representing the

Royal Agricultural Association of Portugal and the Portuguese Industrial
Association. He was accompanied by Lieutenant-Colonel d'Andrade, a
civil engineer. Their mission: to reconnoiter natural resources in Portugal's
colonies.

Also on board was a revolutionary new instrument for the subter-
ranean prospecting of useful minerals and, above all, coal. The instrument
was called an *orygmatoscope,* as developed by Trouvé of Paris. It bore the
characteristic mark *"eurêka."* Senor de Carvalho had come across this
instrument when he was visiting the Universal Exhibition in Paris the
year before. In Greek, *orygma* means "hole made in the earth" and *scopeô*
means "I look at."

The orygmatoscope was a very powerful lamp encased in a metal
cylinder, half of which had a reflector, the other half of which lit up layers
of earth. One of the hemi-cylindrical surfaces constituted the reflector;
the other, in thick glass, allowed the rays of light to pass through, so lighting up, brightly, the layers of earth passed through by the instrument. The
lower part, inclined at 45°, was an elliptical mirror, and the upper part,
on the right-hand side, was open to enable the observer, positioned at the

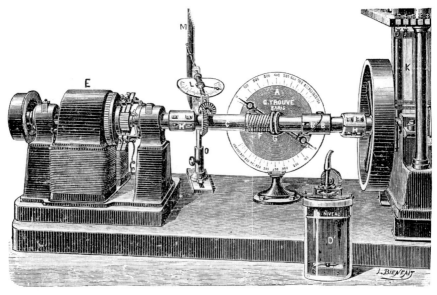

Fig. 2

**Trouvé's universal dynamometric brake for industrial use was fully capable of
direct reading of work and tachometric readings from a distance and on several
points at once (from Georges Barral, *L'histoire d'un inventeur,* 1891).**

entrance to the well and equipped with a powerful Galileo telescope, to see the images of the terrain in the mirror; the light was fixed in such a way that the rays sent upwards could be intercepted. The device was then winched by electrical wires down a borehole to a depth of 200 to 300 meters (650 to 1,000 feet). Lieutenant-Colonel d'Andrade would then be able to look down a Galileo telescope to inspect the layers below.

By July, Trouvé and Doctor Paul Hélot had further perfected their photophore, reducing its weight to no more than 50–60 grams. Instead of being strapped onto the forehead, it rested on the bridge of the nose in the line of the eyes, where it could be used as an otoscope or laryngoscope. Their business agreement read,

> With a view to improvements to the device known under the name of *photophore électrique frontale* Hélot-Trouvé, it has been agreed between the undersigned as follows:
> The modifications will be made by a common agreement according to the indications of Dr. Hélot by M. Trouvé who will support all the eventual costs of study, of construction and of publicity. Doctor Hélot will have the right to returns for his effort for all machines complete with their battery or whatever source of electrical energy, as well as a reduction of 19 percent on all the purchase he will make in his company. In addition the device will carry the name: "New photophore électrique Hélot-Trouvé."

At the base of his copy, Hélot told Trouvé:

> I have just made some new trials. I continue to find the little models superior to the big ones and those whose rays are less divergent…. The battery is certainly the best one, to my knowledge, for the surgery and preferable to all the accumulators in the world, so long as one can receive them all charged up, as in Paris. For transport, does the little battery that you have with you give satisfaction? As for me, I have not been very pleased, as its light fades too quickly. Drop the idea of a little dynamo, for in the town, one always finds someone to turn the little crank-handle during the time required and that will avoid walking around with an acidic solution.[3]

In their brochure, Hélot recalled, "Nearly all the manufacturers, as much as in France as abroad, have more or less imitated it; many have even kept the name of photophore, but most of them have omitted recalling my name. Even though the priority has never been contested, I wish, so as to confirm my rights, to recall that the photophore was presented to the Academy of Medicine in the month of April 1883."

Hélot was not Trouvé's only client. For example, in his 400-page *Manual of Gynaecological Electrotherapy, Operative Techniques,* brought out that year, the 37-year-old Doctor Luc Brivois described a range of hysterometers or uterine sounding devices in carbon constructed for him by Trouvé, as well as a range of bipolar uterine electrodes: "Dr. Brivois observed that the Apostoli hysterometer was often of two weak a caliber with certain patients with uteruses of abnormal dimensions. To apply the method for every case, he asked us to construct a set of varied hysterometers."[4]

With winter approaching and night falling earlier, Trouvé designed and built a carriage lantern consisting of an electric lamp fixed on a plate at the end of the ordinary lantern socket. It could be easily adapted to every type of vehicle. But for newly built carriages, the inventor placed a battery under the driver's seat while the light bulbs were placed in the lanterns themselves. He even placed them in the reflectors or in holders strapped onto the horses' heads. One customer wrote,

> For two weeks, the whole town of Jassy has been astounded, whenever I go out, in the evening, in my carriage. Your electric reflectors placed at the head of my horses, work wonders, and I think that I will have many imitators.
>
> It would be most agreeable, Monsieur, to show my readers, in my newsroom, the numerous masterpieces and curiosities that you showed me during my last trip to Paris; among others, your charming jewels, your luminous walking stick, your shooting stick and your siren-stick, so noisy that it still shatters my ears.
>
> I hope you will be gracious enough to enable me to convince my skeptical fellow countrymen with their own eyes and that you would be able to send these to me as soon as possible.[5]

Universal electric lamp for a carriage headlamp (from Georges Barral, L'histoire d'un inventeur, 1891).

Alongside electric lighting for carriages, Trouvé also developed an electric horse bit for controlling a runaway horse. A crude version of this somewhat cruel device had been invented by M. Defoy in 1866. The bit was connected to an electromagnetic apparatus by metal wires placed in the reins. The rider simply turned the crank of the electromagnet and a current of electricity was sent to the horse's mouth, meant to startle the creature into passivity.

To further improve this, Trouvé worked with a Monsieur Sidos, physical trainer at the Lycée Charlemagne. It was formed of two bits, insulated from each other, that communicated with the two poles of a small inductor, by containing a very flexible guidewire. The appliance and its hermetic battery were contained in a small box placed in front of the splash-board of the carriage. To act on the horse's mouth or neck muscles, it was enough to make the little box pivot or tilt, activating the battery and sending a charge up to the bit. The charge could be decreased or increased depending on the horse's mood. Trouvé's electric bit was successfully tested in the main stud of the state, on the most unruly horses. Mr. Sidos's favorable report to the Society for Encouragement has been lost.

Trouvé had a select number of private sponsors or patrons: Adelina Patti, the world's most celebrated coloratura soprano, and one of the highest paid, resided with her lover, the tenor Ernesto Niccolini, at Craig-y-Nos Castle, Upper Swansea Valley, South Wales. Since acquiring this mansion in 1878, they had considerably expanded it, adding north and south wings, a winter garden, a clock tower and a large conservatory.

But the Patti-Nicolinis were also forward-looking; not only had they equipped their entire house with electric lighting, among the very first to do so in Great Britain, they had also installed an electrically powered Welte orchestra organ (Orchestrion) in the French billiards room. Using paper melody rolls, it had around 146 pipes, including up to 18 trumpets and 33 metal pipes. Driven by a 110-volt DC motor, a blower provided the air to sound the pipes.

More ambitious than this, they had also equipped their private theater with 281 electric lamps and carbon-arc follow spots. So avant-garde was this theater that they organized an official opening on 12 July 1891. Among the invited elite: Prince Henry of Battenberg, the Crown Prince of Sweden, Edward the Prince of Wales, the Spanish Ambassador, and Baron Julius Reuter (founder of Reuter's News Agency).

As part of the celebrations, Adelina and Ernesto had an additional surprise for their guests. In the large glass conservatory was an impressive luminous fountain. The 2.6-kW, electrically driven ornament weighed 10 kg (221 lbs.), and the pool to catch the water measured 6 meters (20 ft.) in diameter. Four incandescent lamps, 300 candlepower each, grouped in front of parabolic reflectors, sent their powerful rays to light up the jets of water playing above them. Ingeniously, as the water fell back down, it turned a little paddle wheel, which then revolved colored glass plates to continuously change the color of the spray of water—like an aquatic kaleidoscope, but a kaleidoscope of fire. The motor used any power source: hydraulic, electric or clockwork.[6] The creator of these fountains was none

1891. Trouvé's ingenious system for a hand-pumped luminous fountain in a floral goldfish bowl (Electropolis).

other than Monsieur Trouvé of Paris. It is not known whether Trouvé, creator of this electric, luminous fountain, had travelled over from Paris to Wales for the official switching-on of his masterpiece.

Illuminated fountains were already popular, even if across the English Channel. In 1884, for the International Health Exhibition in London's

1891. Rare photograph of the monumental luminous fountains designed and built by Trouvé, as commissioned by opera singer Adelina Patti, for display in the conservatory of her Welsh castle, Craig-Y-Nos. The only thing missing is their color effect (Georgia Archives, Alfred Barili Family Papers, ac. 1967–0601M).

South Kensington, Sir Francis Bolton had designed a giant, steam-powered, illuminated fountain. Arc lights shone through colored glass plates with changeable filters, and the whole contraption could only be operated by a team of five men, wearing dark blue goggles. In 1887, the Royal Jubilee Exhibition of 1887 was held in Old Trafford, Manchester, England, to celebrate the Golden Jubilee of Queen Victoria's accession. It was opened by Princess Alexandra, the Princess of Wales (wife of the Prince of Wales, later Edward VII) on 3 May 1887, and remained open for 166 days, during which time there were 4.5 million paying visitors, 74,600 in one day alone. The 120-ft. "Fairy Fountain," designed and built by local engineers Galloway and Sons, largely copied the London fountain, using triple illuminating arc lamps playing on a central jet, while single lamps illuminated 16 other jets. It was a half-hour show operated daily by a similar team. The following year, a similar fountain was admired in Glasgow.

One of the attractions of the 1889 Centenary Exhibition in Paris was the Fountain of Progress designed by G. Bechmann (French), the Water Service's chief engineer, and Jean Camille Formigé, architect of the exposition. The fountain, with neo-baroque sculptures by Jules Coutan, was placed in the center of the open space of the Champ-de-Mars. Beside this, a second illuminated fountain designed by Galloway and Sons was built exactly under the Eiffel Tower.

In a speech given to the International Society of Electricians, Trouvé recounted that he was inspired by the popular success of the luminous fountains at the 1889 Centenary Exhibition:

> Such a success inspired me in the desire to democratize this fairylike divertissement by the combination of fountains which could decorate our drawing-rooms, our dining-rooms, our gardens, etc. And thanks to the adoption of a new principle, both simple and effective, I believe I have fully succeeded. To get this result, the fountains, while becoming light and less extravagant, must keep their power and purity of their brilliance, must be automatic and in harmony with their surroundings.

1891. Trouvé envisioned his luminous fountains being widely used at home, in house and garden, in doctor's surgeries and in public places such as hotels (Musée EDF Electropolis, Mulhouse).

Trouvé's fountains could be constructed in any dimensions: as small as a basket of flowers on the table, their basin being modified with rocks and living fish to swim around in the light. They could be used in a doctor's or dentist's office, public areas, or shops. Placed on a chariot, they could be part of a theater set. They were worked with a pump activated either by hand, foot, clockwork or electric current. Finally, in monumental form, for private gardens such as Dame Patti-Nicolini's, Trouvé's lighting system would enable, if one could obtain sufficient water pressure, constructing luminous fountains rising to *1 kilometer (3,280 feet) in height*. Indeed, he had suggested this to the president of the Organization of the 1900 Universal Exhibition in Paris, due to take place in eight years' time: "With the water jets rising to a staggering height of between 250 and 1,000 meters

1889. This engraving of Trouvé appears opposite the title page of the 600-page illustrated biography of him by Georges Barral entitled *Histoire d'un Inventeur*. It is taken from a painting by Fernand de Launay, admitted to the Salon des Beaux-Arts of Paris in 1889. To date, the whereabouts of this painting are unknown (from Georges Barral, *L'histoire d'un inventeur*, 1891).

[820 and 3,280 feet], their lights could be seen from all the points of the city and beyond. Their colors, as varied and as changing as so desired, could even serve as signals. The only doubt is whether enough water pressure could be created to achieve this.[7]

Although Trouvé's concept of a luminous fountain rising to almost the height of the Eiffel Tower was ultimately turned down, "in 1900, his process was slightly modified for the illumination of the famous Palais de l'Electricité and of its waterfalls which made up 'le clou,' the star attraction of the Exhibition."[8]

In 1891, a very complete and well-illustrated biography of Gustave

Trouvé was published.[9] It was written, in close collaboration with the inventor, by a certain Georges Barral. Six years before, an article about Trouvé written by Wilfrid de Fonvielle had appeared in *The Journal Barral: Revue Universelle Illustrée* (April 1885, number 9). This journal was published on the 10th, the 20th and the 30th of each month with the help of former friends, students and collaborators of J.-A. Barral. Its chief editor was Georges Barral.

In 1864, the young Barral had accompanied the photographer Nadar on a balloon voyage and written it up in *Impressions Aeriennes d'un compagnon de Nadar*. In 1887, he had written the 290-page *History of Science Under Napoleon Bonaparte.*

In Barral's preface to the book about Trouvé, written in Paris on 15 October 1890, he states,

> This *Story of an Inventor* is also a book of attractive science, because M. Gustave Trouvé has touched the artistic, luxurious and amusing side of electricity, while creating the most useful domestic applications and solving the deepest problems of serious electrical engineering…. In finishing this necessary but short preface, we would also have wanted to put any sensitivity over the excessive modesty of M. Gustave Trouvé in the shade.
>
> With great pleasure, we have leaved through this biography of the likeable inventor M. Gustave Trouvé. Usually one is scarcely interested in France in works of this type, so it is none the less curious to follow, so to speak, step by step, the evolution of an ingenious and original mind. The author makes us witness to the successive demonstrations of the unquestioned activity of the inventor. It makes an excellent response to the malcontents who might be astonished at the general character of the work, and it would authorize having a similar biography done. Also, reader, we invite you to go through this book. You will certainly find some novel ideas in it.[10]

In one surviving autographed copy,[11] handwritten on the title page, is this: "Respectful and friendly homage from the author Georges Barral," and underneath, "From the Inventor embarrassed in being totally and so well praised G. Trouvé."

There would not be another biography of Trouvé for the next 120 years. Barral continued to write such titles as *Five Days with Charles Baudelaire in Brussels* (1895). But he would not write about Trouvé's final 12 years of inventiveness when, as we shall discover, both medical instrumentation and theatrical effects would reach their zenith, along with heavier-than-air flight.

That summer of 1891, 20 years after his first attempt, Trouvé relaunched his mechanical bird. He wrote a document, *Study of Heavier-than-Air Aerial Navigation. Tethered Electric Military Helicopter. Aviator Generator-Motor-Propelling Unit*[12]:

I had the honor, many years ago, of being admitted to the intimacy of Messieurs de la Landelle and Ponton d'Amécourt, the fierce defenders, the renewers of the heavier-than-air doctrine whose classical origins go back to Archytas of Tarentum. I was won over and I have since remained their fervent disciple … obstinate admirer of methods used so simply in Nature, wonderfully used by birds to stay in the air and to keep straight.... Nothing has shaken my belief in the possibility of an exclusively mechanical perfect solution to the problem of air navigation.

He examined which motor was best qualified for aerial navigation, combining great power with lightness. He eliminated steam, pure electricity, energy accumulators such as rubber and steel, compressed air and gas motors:

So doesn't there exist today any motor armed with its accessories, generator and propelling device that one can make use of immediately or nevertheless complete for the goal that we have given to ourselves? The comparative experiments that I have brought and that I have controlled with my universal dynamometer seem to attest to this.

And even if the generator and the propelling device, both necessary, are the organs that are hindering us, can we not use a subterfuge? Do not the electric helicopters with which I obtained such good results, present the case of an entirely special adaptation of the propeller to the motor which, like all electric motors, turns at an excessive speed; the liaison is so fortunate that one of the organs is, so to say, made for the other. With my electric boats I have often been struck by this fact that the wash, at the stern, is almost imperceptible. It's that the propeller of my rudder-motor-propelling unit, animated with its great speed/2,400 rpm, twists in the water like a screw turns in its nut. In the same way, my electric helicopter, the propeller does so to say the integral part of the motor, which makes us in the presence of a motor propelling device.

So unable to eliminate either the generator or the propelling device of the apparatus, I incorporate it into the motor and I create a new self-sufficient organism which I call GENERATOR-MOTOR-PROPELLING UNIT.

Trouvé constructed his "generator-motor-propeller" using a Bourdon tube, as was used to measure the pressure in steam gauges. If the pressure of gas in a Bourdon tube increased, the tube bent and tended to spread its branches, but if the pressure decreased, the branches contracted. Trouvé added a second tube inside the first, so increasing the elastic forces of the gases. The chemical combination used was the oxidation of hydrogen:

Hydrogen is obtained easily, rapidly and in great quantity, even more, and oxygen, its combustive, is found ready prepared in the atmosphere; my bird, as those in nature, therefore draws from the air a big part of its food. The explosive mixture can be controlled at will, but it is very close to 25 percent hydrogen for 75 percent atmospheric air, and the ignition is produced by electricity, as in gas engines.

1891. The mechanical bird built by Trouvé to demonstrate the future of heavier-than-air flying machines. With its system of cartridges and Bourdon tubes, it managed a hop of 80 meters (from Georges Barral, *L'histoire d'un inventeur*, 1891).

The compressions and expansions are produced by detonating 12 cartridges contained in the revolver barrel that communicated with the tube. This produces a series of energetic wing strokes that propel and sustain the "aviator," connected to a silk sustaining airplane, in the air.

The departure takes place like this: the light winged device is suspended from a cord fixed at the end of a jib and the pendulum so composed is moved away from the vertical and held by a second cord against the foot of the jib. Two blowtorches, one mobile and the other fixed, placed in the vertical of the mooring point, are designed to set light to these two cords.

With flame, as we burn the first, the aviator, like Foucault's pendulum, begins its oscillation. It makes a circle to come from Position 1 to Position 2, but once arrived there, its acquired speed is horizontal, Flame B burns the cord, the firing pin in freedom comes down, the cartridge explodes, the tube vibrates violently and the wings energetically flap the air by lowering at the same time, the bird leaves the primitive horizontal plane and thanks to the inclination of its tail, takes a slight upwards movement. Then the gases released escape into the atmosphere, in the reverse direction of the movement, to even use their reaction; the vibrator tube resumes its initial shape and the wings lift up a little more slowly than they had lowered.

Promptly, the barrel driven by its clicking brings a cartridge to the firing pin, which strikes it; a second explosion is produced and the previous phenomena occur in the same order. During the third, fourth ... and twelfth explosion, *the bird crossed an overall horizontal distance of 75 to 80 meters*

[80 to 90 yards], in struggling against gravity and rising progressively upwards.

At the end of its flight, the aviator does not drop straight down; the wings, held raised by the closing of the branches of the tube and the silk airplane whose surface is proportioned to the weight of the pseudo-animal, acting like a parachute, and the machine descends obliquely and slowly onto the ground. The airplane, presented in dotted lines, brings together the rudder, the head of the bird, the bends of the wings and the tail. In the future, and whatever the power of the motor, the use of the airplane will remain very useful; its surface constantly proportioned to the total weight will avoid any accident in case of sudden halt of the motive machine.

I repeat, in a bird or a machine of great dimensions, a reservoir of compressed hydrogen will replace the cartridges of the little model and the use of aluminum remains all indicated as much by its specific lightness as by its currently affordable price.

Having presented his experiments with heavier-than-air model flying machines to the Aerostation Commission of the Academy of Sciences, Trouvé left a sealed letter containing all the details. The document is not hand-written but typed, and signed. He concludes:

My contentment will be complete if I have succeeded in sharing with the Academy my absolute faith in the possibility and the coming realization of practical aerial navigation. It's assuredly the first heavier-than-air machine able to be built full-scale and to cross space by its own forces. The extreme experiment of great navigation no longer depends on funds and secondary studies. By bringing together my efforts uniquely of the discovery of light and powerful engine, I have been one of the first—in 1870—to tackle the problem. Its definitive solution will not take long to emerge.

Paris, June 1, 1891, G. Trouvé

Soon after, Trouvé's ornithopter was described in technical reviews. An edited edition of his report, published in 1891 in *Le Monde de la Science et de l'Industrie*, was then translated and published in *Popular Science Monthly* under the title "The Aviator Flying-Machine."[13] Trouvé concludes, "We close by saying with Victor Hugo, 'The future is with navigation of the air.'"[14] This was also picked up by *Scientific American* (1892), by *Prometheus* (year 2, no. 104, Berlin, 1891) and *Luftschiffahrt Trouvésche Flugsmaschine* (Vienna, 1891).

In his book *Progress in Flying Machines*, published in 1894 by *The American Engineer and Railroad Journal*, New York, a retired railway engineer, French-born Octave Chanute, devoted a page to Trouvé's experiment. Among those who read this book were Orville and Wilbur Wright. Indeed, Chanute befriended the brothers and helped to publicize their flying experiments. At his death he was hailed as the father of aviation and the heavier-than-air flying machine.

SEVEN

Healing with Light

By 1892 Gustave Trouvé, 53 years old, could watch and read about the slow progress of technologies he had helped to introduce.

In aviation, a fellow Frenchman, Clément Ader, only managed to make his steam-engined, fixed-winged aircraft *Eole* fly for 50 meters (54 yards) before crashing.

Over in the United States, William Morrison of Des Moines, Iowa, had been testing a six-passenger electric wagon capable of reaching a speed of 14 miles per hour (23 km/h), while the Electric Construction Corporation had set up a virtual monopoly on the almost nonexistent British electric car market. In southern England, German-born Moritz Immisch had set up what was probably the world's first fleet of electric launches for hire (12 of them), with a chain of electrical charging stations established along the River Thames.

The General Electric Company, a merger of Edison General Electric and Thomson-Houston, was about to introduce the first commercial, fully enclosed carbon-arc lamp. Sealed in glass globes, it lasted 100 hours and therefore 10 times longer than previous carbon-arc lamps.

But, true to character, Trouvé was finding other remarkable applications of electric lighting. One of his workmen, for a long time crippled by rheumatism, found himself completely healed after being exposed for several hours to the action of intense light sources used in the production of their decorative luminous fountains at the rue Vivienne workshops. Trouvé, fascinated, began to look into the use of different types of light to heal rheumatism.

Two years before, Dr. François Victor Foveau de Courmelles, aged 28 years, had written in his book *Hypnotism*: "We are surrounded in nature by a subtle force that scientific men call ether.... It would seem possible that this ambient medium may transform the perturbations of nervous power. The nerve cells of the brain vibrate under the influence of different causes, why should it not be thought that this movement does not extend further than the cranium?"

Soon after, Doctor Foveau de Courmelles presented his idea of electrochromotherapy, suggesting that the influence of electric light of such and such a color and temperature could be used to heal neuroses. Before long de Courmelles and Trouvé met up. De Courmelles would later recall,

> I was applying chemical light which had to give me at the Saint Louis hospital, the marvelous results that Marie-Louis Néron has spoken about in this newspaper. He built my radiator with much hesitation because he was only interested in the treatment of rheumatisms by the concentrated heat of incandescent light. It is true that his inventions, his own, captivated him most of all, which is quite natural. But when one is builder, one most not also spurn the wood that the other brings and that will be the seed of new ideas. Thus we had, my having had great difficulty in convincing him, a chemical radiator that then enthused him.[1]

Alongside this, Trouvé continued his services to the theaters, both in Paris and abroad. For example, he created lightning, hail and howling wind for a scene called "The Rescuers" in the play *The Master of Arms* (*Le Maître d'Armes*) put on by Monsieur Rochard at the Théâtre de la Porte Saint-Martin in Paris's tenth arrondissement.

Then for Christmas '92 at the Vaudeville Theatre of the Saint-Hubert Galleries in Brussels, Belgium: "There is the electric sword fight.... In the grand finale, you see slowly rising up from the stage a Christmas tree, 12 meters [40 feet] high, decorated with 250 luminous flowers, of all colors, while two luminous fountains sparkle alongside!" Effect: Trouvé de Paris.

Perhaps one of his greatest theatrical achievements was to create the special effects for a performance of Hector Berlioz's opera *The Damnation of Faust*. The venue was the Opéra de Monte-Carlo, part of the Casino in the principality of Monaco. This was to be the first production of a 32-year-old impresario, Raoul Gunsbourg. Several months before, on the recommendation of Tsar Alexander III of Russia, Gunsbourg was invited by Princess Alice, the American wife of Albert I, Prince of Monaco, to serve as the director of the Opéra de Monte-Carlo. Empowered by Princess Alice's encouragement and support, Gunsbourg had the chance to turn the Opéra into a world-class cultural venue. For the special effects, he had no hesitation in calling on Trouvé of Paris: "It's the eminent engineer, Trouvé, who will direct the various technical maneuvers, in person, for the first presentation of *The Damnation of Faust* on the stage of Monte-Carlo."[2]

The première took place on 18 February 1893. One journalist reported,

There are two ballets. In one of them, Scene VII, the woods alongside the River Elbe—70 luminous roses, made out of petals of colored paper in the middle of each is a little light bulb. Ten Italian ballerinas, carrying in their green velvet corsages a luminous rose powered by a pocket battery, advance to dance the ballet of the sylphs while Faust is asleep.

While Faust and Mephistopheles gallop on Vortex and Giaour, these two black horses as swift as thought itself, represented by two articulated mannequins, as the backdrop of the stage a long canvas is scrolled by, representing the scenery corresponding to the various phases of the race. The effect of lightning is also there!

At the moment that Faust, played by Jean de Reszke, screams, "It is crying blood!," a luminous cascade which is at first a fine green flows down from a height of 8 meters [26 feet], turning red as it does so, thanks to a play of electric lights through colored glass. The audience gasps! An unforgettable effect imagined by Gunsberg in conjunction with Gustave Trouvé. The work received a very warm reception. The music is divine, the words well rhythmic and the set direction wonderful![3]

Another wrote, "Electricity has enabled M. Trouvé to work wonders with the set design like the rose garden or the ballerinas carrying a luminous rose and the ballet of the will-o'-the-wisps in which, clothed in black, they seemed like living flames.... I came out of the Salle Garnier overwhelmed, enthusiastic!"[4]

Often singing lead roles at the Monte Carlo theater was Adelina Patti-Nicolini, still enjoying the luminous fountain created by Trouvé for the giant greenhouse of her Welsh castle, Craig-y-Nos.

Back in Paris, at the Casino de Paris in the rue Clichy, the audience was delighted by the rhythm of flickering lights:

Another type of serpentine dance has just been produced at the Paris Casino. Miss Sita, the famous eccentric singer, accompanies her singing with steps and gracious movements and is all lit up from head to toes, projecting a fantastic electric illumination. These wonderful effects are obtained by 120 to 150 light bulbs, skillfully used and spread around the dancer's clothing which can, at will, be switched off or on.... It's Monsieur G. Trouvé, the skillful electrician, who thought up this imaginative arrangement.[5]

In sharp contrast, 1893 was the year in which Trouvé published a voluminous work aimed at the medical world for the right use of his inventions in this field. Running to a remarkable 788 pages, it contained 273 illustrations of which several had been printed in Barral's biography of Trouvé, three years before. The others, unpublished, are signed either "Trouvé" or again "Bienfait" ("Welldone," a lovely nom de plume).[6] In his foreword, Trouvé explained:

The aim that I have given myself in publishing this manual has not been to enrich the already so opulent bibliography of electrotherapy. In my opin-

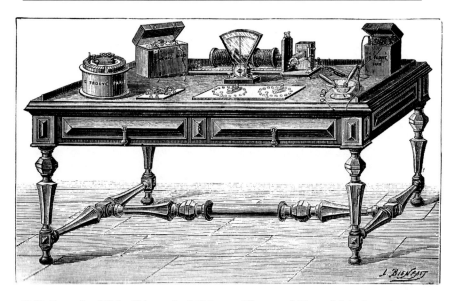

1893. Trouvé published his seminal 788-page illustrated *Manuel théorique, instrumental et pratique d'electrologie médicale (Theoretical Manual and Practice of Medical Electrology)*. Among the many illustrations are his own instruments, such as this "table d'électrothérapie."

ion, a practical and methodical guide was lacking that at once showed the doctor, fixed on the main lines of treatment to follow, which instrument to employ in what operation, and it's this gap that I wanted to fill.... I think that I have scrupulously fulfilled, by application as much as precaution, the programme I set out for myself. May this manual give doctors all the little services that a daily practice demands; for me, this would be a most deserving reward.

In his preface to this book, Doctor Romain Vigoroux begins: "M. Trouvé has honored me by asking a preface from me. I suppose that, despite all his modesty, he cannot believe it necessary that one presents him to his readers. His celebrity as builder and inventor is too well established for him to be even mentioned." The manual presented the wide range of instruments conceived and built by Trouvé in collaboration with the best electrotherapists in France.

One of his more recent, patented on 12 July 1892, was a spring-loaded, handheld medical dynamometer. Medical dynamometers were generally based on a variably-shaped spring on which the patient's fingers reacted so as to measure the muscular effort. In these conditions, the application point was not always the same and gave results that were not always exact. "My dynamometer avoids these errors," Trouvé claimed. It was made up

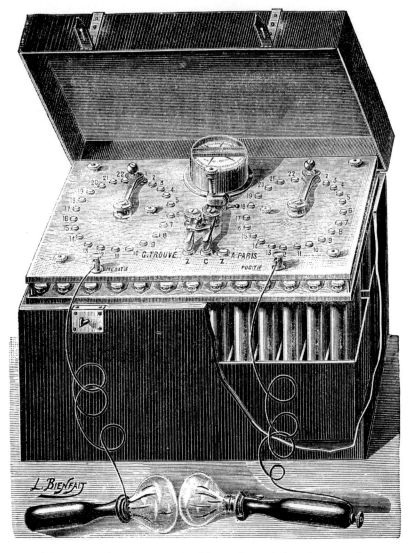

Trouvé's large, portable electro-medical device formed of 44 elements of constant and continuous current, used to stimulate the patient under treatment (from Georges Barral, *L'histoire d'un inventeur*, 1891).

of a spring, which could either be circular or of any other shape; at its extremities, this spring carried two handles or bars that received the efforts of the fingers and so gave a more exactly measurement. A pointier and dial then indicated the muscular effort.[7]

Another was an instrument to relieve patients suffering from hernias.

In Patent N° 223,584, taken out in August 1892, Trouvé and his associate, a Dr. Paul Davidson, describe it as "an electrical hernial ball." The small ball carried an electric generator that, using Trouvé's copper and zinc pocket battery installed inside, switched on once it was placed on the patient's body. Electrical energy was transmitted to two metal plates, which were covered in suede sewn onto the ball to protect it from getting dirty. The suede covering was necessary to avoid the formation of burns under the action of the current, the ball being so designed that when one applied it on the body, the dampness of the skin was enough to create the circuit between the plates and for the electricity to pass from one to the other, while acting not merely on the skin, like previous such instruments, but on the underlying tissues, which they then toned up and brought back to their normal state by suppressing the atrophy. To facilitate the passage of the doctor, one could humidify the electrodes beforehand. Concerned

1893. With these medical dynamometers, perhaps Trouvé drew his own hand holding the instruments (Trouvé).

with the fears of patients on seeing his strange new medical instrument, Trouvé had his pedal-operated, electro-cautery device covered with tapestry to make it looked like an ottoman.

This year, Trouvé was also working with Célestin Contancin, doctor of Montmorillan and senator of the Vienne Department, on creating electrical devices that used hot light applied to patients suffering from tuberculosis, rheumatism and neuralgia.

Trouvé did not abandon his love of aesthetics or his work to further develop the luminous fountains. In March 1893, he made the following proposition to readers of the Bulletin of the Society of Encouragement for National Industry:

> If one feared it hard to push water with these colossal pressures up to 250 or 300 meters [600 to 900 feet], and one can hardly talk of lesser heights since the construction of the Eiffel Tower—nothing would be so easy at least, thanks to this tower, than to establish one or several luminous waterfalls cascading down from its third platform. Four arms, for example, positioned as gargoyles at the four corners, and equipped with my parabolic projects and accessories, would vertically launch, from top to bottom, their cones of multi-colored light and the falling water spray, directly lit, would come towards the ground, blossoming and dividing up into a seedbed of stars and precious stones that, little by little, would dissolve into a colored cloud enveloping the foot of the tower and the spectators. It goes without saying that one could simultaneously set ablaze the edifice or mix with luminous projections of sections the different tiers of waterfall. The spectacle would certainly be very novel and grandiose.

He did not miss out telling his readers about his great experiment with special effects in many theaters: "Gentlemen, allow me again, before finishing, to tell you about some electrical effects, some tricks, used at the Porte-Saint-Martin to represent a lightning bolt."[8] In the same article, there was an illustration of a domestic luminous fountain with multiple jets and changing multi-colored lights, "built for M. Eiffel."

That July, M. Le Général Sebert reported on behalf of the Committee of Economic Arts, of the Society of Encouragement for National Industry, on the claims of M. Gustave Trouvé to the prize founded by Mme Melsens in memory of her husband. This was the second time the prize had been awarded. He wrote,

> This choice hardly need be justified. The numerous works and the multiple inventions of M. Trouvé are too well known for it to be necessary to recall them in detail, and it will be enough to mention summarily those which enter into the categories that the Melsens prize has especially in view.
> Monsieur Trouvé is an indefatigable worker who has explored innumerable subjects among those that offer themselves to human activity; he is a

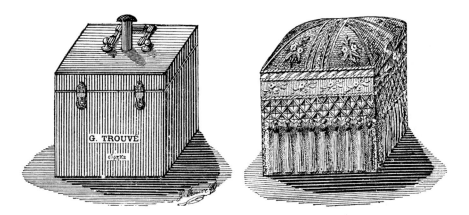

Concerned with the fears of patients on seeing his strange new medical instrument, Trouvé had his pedal-operated electro-cautery device covered with tapestry to make it looked like an ottoman (from Georges Barral, *L'histoire d'un inventeur*, 1891).

researcher always on the alert and always ready to put his ingenious mind at the service of those who present him with a problem whose solution can be of interest to humanity or the greatness of the country. The distinction that the Society for Encouragement awards him today will only be a feeble reward for the services he has given.

The prize in question was some 500 francs, equivalent to today's $4,500.

Trouvé's *Manual of Medical Electrology* did not include his electric trigger mechanism for chronophotography on a unique plate, built between 1892 and 1893. This object can still be found in the reserve collection of the museum of the Conservatoire des Arts et Métiers in Paris. Most of the objects currently conserved by the CNAM have a provenance. But, exceptionally, the provenance for this electric trigger (Inventory N° 16961–0002) does not exist. The description simply reads, "The Electric Dispatcher of the Machine for Chronophotography on Londe's Unique Plate; Item N° 16961–0001 portable stereoscopic photographic chamber called the 'stereocycle.'" Nor did Trouvé patent it.

A photographer by profession, Albert Londe was working at the Paris hospital of La Salpêtrière under its director, Jean-Martin Charcot. He was taking photographs of female patients that served as evidence for the Salpêtrière doctor's specific theory of hysteria. In reality, these were wholly staged representations in which doctor, patient, and photographer all collaborated.

Londe designed and built a camera with nine lenses that were tripped by electromagnetic energy, with a battery provided by Trouvé and a

Fig. 2. — Chambre noire.

Fig. 3. — Distributeur.

Fig. 2 et 3. — Fig. 2. Chambre noire. — A, Platine portant les objectifs, les obturateurs et leurs déclenchements électriques. — B, Contact à treize fils. — C, Chambre noire. — D. Crémaillère de mise au point. — Fig. 3. Distributeur Lucien Leroy. — A, Platine. — B, Balai. — C, Rondelle en ivoire isolatrice. — D, Un des douze contacts. — E, Tube isolant renfermant les douze fils. — F, Les douze fils en relation avec les douze bornes G, G. — G', Fil de retour en relation avec le balai. — H, Echappement. — I, Armature. — J, Electro-aimant. — K, K, V, V, Butoirs de l'armature. — L, Réglage du ressort antagoniste. — N, N, Bornes recevant le courant de l'expéditeur. — O, Remontage du mouvement d'horlogerie. — P, Poussette pour la remise au zéro.

Fig. 4. — Le nouveau laboratoire photochronographique en plein air de la Salpêtrière.

1893. The camera used by Albert Londe to take a sequence of nine time-lapse photographs of hysterical female patients at La Salpêtrière Hospital in Paris. It was electrically activated by a machine commissioned from Trouvé. It is considered by some as a precursor of the cinematographic camera. But while Londe is credited, Trouvé is not (Musée EDF Electropolis, Mulhouse).

metronome to time the release of the shutters. This camera took photographs on a glass plate in rapid succession.

Now known as a photographer who added to the further study of stop-action series photography, Albert Londe must be acknowledged for his overall work within medicine using photography. He would use his talents in the study of animal movement and the action of waves. Adding three more lenses to his camera of 1882, Londe used 12 lenses to photograph a succession of images of patients in a variety of movements. The purpose: the study of muscle-movement. Exposures lasted from one and a half seconds to several seconds. But he had Trouvé to thank for the essential mechanism.

At the same time, the Lumière brothers were beginning to make their very first experiments with cinematography using the principle of the projection of a succession of images onto a screen. With his *auxanoscope* projector, his photographic trigger, and his audio-visual tricks for the theater, the play of sound and light of his luminous fountains—all electric—Trouvé was really in the spirit of an epoch when the very foundations for a revolutionary picture technology were being laid down.

For the industry, in July 1893, Trouvé took out Patent N° 229,314 for what he called "a dynamo ventilator," for the input and output of air or gas under pressure. It was an ingenious combination of an electric motor mounted on a mobile armature and linked to the axis of a ventilator, the small blades of which could vary depending on use. This configuration resulted in the air-cooling of the motor, enabling it to work with a stronger current than usual for all types of bellows, blowtorches, lighting equipment and in general for machines needing air or gas at a feeble or average pressure.

In sharp contrast, that same summer, Trouvé patented[9] a deceptively simple device for automatic fishing. He conceived of a net, around the edge of which was inflatable India rubber tubing that could be used to lower and raise the net from a distance. The inflation and deflation of the tubing was carried out by means of a switch-controlled, compressed-air generator, which was either on board the fishing boat or on shore. The inflatable net was also attached to a buoy, which carried an electric lamp fitted with a reflector so the fisherman could see his net at night. In addition, the tinkling of a bell attached to this device indicated the entry of fish into the net; then by using a balance linked to the net, the fisherman could gauge the amount of fish he had caught that night. This was granted home and foreign patents by 1894 and was publicized in a booklet entitled "A New System of Fishing."[10] Several years later Georges Dary would write, "The idea of using electricity for fishing and of attracting fish by submerg-

1894. The nocturnal automatic fishing that Trouvé developed was almost complementary to his electric rifle, which he had now equipped with a directional light on the barrel for hunting in dark forest or at night (Georges Dary, *A travers l'électricité*).

ing electric light dates back several years. But it's impossible to give a definitive decision about the excellence of this process, sometimes successful, sometimes useless."[11]

Trouvé, a seasoned hunter, also developed an "electric lance," which in a hand-to-hand fight with a wild boar or other dangerous animal gave the hunter precious help and which, without killing the animal, stunned and shocked it to enable its adversary to make use of his weapon without danger. In short, this was the first stun gun, or Taser, developed 70 years later by a NASA researcher, Jack Cover.

He simply could not leave his light fairies alone! He was still concerned about the weight and autonomy of the batteries to power those wearable luminous electric jewels. According to his patent N° 236,921 of 10 March 1894, during the show, the artiste would wear a belt of supple material to which various light bulbs were fixed, protected by reflectors.

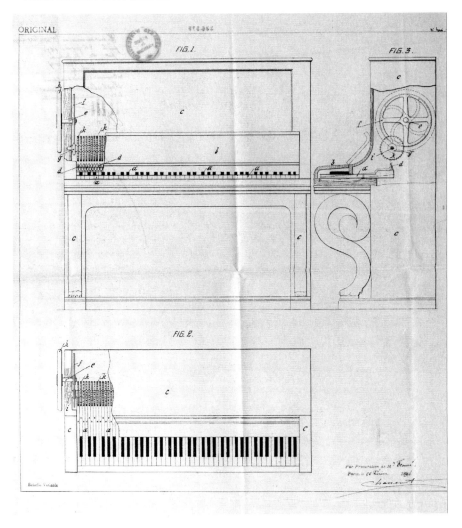

1894. The patent drawing of the Savart-wheel piano with the option of electric/clockwork propulsion makes Trouvé the inventor of one of the first electrical musical instruments (courtesy INPI archives).

She (or he) would then be wired up as follows. At certain points on the stage floor were two conductive plates, linked to an electrical supply source beneath. The artiste wore special shoes, the toe and the heel of which were fixed with conducting metal plates. In the empty place between the heel and the toe, this shoe carried a little metal socket that engaged with the conductors to which wires were attached.

Whenever the artiste placed her two feet on the plates, the electric current passed through the electric sole, following the wire hidden in her clothing to light up the colored bulbs and then returned to the electrical source via the second electric shoe sole and the plate. This freed the artiste from having to carry a battery hidden in their clothing. By using a switch held in her hand, the artiste could also vary the color of the luminous rays and instantly produce different effects. A wire extended into her hair could also light up a luminous diadem.

During that winter, Trouvé and his small team worked on something totally new—an electrically powered keyboard instrument. It was based on a physics machine called Savart's Wheel.

French physicist Félix Savart was the co-discoverer of electromagnetism. His main interests had been acoustics, vibrating bodies and music. He gave his name to the savart, a unit of measurement for musical intervals. In the 1830s, while investigating human hearing, Savart had constructed large, finely toothed brass wheels that, when fine blades were applied to their revolving teeth, depending on the rpm, produced a whole range of sound frequencies, up to as high as 24 kHz. They are considered to have been the world's first artificial ultrasonic generators. Working with a Parisian musical instrument maker, Savart had attempted to incorporate his wheel into a musical instrument but had failed when they disagreed over the determination of the lowest frequency.

According to Patent N° 236,575, taken out on 18 May 1894, Trouvé's innovation was to take Savart's Wheel and configure it into a new form of keyboard instrument whereby for every one of the 88 notes, there was a blade-to-wheel effect geared up to a single, horizontal shaft. The number of teeth on each wheel and the speed at which they turned were proportional to the number of vibrations of the chromatic range.

For example, the wheel corresponding to the key to give the note must run at 870 teeth per second. Loudness was based on the extent of the contact between the blade and the toothing of the wheel. As with all keyboard instruments, it would be possible to play chords on Trouvé's novel instrument.

With the aim of teaching the student, each key could carry an indication of the number of vibrations to which it corresponded. The timbre, or sound quality, depended on the material of which the blade was constructed: fine metal or an equally flexible material. The form of the toothing could vary depending on the effects desired, but in principle, saw-toothing or ratchet teeth were the best suited.

The wheeled transmission could be replaced by any other type of noiseless drive system, such as a belt or cord with sheaves. The shaft could be driven either by clockwork *or by an electric motor*, and positioned either inside or outside the piano box. The instrument would be equipped with accessories such as a clutch enabling the user to stop the movement of the shafts at will, or to use the pedals regulating the contact of the blades with the wheels, to enable the execution of *forte* and *piano*. Trouvé noted, "My invention can also be applied as much to instruments played by hand as to automatic instruments, to perforated cards; I also reserve the faculty to transmit the vibration produced by my system to any body susceptible to vibrate and notably to harmonic chords."[12]

In an attempt to see whether the Trouvé musical instrument was ever built, various musical instrument museums were approached and the French national database for musical instruments conserved in some 230 regional museums was consulted. These collections together encompass 4,500 instruments. No such instrument was found.

While it is not known whether the Trouvé instrument was built, two years later, in 1897, Thaddeus Cahill of Holyoke, Massachusetts, built his Telharmonium (also known as the Dynamophone). He became convinced that music could be made with electricity. (He also worked on an electric typewriter.) An electrical signal from the Telharmonium was transmitted over wires; it was heard on the receiving end by means of "horn" speakers. Like the later Hammond organ, the Telharmonium used tone wheels to generate musical sounds as electrical signals by additive synthesis. It has since been considered the first synthetic instrument due to its ability to generate sounds electromechanically, because the sound is produced by moving parts rather than electronic oscillators. Cahill showed his first Telharmonium to Lord Kelvin in 1902. Cahill had tremendous ambitions for his invention; he wanted Telharmonium music to be broadcast into hotels, restaurants, theaters, and even houses via the telephone line. At a starting weight of 7 tons (and up to 200 tons) and a price tag of $200,000, only three Telharmoniums were ever built, and Cahill's great vision was never fully implemented

In short, Trouvé would appear to have developed an electrically powered vibraphone, 40 years ahead of legends such as Hammond, Martenot, and Wurtlitzer. What might he have called it? A Trouvéphon?

Trouvé's pioneering of electric boats continued to make steady progress around the world, even if he was not involved. In 1893, the World's Columbian Exposition was held in Chicago to celebrate the 400th anniversary of Christopher Columbus' arrival in the New World in 1492. Its scale and grandeur far exceeded the other world fairs. The iconic centerpiece of the fair, the large water pool, representing the long voyage Columbus took to the New World, worked beautifully. A fleet of 55 34-ft. launches, built by the American Electric Launch and Navigation Company (ELCO), silently carried fair-goers around the site. It was claimed that a million people had ridden in them for a total distance of some 200,000 miles before the exposition closed. Ironically, the buildings were destroyed soon after, due to an electrical fault.

From the 1850s, increased industrial trade had led to a growing population in Bergen. In 1894, an engineer called Jacob Trumpy saw the need for a ferry across the harbor. Inspired by idea of an electric ferry during his stay in Westphalia, Germany, he introduced idea of electric propulsion to the Bergen government. On 15 May 1894 Bergens Elektrische Faergeselskab (Bergen Electric Ferry Company) was formed.

Despite protest from politicians that the e-ferries would take away their livelihood from ferrymen, two ferries started operation in August 1894. It was "the first regular passenger service of electric boats."[13] By the end of that year an additional six ferries were employed on different routes, linking the six different districts which surrounded the port. The ferries were not given names, simply numbers, "BEF 1," "BEF 2." Each BEF measured 8 meters long by 2 meters wide, with a draft of 0.8 m. They had a tonnage of 6 metric tons and could transport 18 passengers (including crew). They were open at the front and aft with only a canvas roof. This gave passengers little protection against the rainy Bergen weather.

In the Norwegian tradition of double-enders, they were constructed symmetrically, with a propeller at each end, so that when leaving a station they did not have to turn about. The two propellers were mounted on a common shaft that was coupled directly to a 3-horsepower electric motor with a weight of 300 kg, placed in the center under the planking. The Hagen batteries were distributed under the seats and weighed 1,400 kg. Their capacity was 20,000 watts-hours and the speed obtained with an output of 2,300 watts was 10 kilometers per hour, speed sufficient in a crowded port like that of Bergen. The ferries were soon providing frequent service: "One of these eight boats leaves every 5 minutes from 7 o'clock in the morning until 9:30 pm, carrying out a daily course of 40 sea miles and transporting an average of 1800 passengers."

During the night, placed in a special station at Bradbenken in Vagen, the BEFs did their main battery recharge with the aid of a 30-horsepower dynamo. They could also receive a 4-minute "topping up" between trips. During 1896, the BEF fleet transported a total of 486,000 passengers, or 40,500 per month. This service went on for 30 years.

Trouvé continued to explore the spectacular theatrical effects of his luminous electric jewels. In September 1894, he obtained Patent N° 239418 for a luminous, electric skipping/jump rope. Colored, faceted light bulbs or light tubes were wired along the rope, protected by intervening rubber washers. The electric current came either from Trouvé's zinc-carbon batteries hidden in the handles, or from static electricity generated by the metal soles on the shoes worn by the artiste and wired up to their hands. One can only imagine the effect of a troupe of electric light jumpers.

He continued to supply to a wide variety of users. When engineer Charles Jeantaud built his first electric car, he called on Trouvé for advice. The result was a neat two-seater carriage, with a battery of Faure accumulators weighing 450 kg mounted beneath the seat. The 4-hp motor, which could develop 1,500 rpm, was in-unit with the rear axle, which it drove through a double-reduction gearing.

Jeantaud, Faure and Trouvé then worked on a transmission system whereby a rheostat and a transformer would change the DC current generated by the transformer to the AC current needed to start the engine.

A Jeantaud four-seater brake with a surrey top took part in the 1895 Paris–Bordeaux race, the only electric vehicle to do so. Although Jeantaud had arranged ample supplies of spare batteries en route, the car was eliminated during the early stages of the race by axle trouble near Orléans.

In Vienna, a 58-year-old Russian inventor, Wilhelm Kress, used a ⅓-hp Trouvé motor for his ⅓ scale model of a helicopter. Seven years later, financed by the Emperor Franz Josef, Kress would build an unsuccessful full-scale waterplane.

On the evening of 6 February 1895, at a Session of the International Society of Electricians, Monsieur R.-V. Picou gave a talk about AC electric motors. He spoke of Tesla's hydro-electricity-generating system at Niagara Falls, and of his firm Westinghouse's complete 11,000-kW polyphase generation and distribution system with multiple generators, used at the Chicago World's Fair, and its electric boat fleet.

At the end, Trouvé asked Picou if, to his knowledge, there existed electric motors that could be supplied by either direct current or alternating current.

Picou replied in the negative. DC dynamos with laminated inductors could, under certain precautions, turn under the action of an alternating current, but their working in these conditions was not practically acceptable; from the industrial point of view, Picou did not see the interest that such "omnibus" machines would present.

Trouvé, on the contrary, stated his belief that this type of motor, of which he had made a version, would be likely to render important services at least in certain particular cases. Gradually, the future would prove him right, and so one can consider him as one of the inventors of the universal electric motor.

The 1890s was "the Golden Age of Bicycles," or over in France, "la folie de la bicyclette" ("bicycle madness"). Many improvements were being made and patented—pneumatic tires, the rear freewheel, coaster brakes, derailleur gears and hand-operated, Bowden cable-pull brakes. In his patent for a new velocipede, granted early in 1895, N° 243016, Trouvé observed how the stability of normal bikes depended on gravity and steering. By reconfiguring the most advantageous points for these two actions, he designed a steel-framed bicycle whose shorter framework made it lighter and so easier to ride, in particular when climbing gradients. By making the junction of the saddle-bearing tube in front of the rear wheel, his bicycle became easier to steer. Instead of a standard bicycle with its 18 × 8-tooth gearwheel, Trouve's bicycle had a 21 × 7-tooth unit. If it had ever been made, perhaps it would have been called the Eureka.

Also during that summer, he developed a handheld instrument for massaging the human muscles, perhaps such as calf muscles tired after a day of cycling. It could be worked by hand-cranking and/or powered by any source of electricity: battery, induction coil, a static machine or a machine supplying high tension and high frequency currents. It was made up of two units called strikers or hammers that alternated in pummeling the part of the body being massaged. The pummeling could be straight or rotary. The massage machine could also use an electrode plate for applying heat to various parts of the body. He was granted Patent N° 249231 on 27 July 1895.

Eight

An Alternative Light Source

In 1892, Trouvé was among those beginning to wonder whether electricity might not be the only solution for domestic lighting in the future.

Some three years before, in 1892, a Canadian called Thomas Wilson and a Frenchman called Henri Moissan both had made the discovery that the immersion of calcium carbide in water produced acetylene gas, which in turn gave out a brilliant white light. The scientific world was becoming excited about acetylene as the lighting of the future. Requiring neither batteries nor wires, it offered greater reliability for places where electric power was not available, such as an isolated chateau or a buoy out at sea. Trouvé immediately saw the advantage. "Practice was not long in convincing me that the first condition to fulfil to supply lighting with acetylene was to have this gas absolutely dry and cold."

He began to experiment in his Paris workshop, first with a simple laboratory glass bottle inside a large vase and a little basket with fragments of calcium carbide. He then progressed to making both a portable acetylene lamp and a bigger version for electric lighting,

> but not without long and patient researches to make this new type of lighting practical. Just to assemble the portable lamp like a simple hydrogen burner, which was a device known by all chemists, one obtained practically no usable result, because the production of acetylene gas by pure and simple immersion of calcium carbide in water is so turbulent that there is a considerable production of water vapor, which, mixed with the gas, hinders its combustion.[1]

To graduate the attack of calcium carbide by water, Trouvé replaced the ordinary bell jar with a flask pierced by a hole in its bottom and placed the pieces of solid product in a wire basket in distinct layers separated by glass washers. To remedy the production of water vapor, above the basket he then placed a metallic disc serving as condenser. He then passed the gas so produced through two concentric tubes forming a sort of siphon.

This completed the condensation of the vapor and ensured that the acetylene stayed dry and then burned in perfect conditions. Although this was in glass, the body or external envelope of the lamp could easily be made in materials other than glass, such as porcelain, china or metal, so as to give it a more decorative aspect.

Trouvé was enthusiastic as ever: "The flame of the lamp, with a lighting power of 5 Carcels [9.5 candles] is remarkable for its striking whiteness, its steadiness and one feels a sort of wonder to see this superb flame produced by the dipping of a blackish body, somewhat like coke, into simple water."

To supply larger lighting systems, Trouvé developed a system of gazometers, from one up to four, depending on the demand. He went on to perfect an automatic device for producing and bottling acetylene, which included a generator and a gazometer and where production was controlled by consumption. This would not only enable the consumption of calcium carbides from all sources, pure and impure, at a low price, but also the easy installation of a practical production of gas lighting at home.

Indeed mid–1896 saw publication of a 16-page brochure entitled "Eclairage General à l'Acetylene: Par les Appareils bretevés en France et à l'Etranger de l'ingenieur G. Trouvé. (General Acetylene Lighting: By the Appliances Patented in France and Abroad by the Engineer, G. Trouvé)." It was published by the General Company, located on 94 Boulevard Richard-Lenoir, in Paris, for the sale of acetylene lighting appliances. This was a historic, scientific and practical publication. The list of principal magazines having published articles about Trouvé's acetylene appliances, from November 1895 to May 1896, totaled 91; although the majority were French, magazines in New York, Turin, Milan, Dresden, Barcelona, London and Brussels reported on Trouvé's acetylene lamps. At the end of the brochure, there is a reprint from *Le Petit Journal* (illustrated supplement) N° 284 of 26 April 1896. Written by Émile Gautier, and entitled "Eureka, L'éclairage à acetylene (*Eureka, Acetylene Lighting*)," it reads:

> I will astonish nobody in adding that the one who therefore holds the record in this race towards the light is Mr. G. Trouvé, whose name (in Greek: Eureka) is an entire program. Every time there is a problem to solve, a difficulty to overcome, a new path to open up, one can be assured that Mr. G. Trouvé will emerge with a solution. This devil of a man whose works, all as curious as each other, can no longer be counted as just one idea per day. Just for the exhibition of 1900, he has prepared four surprises for us! Already accepted by the commission, and therefore the most banal is the setting up of a luminous cascade of three hundred meters.... Ah! He has not stolen this nickname of his, "the French Edison," except for that fact that he himself is the inventor.

Always attentive to detail, three years later, on 9 March 1898, he even patented—N° 275,794—a system of hermetic closing for cans, drums and other containers, specifically metal barrels for carrying calcium carbide. "These are the particular details which alone enable the good functioning of devices, and it's their invention which for M. Trouvé ensures the glory of having put the use of acetylene gas within everyone's range of, and of having perhaps prepared a real revolution in the conditions of home lighting."[2]

Characteristically, Trouvé did not follow up industrially. He left that to others. Two years later, a 23-year-old engineer set up a factory at Neuilly that he called "Blériot Headlamps," based on *his* patent for portable acety-

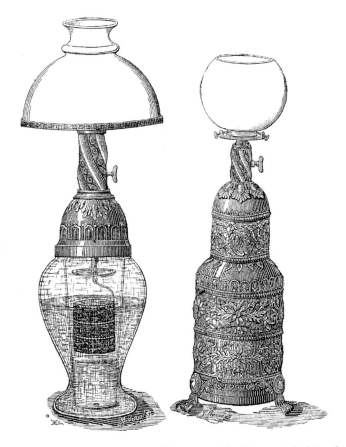

1895. Trouvé had very soon mastered the potential of domestic lighting by acetylene gas and characteristically reduced the size to compact and portable dimensions. As usual, he never thought of industrializing his innovation (Musée EDF Electropolis, Mulhouse).

lene headlamps. His target audience: the nascent automobile industry. The success of the company would make Louis Blériot wealthy enough to indulge in a series of flying machines, in one of which, on 25 July 1909, he would be the first man to successfully fly across the English Channel.

The 1896 directory of the telephone network for the Paris region shows a strong increase in subscribers. The Trouvés who were embroiderers had been joined by one Alexis Trouvé, secretary-general of the Havas Agency. But again G. Trouvé was absent.

At the session of the International Society of Electricians, held on 8 January 1896, the theme was "Calcium carbide and acetylene: their applications": "M. G. Trouvé recalls the applications of lighting by acetylene, which he has already realized and presented to several scientific societies; he gives some information about the results of this lighting and its cost price."

On 2 September, Dr. Paul Hélot, co-inventor of the photophore, who had been running his pioneer ear, nose and throat clinic in Rouen, giving free consultations, died suddenly, at the early age of 51, after scarcely 48 hours of illness. Food poisoning or an acute nephritis were given as the possible causes. He had been interested in exotic fish, installing an aquarium with a thermostatic system thought up for the breeding of Chinese macropedes. (Today, in Rouen, there is still a Paul Hélot surgery, specializing in ENT: ear, nose and throat). Apart from the letters Trouvé wrote to Hélot, in the family papers, there was the following touching poem:

Poème à Gustave Trouvé
(auteur inconnu)

Toi dont le nom vainqueur, retentit aux oreilles
De paris à Pékin, de Rouen à Kamchatka
Très illustre Trouvé, toi qui fait des merveilles
Et les signe Euréka

Glorieux héritier de ton père Archimède
Pourquoi me faire attendre et me laisser souffrir
Quand tu pourrais si bien m'envoyer le remède
Qui saurait me guérir ?

Qu'on me parle migraine, abcès ou pneumonie
Je réponds Photophore et tout va de travers
Depuis qu'a commencé cet accès de manie
Tu vois, je fais des vers!

Poem to Gustave Trouvé
(unknown author)

You whose name of victor, retained in ears
From Paris to Peking, from Rouen to Kamchatka

Very illustrious Trouvé, you who work wonders
And sign them Eureka

Glorious inheritor of your father Archimedes
Why make me wait and let me suffer
When you can so well send me the remedy
Who knows how to heal me?

That one talks to me of migraine, abscess or
    pneumonia
I reply Photophore and all goes across
Since once has begun this access of mania
You see, I make verses!

In 1897, Trouvé patented a lens device whereby the exterior lamps for vehicles could simultaneously light up the vehicle's interior. Prior to this, in an omnibus for example, lighting inside and outside were separate. Trouvé's simple device used a condenser mounted in the angle of the lamp to light up a portion of the interior by causing a portion of light ray emitted by outside lamps to converge at such a point to enable a passenger to read without being inconvenienced by the glare and without being seen from the outside. Trouvé wrote, "My invention can be applied to lamps for all kinds of vehicles."[3] Alongside the 15,000 horse-drawn cabs, electric taxis built by Louis Krieger started to appear on the streets of Paris. Among Trouvé's creditors at the end of his life was the Chambres Syndicale des Voitures de Place, or chauffeur-driven cars for rent.

In England, Walter C. Bersey designed a fleet of such cabs and introduced them to the streets of London in 1897. They were soon nicknamed 'Hummingbirds' due to the idiosyncratic humming noise they made. In the same year in New York City, the Samuels Electric Carriage and Wagon Company began running 12 electric hansom cabs. The company ran with up to 62 cabs operating until it was reformed by its financiers to form the Electric Vehicle Company. Andrew L. Riker of Elizabethport, New Jersey, introduced the first electric tricycles to the United States.

There was still a fashion for luminous, electric fancy dress: "Electric blue satin, covered with silver zigzag flashes; silver cords are wound about the neck, arms, and waist; to typify the electric coils. Bodice of blue satin draped with silver and crepe de chine; wings at the back; an electric light in the hair. A staff carried in the hand with coils encircling the globe which surmounts it."[4]

Trouvé's interest could range from the most wacky to the most industriously sophisticated. Perhaps nostalgically recalling the little windmill he had built in his childhood, in 1897, he patented (Patent N° 263797) a toy that he called a "tourniquet" but that has nothing to do with tightly bandaging a wound. A fragile little windmill, it could be fitted to either a hat or a walking stick; it spun round no matter the wind direction, and while on a hat, it still moved while its wearer was walking, or even cycling. To make it spin better, Trouvé had fitted little half spheres or cups to catch the wind; these could be made of materials such as cardboard or celluloid. On one tourniquet, with 12 arms, half of them would turn one way, the other in the opposite direction. The little spheres could be transparent, colored, opaque, and fitted with figurines, animals or other motifs.

We do not know whether Trouvé ever offered his electrical skills to helping the Lumière Brothers with their patented, hand-cranked cinematograph camera. On 4 May 1897, one of their film shows was put on to raise money at the annual Bazar de la Charité organized by the French Catholic aristocracy in Paris. That year, it was held in a large wooden shed, 80 by 13 meters (260 by 40 feet), at Rue Jean-Goujon 17, in the eighth arrondissement of Paris. Inside this shed, a fantasy medieval street was built with wood, cardboard, cloth and papier-mâché. In one of the booths, for 50 centimes, their ladyships could watch the world's very first film shorts, each one lasting less than 50 seconds: "Coming Out of the Lumière Factory in Lyon," "The Arrival of a Train at Le Ciotat" and "The Sprinkler Sprinkled."

These films were screened with a 35-mm Normandin and Joly projector using a system of ether and oxygen rather than electricity. That afternoon of 4 May, the second of the planned four days of the bazaar, the projectionist's equipment caught fire. Exits had not been properly marked. In the resulting panic, some 126 women were burned to death or asphyxiated, many of them aristocrats. Perhaps the most eminent was Her Royal Highness the Duchess of Alençon, née Sophie Charlotte of Bavaria, sister of the famous Empress Sisi. The fire almost killed off the fledgling cinema industry. Soon after, the Lumière brothers put together an electrically driven projector.

In March 1898, Trouvé, ingenious as ever, patented a small universal water pump that could be used as a lifting pump for wells, an emptying pump, a fire pump mounted on a bicycle, and a transferring pump—and even to propel a boat. With the boat, the water was sucked up a pipe at the bow and thrust out via a pipe at the stern. In short, this was a waterjet-powered boat, although not a world first. Depending on the use, Trouvé's pump could be hand-cranked or electrically driven (Patent N° 276,467).

The following year, working with a Paris-based civil engineer called Louis François Bellot, Trouvé increased the sophistication of his gyratory pump, again hand-cranked or mechanically driven. Its generators could be rectilinear, converging, diverging or curvilinear. The patentees suggested their pump could be used in either civil or military engineering, or for wells, mines, agriculture, and again boat propulsion (Patent N° 286,274).

On 30 August 1899, Gaston Tissandier, who had once written so favorably about Trouvé's latest inventions, died in his home at N° 3, rue Bleue, Paris. His brother Albert continued to take part in the editing of *La Nature* until 1905, dying the following year.

As the century came to an end, Trouvé attempted to apply his mind and skill as a constructor to a diversity of applications. The rise of the internal combustion–engined automobile on both sides of the Atlantic has been exhaustively chronicled elsewhere, and to a lesser extent the demise of the modest battery-electric car fleet. Trouvé was of course fully aware of this changeover. Among the hundreds of manufacturers that were pioneering the horseless carriage was the French firm of De Dion-Bouton. In 1883, the Marquis de Dion and his colleagues Bouton and Trépardoux had used a Trouvé-Hélot frontal headlamp for ballooning experiments. In 1894, they added a gasoline-engined tricycle to their best-selling steam car range; a two-seater four-wheeler soon followed and met with much success in the United States. These were soon fitted with acetylene lamps, indirectly adapted from Trouvé's compact models.

In 1899 the race for "Automobile Boats" organized by the Hélice Club de France ("Helice" = propeller) saw 23 entries, of which 14 used gasoline, seven steam, one naphtha—and one electricity. During the 31 km (19 miles) from Argenteuil to Bezons and return, the top speed was obtained by the 12-m *Phoenix* with a 16-hp Panhard and Levassor internal combustion engine. Four years before, Émile Levassor had won the world's first petrol-engined automobile race.

Aware of the increasing popularity of the automobile, Trouvé tried his hand at a constant and variable level carburetor for internal combustion engines, although this was soon surpassed by simpler and more efficient carburetors (Patent N° 295,103). He also took out a patent for mixing liquids using a pair of hollow, truncated cones mounted on a shaft and rotating with a case.

On 19 July 1900, during the Paris World's Fair, the official inauguration was held of the first Metro line between Vincennes and la Porte Maillot. The Metro was engineered by Fulgence Bienvenüe, and the entrances to the stations were designed in art nouveau style by Hector Guimard.

Trouvé, aged 60, exhibited[5] his latest luminous fountain system, which used solid bodies such as rice, semolina, corn, sand, confetti or celluloid chips, so replacing the liquids and steam used up to the present. He had been developing his patented system for the past couple of years, perfecting the fan, the ejector and the centrifugal pump, so putting this material into movement in such a way as to obtain the appearance of an indefinite fireworks display, using a play of colored lights (Patent N° 256,688).

It is interesting to note that for the same exposition, Eugène Hénard had created the Hall of Mirrors, an incredible combination of lights and mirrors. One recalls one of Trouvé's patents of 16 years before for using mirrors to multiply the effect of dancers and artistes wearing his luminous jewels. Outside the hall, there was a breathtaking, crowd-pulling exhibit: the luminous fountains in the Champ de Mars, recalling the previous exposition:

> By day, the numerous water jets, sprinkling the waters making up the end of the garden, produce a very pretty effect. It is even better in the evening. Whenever the electric beams begin to turn copper, silver or golden the gushing fountains, the waterfalls and the front wall, the visual effect is fairy-like. We would applaud without reserve if we did not recall luminous waters of 1889, which were much livelier, much more graceful and which achieved a much greater success. We are far from the enthusiasm of 11 years ago.
>
> Monsieur Trouvé, who is, I believe the inventor of luminous fountains, had a great idea that was turned down. He proposed placing illuminated jets under the first platform of the Eiffel Tower, which would have completed and prolonged them. But such an ingenious combination evidently could not please those engineers who had had the idea of destroying the Eiffel Tower itself and who, consequently, could not understand the interest one had in making the new center of the attractions out of it. Monsieur Trouvé's plan, which did not belong to any administration, not even those of the Ministry of Works, was pitilessly brushed aside. This is why our illuminations of 1900 are really far from those that honorably preceded them. Official scientists too often have the detestable habit of forgetting that it is not only in geometry that the straight line is the shortest distance between one point and another.[6]

As for the theatrical effects, Trouvé simply could not resist keeping in his hand. On 7 February 1900, a new opera opened at the Paris Opera, Palais Garnier. *Lancelot du Lac* was a lyric drama in four acts and six scenes, with the libretto by Edouard Blau and Louis Gallet, music by Victorin Joncières, and the special effects by Trouvé, included a magically lit boat. One society reporter mentioned, "There is a beautiful green light in 'Lancelot.' It is that of the little lanterns that the dancers carry on their heads in their role as glow worms. The battery for these electric emeralds is hidden in their hair. All these lights glittering above the white models give the impression of an immense necklace of shining precious stones on bared shoulders."[7]

Perhaps more mysteriously, the same month, on 8 February 1900, a

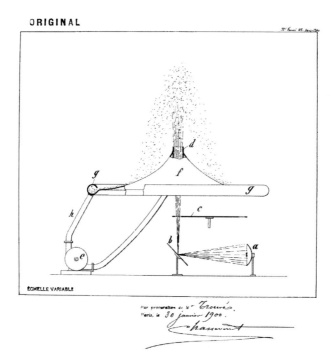

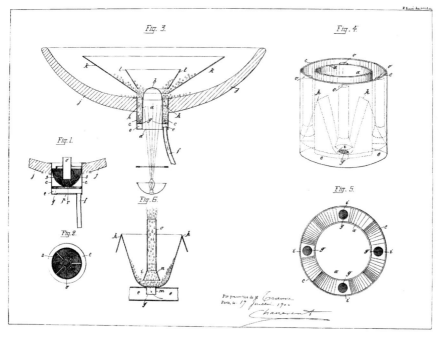

1900. Trouvé adapted his luminous fountains for solid bodies such as rice (author's collection).

"Trouvé" was granted Patent N° 293664. But rather than Gustave, it was his brother Jules Albert Trouvé. Moreover, Jules Trouvé's patent agent was not the faithful Chassevent, but Messieurs Boramé et Julien, engineers at N° 8, rue de la République. Even stranger, Gustave's and Jules's brother Paul Auguste happened to live at N° 84, rue de la République.

At any rate, the patent concerned a new type of lifejacket for passengers on ships in distress. At the time, most lifejackets were crude, bulky affairs composed of chains of cork or kapok. Trouvé's lifejacket, inflatable, would be made of a weatherproof envelope, worn using a simple pair of shoulder braces. It incorporated small, rubber-insulated maritime electric batteries not only to inflate the jacket, but also to power a light to transmit and receive SOS messages and to launch a distress flare. There was also a reversed funnel device for catching rainwater for drinking, and small cans containing crisp bread, rescue rockets and drinking water. Although its versatile compactness seems to point to Gustave Trouvé, we shall never know why Jules applied for and was granted this patent, for a device very similar to those indispensable on every passenger aircraft flight today.

Back in the medical world, "L. Bienfait's" main preoccupation was in developing instruments whose light rays could heal, among other things,

1899. Dr. François Victor Foveau de Cour-melles encouraged Trouvé to adapt his instrument-making to using electric lighting to heal skin diseases (Musée EDF Electropolis, Mulhouse).

skin diseases. In 1897 Dr. Foveau de Courmelles had written a treatise on medical radiotherapy. Three years later, he wrote about electricity and its applications. By this time he had begun to work with Trouvé on an electric light therapy instrument. Up to that time, a Professor Niels Ryberg Finsen of Copenhagen had developed his phototherapy machine, "light that heals." Finsen himself suffered from Niemann-Pick disease, which inspired him to sunbathe and investigate the effects of light on living things and the way in which certain wavelengths of light can have beneficial medical effects. His most notable writings were *Finsen Om Lysets*

Indvirkninger paa Huden (On the Effects of Light on the Skin), published in 1893, and *Om Anvendelse i Medicinen af koncentrerede kemiske Lysstraaler (The Use of Concentrated Chemical Light Rays in Medicine)*, published in 1896. These papers were rapidly translated and published in both German and French.

The Finsen lamp was a bulky machine, suspended from the ceiling by a system of pulleys. UV light was projected through each of the four telescopes so four patients could be treated at once. One nurse wearing dark glasses was responsible for one patient.

In December 1900, Trouvé presented the Academy of Sciences with his instruments based on increasing the intensity of light bulbs using parabolic mirrors: colored light, notably red, which could be used to prevent the scars from smallpox; cold light, obtained by absorbing heat rays by means of a solution of potash alum placed in their path and, if need be, surrounded by a flow of cold water; and chemical light, which Finsen had advised in radiotherapy for treating lupus (until now incurable and requiring very intense light).

Trouvé constructed a number of different instruments. One providing cold light was built to be worn over the ears and project a light of 10–12 volts with the auricular interposition of a glass recipient filled with alum. Using this, a Doctor Paul Garnault achieved positive results with patients suffering from deafness and tinnitus.

The Foveau-Trouvé system was made up of a lamp placed inside a conic trunk finishing with a quartz lens so as only to allow the passage of ultraviolet light. The source of light could be normal, carbon, acetylene or metallic. It had an external sleeve around which a current of cold water circulated, and an internal sleeve containing a cupra-ammoniacal solution aimed at preventing the passage of chemical light. Hot air surrounding the incandescent lamp escaped through small holes. "We have been able to limit the quantity of water used—a pump circulating the same small quantity of water which is kept cool by an external recipient," Trouvé explained.[8]

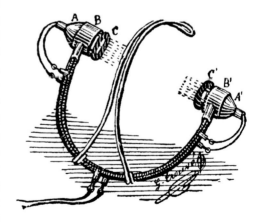

1900. Trouvé constructed this instrument for a Dr. Garnault for the phototherapy of an inflamed area, after the removal of a tooth, passing by the ears (ASPAD).

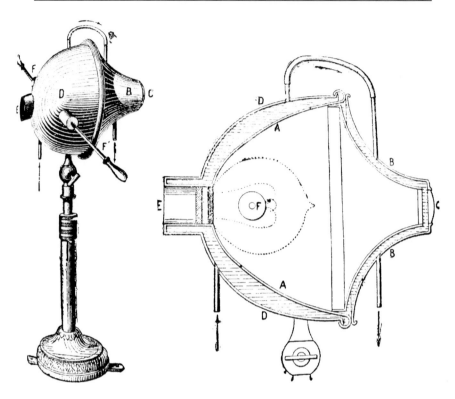

The Foveau-Trouvé "Finsentherapeutical" device (*L'Année Electrique*, 1904 [Libraririe Polytechnique, Ch Béranger]).

Once again, Trouvé had reduced Finsen's bulky process down to the Lilliputian, compact and practical. Foveau and Trouvé published their instruments in Foveau's *L'Anneé Electrique* of this year, and their presentation to the Belgian Royal Academy of Medicine was published in March 1901. They announced remarkable therapeutic effects, obtained without burns or side effects, on patients suffering from lupus, epithelioma, pulmonary disease or various tuberculoses. Trouvé's 10-amp arc-lamp was used for 10 minutes at 70 volts, or a 5 amps for up to 45 minutes. The results obtained by the Foveau-Trouvé machine showed that luminous radiation, judiciously employed, could enter into serious therapeutical practice:

> The curative effect of chemical rays is therefore certain for phlegmonious fluxion, since it enables, with the conservation of the sick organ, the healing of phlegmacy, in a period of time more restrained than that which it takes to disappear after the extraction of the tooth…. On the superior and temporal part of the jawbone, one would be able to work through the ears and

use the radiator built for these by G. Trouvé on the indications of Dr. Garnault.[9]

But as usual, others were soon trying to outshine them. In March 1901, Professor Charles-Émile Lortet, doyen of the Medical Faculty of Lyon, and Dr. Genoud, head of works at this faculty, presented details of their phototherapeutical instrument to the Academy of Sciences in Paris, again to the National Society of Medicine at Lyon some three weeks later, and again at a session of the Society of Dermatology and Syphilography. They made no mention of the Foveau-Trouvé instruments. In *L'Année Electrique* for 1902, Foveau stated that the only difference applied by the Lyonais was to place a bowl of colored water in the path of a voltaic arc lamp. The Lortet-Genoud instrument was tested alongside the Foveau-Trouvé instrument at the Saint-Louis Hospital in Paris. It was found that the former device consumed more electrical energy, burning the patients, thus slowing down the treatment, and that its operator was blinded by the light.

The first ever use of radium for cutaneous therapy was made the following year, also at the Saint-Louis Hospital, by dermatologist Henry Danlos, with radium supplied him by Marie Curie. One wonders whether Trouvé was called on for the electromechanical assistance.

Louis Lépine, prefect of police for the Seine, responsible for the use of modern forensics by the French police force, created a competition-exhibition, with a prize of 100 francs for a small manufacturer of innovative toys or ironmongery. It was aimed at bringing out the small Parisian manufacturers from the current economic stagnation. The first expo took place at the Palais des Exposés from 24 November to 8 December 1901. The annual competition is still run today. Trouvé could not help but take an interest in this challenge to making small and useful items, even toys.

In the complete directory *Paris Tout Entier Sous La Main* (*The Whole of Paris in Your Hand*), published by Hachette in Paris, part 4 printed a complete list of streets and house numbers of all company and business addresses. It included "Trouvé (G.) *appar électriques*. Vivienne 14." Others with the name Trouvé are: a provider of party accessories, a gilt jeweler, a decorative embroiderer, a clothing maker, a greengrocer, a fruiterer, etc.; but Gustave is still absent from the telephone directory.

In March he patented a small hand-cranked tool for speeding up the making of helical springs, flexible helical shafts.

Work on battery power continued: "It's already a long time since one found ['*trouvé*'] the way to make electric lighting portable, for lighting up minuscule bulbs—tie pins, jewels or various parts of clothing using miniature bulbs. At the theater one has made curious applications of this process."[10]

Stating that the latest batteries were lighter and more powerful, a company called M. Mathieu, N° 29 rue Valois, Paris, launched a range of electric gadgets:

An electric torch walking stick	35 francs
A pocket torch	12 francs
A tie pin	10 francs
A carnival "Cyrano" nose	9 francs 50
Replacement batteries	2 francs 25

Even at the beginning of the twentieth century, it was still uncertain whether electrification would really replace gas lighting. In January 1902, Trouvé patented a portable, hand-cranked, electro-pneumatic device for lighting up gas lamps in streets where lighting was difficult to obtain with the primitive means then in use. It was basically a hand-cranked electric spark plug, using a Siemens coil.

During the next two months he tinkered with two toys in the knick-knacks class. (He had already come up with his windmill hat!) The first was a system for propelling any toys floating on the water or in the water.

Left: 1901. Engraving of Trouvé towards the end of his life (collection Musée de l'Air et de l'Espace–Le Bourget). *Right:* 1901. Rare photogravure of Trouvé as it appeared in an Italian publication. He is proudly wearing the medal of the Chévalier de la Légion d'Honneur (author's collection).

For example, a toy submarine, filled with calcium carbide, coming into contact with water, produced acetylene in the form of water bubbles which, rising to the surface, then propelled the toy along (Patent N° 319719). Half a century later, the baking-powder submarine toy would become available in packets of Kellogg's breakfast cereal. It gave the author of this biography, then five years old, a lot of fun in the family bath.

The second toy was a spring-loaded harpoon or spear gun for hunting or fishing, either on the land, in the water or in marshland. The harpoon could be attached to a cord that could then be used to pull back the prey. It could also launch a parachute (Patent N° 319,755).

Compared to his more heroic inventions of 20 years before, for one reason or another, Gustave Trouvé was no longer involved in the great challenges of the period, such as automobile, aeronautics, and cinematography, even if Foveau de Courmelles wrote, "Very recently, he had turned his mind towards balloons! He held the solution! He was sure of the result. He spoke about it with such an ardent passion and conviction!"[11]

On 3 June, there was a massive thunderstorm in Paris, and for the first time the Eiffel Tower was struck by lightning.

In July 1902, still at the same workshop he had occupied for the past 24 years, Trouvé was fixing a chemical radiator that had served for treating lupus when the saw he was using slipped, cutting his thumb and his index finger. The thumb became inflamed. Accustomed to small injuries like anyone using their hands to cut, to saw, or to plane, Trouvé at first paid little attention to this. Faced with a growing infection, he was soon unable to ignore its threat.

"We immobilized him," wrote Foveau de Courmelles. "We nearly amputated his hand. He refused, saying it would have stopped him from working. Then everything got better. But this man, for whom illness did not count and didn't even care about it, ignoring it, went to see some friends on the 14 July, drank some ice drinks, caught cold in his bed the following night and woke up with both a stroke and congestion of the lungs, which immediately got better, but then his arm became inflamed again.... We could not save him."

Gustave Pierre Trouvé died at 11 o'clock in the morning of Sunday, 27 July 1902 in the Saint-Louis Hospital, Paris, where he had been admitted on 18 July for a phlegmon of the hand and a high fever. Two days later, at 4 o'clock in the morning, a train pulled out of the Gare d'Orléans station, with Trouvé's corpse on board. Destination: La Haye–Descartes, his birthplace. "His funeral took place on Thursday 31 July in La Haye–Descartes, where his corpse had been transported."[12]

On 1 August 1902, Foveau de Courmelles's obituary of Trouvé was published on the front page of a journal, surprisingly not in Paris but in Luxembourg:

> The ingenious electrician Gustave Trouvé has just died and the newspapers of the capital, who, however, often spoke about him and his life, are dumb over this premature death. This man who throughout his life worked for humanity, does not find a *post mortem* biography. He died aged 63, having the appearance of a man of 45, with his abundant black hair scarcely showing any white strands. He was Chevalier de la Légion d'honneur since 1881. It's true that governments do not favor independent scientists, those whom one doesn't see in the ministerial antechambers or others. When one meets them, sometimes one pushes the condescension—even though they ask for nothing but to be told what they would merit, even to promising them, except only to think of self and to leave them indefinitely in the dark! It's true that this dark, suitable for laboratory work, is what best pleases them, which is suitable to them essentially so as to work their meticulous and fertile researches for ungrateful humanity. Thus, Gustave Trouvé died simple Chevalier de la Légion d'honneur, grade acquired at the Electricity Congress of 1881, after a hard-fought struggle.
>
> It would need a volume, alongside the volume that Georges Barral devoted to him in 1890 and to increase it with his work of 12 years, to relate in minute detail the discoveries of this electrician, contemporary of Ruhmkorff, Breguet, Gramme, Planté, of this fertile Pleiades that went before him in his career and close to whom he holds the most honorable place. If Buffon was able to say of genius that it's a long patience, how much he would have said this of Trouvé, who spent 40 years of his life in his laboratory in the rue Vivienne, well known to researchers, and who did not take the time to marry, and scarcely even to eat ... and despite this, welcoming, friendly, even chatty, spiritual, on occasion a great hunter.
>
> Who will take up this heavy succession of useful inventions left by Gustave Trouvé? It will need the intellects of several doctors, of engineers, so as not to drop into escheated inheritance, these works that go from the electric explorer, to electric boats, to aerial navigation, passing by so many useful intermediaries, electric jewels, pumps launching liquids up to crazy heights, luminous fountains with or without water, electro-medical devices. I plead with the poor inheritors, his family besides, that they surround themselves with competent minds for the use of his really heavy legacy and about which one must not disappoint humanity!
>
> Apart from a personality perhaps a little oversensitive and that distanced him from so many capitalists who would have been able to turn into the French Edison, he was a hard-working man, good and really useful. Scientific bodies did not have a more precious collaborator and for a long time of interest more powerful than the countless discoveries, progress and even simple improvements that Gustave Trouvé brought to them. Alongside so many rogues of science, taking credit for the work of other people and hoisting themselves up to the highest situations, it is good and soothing to note the fine and big face of Gustave Trouvé working for science, for Her alone, and to wish him, beyond the tomb, a moving adieu![13]

Here is a selection of comments on Trouvé's life and work:

The fame of Gustave Trouvé, great in France, is universal abroad, where all the scientists of the two worlds are unanimous in paying homage to the ingenuity of his mind and the capital importance of his works. The simplicity of his tastes and the generosity of his heart have only given him a simply golden ease. Graham Bell was very astonished when he visited him to learn that he was not a millionaire several times over like all his colleagues in the United States. In France we do not yet know how to completely honor those who are inventors and scientists.[14]

∼

It was enough to propose a problem and Trouvé did not delay in bringing an always pleasing and original solution. Once the solution was found, he most often neglected to exploit it commercially and passed on to other researches.[15]

∼

M. Trouvé was gifted with a happy personality, with a great skill in elocution; he has left many friends; also his loss will for a long time be felt by people who are cultivating the different branches of applied science which he himself studied with so much activity during his so short a career.[16]

∼

Apart from numerous electro-medical instruments devised by Trouvé, his electric engines for pleasure boats and a crowd of instruments which it would be too long to enumerate, the ingenuity of this exceptional inventor was given free rein in the artistic and fantastical world. One always finds in him the child who at seven years old conceived of building a steam engine with umbrella rods and an old hunting box; and it worked really well. His rapidity of conception only had as a rival his skill as constructor, and to the aid of these two master qualities, he knew how to realize everything about which the most overflowing imagination could dream.[17]

∼

One understands that, turning over the ideas by hundreds, in having the skill necessary to immediately put them into execution, the multiple inventions of Gustave Trouvé could not present equal merits, merits that his father's heart had a natural tendency to exaggerate, but it is not less certain that a good number of them, of a practical nature and of an incontestable originality, will follow and transmit the name of Gustave Trouvé to our grandchildren.[18]

∼

If he, as independent scientist, most often met with ingratitude, he has, in return, more than his conscience and satisfaction of the useful effort accomplished, so many witnesses of great or humble minds, minds living in unison with him, sincere and unselfish friends. The fertile mind of Gustave Trouvé, where vibrated the microbe of invention in innumerable colonies, was showing itself here last December, and this brain is no longer![19]

∼

Gustave Trouvé was, in private life, very obliging, very good, of an inexhaustible kindness and with an indulgence towards others at least equal to that which he had for himself. Those who have known and been associated with him will regret the premature disappearance of this relentless worker, of this fertile inventor who will leave a name in the history of inventors of the end of the XXth century.

He was one of those rare inventors to physically build what they had conceived. He was a skillful mechanic, at the same time an ingenious inventor and an inventor full of resources. He has died without having finished his work; beside, no inventor ever finishes his, because the inventor, however unfortunate, is always searching.[20]

Aeronautics has suffered a heavy loss. Gustave Trouvé was one of the oldest, the most inventive and ingenious aeronautical engineers of all time. He was not only, simply, ingenious when occupied with aeronautical questions, but also by other technologies; he took out no less than 300 patents![21]

On 4 August 1902, Paul Auguste Trouvé, a younger brother, also living in Paris, arrived at Trouvé's Paris workshop, 14 rue Vivienne. He and a notary, Marcel Cocteau, made an inventory of items Gustave had left to him, his elder brother Jules, living in Le Dorat, in the Haut-Vienne region, and his sister Marie-Clarisse Jahan, living in Sainte-Maure, in the Indre-et-Loire region, widow of François Jahan.[22]

The inheritance included a collection of electrical precision instruments, some medical; personal belongings located at home; personal belongings at Chatou; 11 patents, two applied for just before his death; and shares in the Channel Bridge and Railway Company, the Panama Canal Company, and the Eiffel Tower Company.

Then there is a revealing list of the wide variety of individuals and companies owing him various sums of money, including doctors, medical and dental instrument manufacturers. Some of these were mentioned earlier in this biography—such as the Colonial Ministry (for the sultan's electric boat), the Grévin Museum (444 francs still owing for the 1895 Mouche d'Or waxwork statue), the Ligue d'Enseignement (perhaps for the auxanoscope), Dr. Vigoroux (head of the Electrotherapy Service at the Salpêtrière and writer of the preface for Trouvé's *Manual*), Doctor Davidson (for their hernial ball of 1892), and the Bichat and Salpêtrière hospitals.

But there are other intriguing names, too. We have not yet been able to discover exactly what electrical device he constructed for them, although we can guess: the Chambre Syndicale des Cochers et Chauffeurs de Voitures (taxis) of the Paris region; the Lycée Fenélon (the first girls' college in Paris); the Paris Fire Brigade; Lacarrière Delatour et Cie (specialist in monumental bronze lampstands and chandelier holders for gas, then electric, lights); Saget et Cie (pharmaceutical suppliers, including surgical instruments); Schneider et Cie (an armaments specialist recently launched into electricity); Réné-Augustin Poitrimol (who took out a patent in April 1896 for an instrument gasifying mineral oils and consuming the gas as carbureted air), to mention just a few.

Trouvé's total assets came to 23,244 francs (equivalent to today's $110,000). He had always been the tenant at 14, rue Vivienne, the workshop where he had conceived and constructed so many extraordinary instruments, and his rent was paid up for the next six months.

Trouvé's inventions were soon copied and adapted by others. Later in 1902 a certain Monsieur Judic, a trained electrician who was also a director of Le Châtelet theater in Paris, used electricity to fake a steamboat for a performance of *Le Voyage de Suzette* (music by Joncières, for whose *Lancelot* Trouvé had created the special effects a couple of years before). Judic took up Trouvé's invention of *fontaines lumineuses* to give the on-stage impression of a cascade of precious stones of every color by means of thousands of incandescent light bulbs. By rotating a switching system in one direction, this gave the impression of a waterfall, and in the other direction, of a firework display. This special effect was so impressive that Judic was invited to the Drury Lane Theatre, London, to create the same effect.

To take Trouvé's *bijoux électriques* one stage further, Judic equipped 60 dancers at Le Châtelet *each* with some ten light bulbs in their costumes and headdresses. It had already been done some 20 years before by Trouvé at the Paris Opera and at Le Châtelet, but with less dancers and to less effect. Judic formed his dancers into groups, each personifying a precious stone of a different color. To power the assembly of 4-volt lights, each dancer wore a rubber bag containing a small battery hidden at their back of her clothing. There were two circuits, one for the headdress and the other for the costume, both worked by a switch placed within the dancer's hand-range. At given choreographic moments the 60 dancers switched on and switched off. The effect was magical. When these effects were written up in *La Nature* magazine,[23] no credit was given to the late Trouvé.

There was a French actress called "Anna Judic," whose real name was Anne Marie-Louise Damiens. From 1876 to 1896, Mademoiselle Judic was the star of the show at the Théâtre des Variétés, dressed by Alfred Grévin and ornamented by Trouvé's ingenious electric jewels.

Trouvé's company did not disappear: "We are happy to learn that the firm he founded and which arrived at a great degree of prosperity will be continued by one of his friends, the principal confidant of his projects, of his hopes and the witness of all his works."[24] In fact in Foveau de Courmelles' *L'Année Electrique* (1904), there appeared the following half-page advertisement:

> Instrument Manufacture Electro-Medical: **Maison Gve Trouvé,** Engineer-Constructor, Chevalier de la Légion d'honneur: **A. de Sainville Successor,** 14, rue Vivienne, 14, Paris: Medical Instruments of all types, new Finsen-style instrument "the Foveau-Trouvé" for the treatment of lupus and other cutaneous illnesses; electrical massage instruments; Light baths, etc.; New silver-lined cauterizers which can be passed through a flame and put in any liquid for sterilization.
> Manufacturer's Marque εὑρηκα
> Catalogue sent on demand postage paid
> Telephone: 518.11[25]

Indeed in the *Bottin de Commerce*, trade directory for Paris, Gustave Trouvé was indicated until 1907.

And it was the name Eureka that was used to promote an ingeniously simple and compact little instrument that bore all the hallmarks of "L Bienfait." This was an electric fan. The electric fan was an American invention. Between the years 1882 and 1886, New Orleans resident and Edison employee Schuyler Skaats Wheeler perfected his two-bladed desk fan powered by electricity. It was commercially marketed by the American Crocker and Curtis electric motor company; a man called Philip Diel introduced the electric ceiling fan. At that time, electric fans were most often used in commercial establishments or in wealthy households. They were bulky, heavy and costly. "In this case it became necessary to find a device that was low-cost, low consummation, compact and easy to install. This problem has been very happily solved by the Ventilateur, Eureka brand." With its removable and interchangeable cap system, it could be inserted into either screw or bayonet sockets and use any electrical system. Its light weight and its compactness, as well as its elegant shape, enabled its adaption, without lowering their value, to the richest and most artistic holders. According to the makers, the consummation of this little venti-lator, despite its big air output, did not exceed one-tenth of an amp and its heat output did not exceed 10° above ambient room temperature, even after working for 100 hours without stopping. It was supplied as a 100-volt and a 220-volt unit, DC or AC, at a price range of 35 to 55 francs per unit. It was patented and made by K. B. Paris.

With both Hélot and Trouvé dead, and nobody to defend the rights of their photophore, others began to manufacture it. In England, for example, the Holborn Surgical Instrument Co. of London manufactured it as "The Holborn." Another maker was "Kohinoor." The 108.93-carat Kohinoor diamond belonged to the Crown of England; the use of the name recalls Trouvé's adaptation of the photophore to his *bijoux électriques.* Yet another was K. Schall, an electro-medical instrument maker of Cavendish Street, London. Ironically, another instrument maker to use the Trouvé headlights was Leiter and Co.; let us not forget that Leiter claimed to have invented the endoscope—several years *after* Trouvé!

NINE

Rehabilitating Trouvé

During researches for this book, I contacted a great many archives and museums in the hopes of finding additional material. Although a number of these were able to find documentation, I became more and more surprised and frustrated to encounter a lack of surviving information about my chosen subject in certain archives that ought to have been the most logical and the most fruitful to consult. These include the French National Library (Paris), apart from two small mentions and one engraving; Musée des Arts et Métiers (Science Museum in Paris); Carnavalet Museum (Paris); Musée de la Marine (Maritime Museum) (Paris); Siemens Archives (Germany); Thomas A. Edison Archives (USA); Tesla Archives (Serbia); Joseph Swan Archives (Newcastle-upon-Tyne, UK); European medical museums (following a published appeal which received no response); the Archives Municipales de Tours; Laboratoires de Roscoff et de Banyuls; and the Austrian National Archives.

Very few portraits of Trouvé have survived and only four engravings. One is based on an oil painting by Fernand de Launay that was admitted to the Salon des Beaux-Arts de Paris in 1899. To date, its original canvas has not been relocated. The other three are certainly based on photographs, none of which have been located despite exhaustive research.

Well-known historic photo agencies such as Roger Viollet and Rapho have found nothing in their exhaustive archives. The National Archives Collection at Saint Cyr has nothing, even in the exhaustive collection of portrait photos taken by Nader of Parisian celebrities, including several of Trouvé's colleagues, in the nineteenth century. The Bibliothèque National de France has no photos of him either. The Musée Carnavalet, Paris's museum, has not found a portrait of him in its collection of over 15,000 "cartes de visite."

There is just one possibility. In 1883, a photo was taken of the Tissandier brothers in the nacelle of their aerostat, before takeoff. Standing beneath are a group of people, the team. One is definitely battery pioneer Gaston Planté. But who is the other, bearded, with straw boater and hands in his pockets? He does appear very like the portrait engravings of a certain Gustave Trouvé.

Fortunately, thanks to the responsible approach of certain archivists concerned with the heritage of electricity, of medicine, of aviation, of the theater and of the City of Paris, extracts from books, articles in magazines, press cuttings, and correspondence have been assembled to create a picture, albeit incomplete, of the brilliant electrical engineer of 14 rue Vivienne.

But there are still gaping holes in the puzzle. As already indicated, no definitive portrait photo exists—only the four engravings (most probably taken from photos) as mass produced in technical journals. Apparently, only a scattered dozen of the ingeniously conceived and meticulously constructed instruments he built have survived. There is no grave, let alone bust or statue, only a street name, and that not even in Paris, but a backstreet in La Haye–Descartes, his hometown.

Contrast this blatant anomaly with Trouvé's colleague and friend, Gaston Planté, the very modest pioneer of the rechargeable lead-acid battery. Streets and alleys in over 20 towns all over France are named Gaston Planté. The Bulgarian Academy of Sciences presents the coveted and prestigious Planté medal every three years in his memory. There is not a dictionary or encyclopedia, French or foreign, that does not include a reference to Planté. There are photos of him, and a grave and, very recently, a statue.

In an age of the popularity of the conspiracy theory, does one dare ask whether somebody, a few decades ago, went about deliberately destroying information about Trouvé? If so, who were they? Was it a jealous enemy or rival? Did the modest Trouvé himself plan and ask to be forgotten by posterity? Or was his family simply not interested in their relative's remarkable discoveries?[1] People simply and incorrectly fall into the trap of thinking that Trouvé, worthy of admission into the pantheon of scientific giants, is simply the past participle of the French verb.

The recent literary rehabilitation of Gustave Trouvé began in 1995, when Alain Ségal, a gastroenterologist from Reims, published "The Place of the Engineer Gustave Trouvé in the History of Endoscopy." This was published in volume 29 in the journal of the Society for the History of Medical Science.

Six years later, 2001, Trouvé reappeared in a book by French professor and technical journalist Georges Ribeill. It was called *De l'objet technique a l'utopie sociale: Les ressorts de l'imaginaire technologique des ingénieurs au xixe siècle (From technical object to social utopia: The roots of techno-logical imagination by engineers in the nineteenth century)* (La Découverte, 2001). Ribell comments,

> This great electrical market where Trouvé accumulated his findings finally brings together objects functionally dedicated to various fates. If in fact his universal safety lamp, portable, automatic, reversible, can be recognized as today's present-day battery powered pocket torch, still very useful, his extraordinary luminous electric jewels decorating ladies' hairstyles and the corsages, will not on the other hand pass into posterity, joining those objects put aside. On the contrary, his shows of Amazons and gymnasts adorned with bright jewelry, living chandeliers, anticipate some contemporary special effects! Before the letter, Trouvé in short excels in the invention of practical and decorative household items, gadgets with which he would like to furnish the everyday world. His quest for inventions in all fields of transport, com-munications, medical and military techniques, should make up a hero both patriotic and pacifist....
>
> However, the paramount importance of his dynamometers and gyro-scopes, or the philanthropic nature of his medical instruments, which merits universal gratitude, was not necessarily recognized by his contemporaries! More consistent than utopian construction, Trouvé's electrical bazaar holds the magic shop of accessories and electrical decorations, a kind of Ali Baba's cave, where from the trivial to the serious, he accumulated overall the find-ings with which he wanted to saturate our civilization.[2]

As explained in the preface to this book, my own crusade to publicly rehabilitate Trouvé began with a single-column entry about him on page 16 of my book *The Guinness Book of Motorboating Facts and Feats*, pub-lished in Guinness Superlatives Ltd. in 1979. In 1996, having resumed my research, I was able to publish an enlarged article about him in *Neptunia*, the journal of the Friends of the Naval Museum in Paris.

Another 11 years were to pass before, in 2007 I was able to place a four-page article, "Found in France," in several British specialist publica-tions. On 17 February that year, I received a letter from Monsieur Yves Garnier, director general of Editions Larousse: "After consultation with our scientific advisers, we are pleased to tell you that Gustave Trouvé will be inserted in a coming edition of the *Petit Larousse*."

Unknown to me, in 2010, Trouvé was included in historical fiction. In 2010, Gail Carriger, a British American steampunk novelist, published the third in her popular Parasol Protectorate series, *Blameless*. In this book, Trouvé invents and provides various mechanical objects integral to the plot, including, in 1874, a full-scale, steam-powered, passenger-carrying ornithopter. His clock shop in Paris features prominently. In 2012, Carriger wrote the final book in that series, *Timeless,* in which Trouvé

The unveiling of the commemorative plaque to Trouvé in his hometown of La Haye–Descartes in 2012. From left, the author; Gérard Henault, president of the Community of Communes of South Touraine (rear); Bruno Méreau, deputy mayor of Descartes; Jacques Barbier, mayor of Descartes; historian Jacques Callu; Jacques Barbot, former mayor of Descartes; Noëlle Baranger, deputy mayoress of Descartes; Monsieur Villeret, deputy mayor of Descartes (author's collection).

once more assists her main character, Lady Maccon. As Carriger wrote to me in an e-mail dated 29 June 2014, "Few of my English-language readers realize that he was actually a real person." She explained that she knew of him due to her to research into inventors in 1870s France.

Finally, in 2012, my full biography, *A La Recherche de Trouvé: La Quête d'un génie français oublié* (*Looking for Trouvé: The Quest for a Forgotten French Genius*) was published by Pleine Page of Bordeaux. It runs to 200 pages with 80 illustrations. Following its publication, on 13 October 2012, Monsieur Jacques Barbier, the mayor of Descartes, unveiled a commemorative metal plaque in the Saint Lazare Square, former site of Trouvé's birthplace. Two months later, the Académie Nationale des Sciences, Belles Lettres et Arts de Bordeaux, founded in 1712 by King Louis XIV, presented me with Le Prix Jacques Paul, "pour couronner votre oeuvre (to crown your work)." In my acceptance speech I stated that the prize was as much for Trouvé as for me.

Inspired by my work, others began to write about Trouvé. *Gustave Trouvé, the French Edison?* by Professor Jacques Cattelin of the Touraine Academy, France, was published in 2012. Professor Cattelin concludes:

What did they have in common? They were incredibly creative and this in various fields of research. Electricity occupied the top spot for the two inventors. They are also interested in telecommunications, and the arts (Edison in phonograph and cinema). They both had one consuming passion dedicated to research. Trouvé remained unmarried and it seems that Edison devoted little time to his family.

Trouvé filed 300 patents and Edison more than 1,000. But while Trouvé worked with a small entourage, Edison already had two partners and a team of 60 paid researchers by 1874. The latter knew how to find investors: for example, the development his incandescent lamp necessitated testing 6,000 plant substances for the filament, finally costing some 40,000 dollars. He surrounded himself with financiers and industrialists, which enabled him to employ 35,000 people.

From the point of view of intellectual honesty, while Trouvé was irreproachable, Edison did not hesitate to appropriate the work of other researchers. He lost his case against Joseph Swan, pioneer in the development of the electric incandescent lamp. He even shamefully pirated the film by Georges Méliès, *A Trip to the Moon*, and exploited its diffusion to his advantage.

Both inventors are symptomatic of their epoch, which was a turning point for research: Trouvé, representative of the inventor-scientist-craftsman, and Edison, forerunner of the modern scientist-entrepreneur who did not work alone. Perhaps Edison's greatest invention was the modern research and development laboratory. Edison had also been anxious to ensure his posterity, and indeed many places and objects bear his name.

Commenting on the obituary of Gustave Trouvé published in *Electrical Industry* in 1902, Damien Kuntz, director of Collections and Documentation at EDF's Electropolis Museum, France, has written:

> Despite the fact that he shows respect for his late colleague, the writer considers his inventions in an almost ironic way, saying they were of uneven quality and, like a father towards his children, Trouvé considered them all with the same love, even giving them a value that they did not have. Indeed, among his many inventions, it is clear that there is a huge difference between the electric vehicle or boat, for example, and his small "gadgets." This probably discredited him in the eyes of "more serious" electricians.
>
> Reading between the lines, I also believe that for both electrical engineers and industrialists, Trouvé was considered a case apart, a little wacky. It is even possible that his personality did him no good, preventing him from exerting any real influence in the milieu where decisions were made and things done. Trouvé does not seem to have been a stickler for propriety. His manners were not in line with the social codes of the world of the electricians. In addition, Gustave Trouvé did not reason in terms of market, trade, industrialization or profit. He also seems to have never really taken advantage of his work, only pursuing an invention for its own sake. So he did not at all speak the same language as those regarding themselves as professional electricians.

We can therefore deduce that he remained socially "apart" from his colleagues. In other words, I am convinced that he "was not part of the band." So electricians at the time did not have to go beyond the appearances of this rather eccentric character to really look at his inventions and judge them objectively.

This is a great pity because, prisoners of their social conventions, and perhaps for other reasons which escape us, they missed the opportunity to appreciate such a valuable man. The apparent simplicity of some of Gustave Trouvé's inventions hide many applications that have now become very topical, used daily or which one regularly believes reinvented. As such, he certainly deserves to reappear in our collective memory.

The availability of his biography in English is a step toward increasing his renown, but for Trouvé to become the household name he was some 120 years ago, there are still many actions that might be taken. The most obvious would be a museum. Unlike for recognized giants of electricity such as Tesla and Edison, there is no permanent exhibition devoted to the life and works of Gustave Trouvé, perhaps because of the paucity of items left in the world.

In 2015, a graphic novel entitled *Electropolis: A Fairly True History of Electricity* (Strasbourg, France: Editions du Digne) with the scenario by Lionel Courtot and drawings by Curd Ridel makes mention of Trouvé's electric tricycle and boat. This is the first graphic novel ever to do so.

As previously described, after Trouvé's death, his archives and possessions were transported by train from his downtown Paris workshop back to his family hometown of La Haye–Descartes. When that home became the town's secondary school, they were then transferred to the town hall. But then at 5 p.m. on Saturday, 19 February 1980, a fire ravaged Descartes Town Hall. According to Lieutenant Jean-Pierre Begenne of the town fire brigade, who was on duty, the first floor and the loft were totally destroyed, including Trouvé's archives.

In addition, there is no longer any grave. Jean-Francois Trouvé reported:

> Having visited the cemeteries of Descartes, Abilly and Sainte-Maure, I did not see GPT's grave; on the other hand, to my great surprise, I discovered the grave of his sister, Clarisse Jahan. A widow at 46 years old, she lived on until 1916, to the age of 82. I must say that I was surprised to come across the tomb. It's rare to see such old graves. Many no longer have an inscription, without name; some have collapsed, torn open, what a sight![3]

Monsieur Joël Galland, in charge of parks and the cemetery at Descartes, embarked on a separate search in the late August of 2007. Despite his thoroughness, Galland found no trace.

Initial researches elsewhere have found some 19 instruments in the reserve collection of the Museum des Arts et Metiers in Paris. There are four electric motors—one at EDF's Electropolis museum in Mulhouse, and three in the museum stores of Parisian high schools.[4] Otherwise, there is a cautery cutting handle with extensions and a polyscope in the Fauchard Collection of the Paris Hospitals Museum, a frontal headlamp in the reserve collection of the London Science Museum, and a universal safety lamp at the Teyler Museum in the Netherlands.[5] In what may be the only receipt for a Trouvé instrument, we can see that the latter was purchased for Dfl 46 on the 10th of November 1884 in Haarlem, from a factory/shop owned by F.W. Funckler. The shop sold barometers, thermometers and microscopes. The lamp had more or less the same price as a barometer. On the receipt dated April 1885, it says in Dutch that the shop supplied a workman who worked 224 hours at 20 cents per hour. This made the lamp rather expensive.[6]

In an attempt to increase this virtual collection, I published an article-appeal in *The Bulletin of the Scientific Instrument Society* (N° 115, 2012). Although this is read by dedicated collectors and curators, there was absolutely no response. Alongside this, direct searches of such museums as the Science and Technology Museum, in Milan, Italy, met with a similar negative response.

During World War I, the citizens of France donated many metal objects, which were melted down to make bullets, shells, canons and tanks. Many of Trouvé's instruments may well have been sacrifices in the cause of war.

In terms of original vehicles, neither the electric tricycle or the electric boats have survived, although searches were made. For example, with the help of the Friends of Pierre Loti, an attempt was made to find the electric launch sent out to Fez in Morocco in 1889 as a gift to the Sultan Moulay-Hassan. All that was found was the word-of-mouth memory that a similar boat may have ended up in a garage covered in pigeon droppings, but without its original machinery.

Contact was also made with an association called Sequana, concerned with the pleasure-boating heritage of the River Seine near Paris, particularly Chatou. Although Sequana had been collecting traditional sailing dinghies, canoes, and engines, they had never heard of Trouvé. Following my sending them information, they formed an ambitious plan to build a working replica of Trouvé's electric launch, which he tested on the Seine in May 1881. The Sequana technical team's visit to the Paris Science Museum's reserve store to photograph and measure its rare Trouvé engine for replication was positive.

But then they came up against the problem of the battery. A very

The road named after Trouvé in La Haye–Descartes (author's photograph).

precise article published in *La Nature* reported that these batteries were two in number, each one weighing 33 kg (73 lbs.) and containing 1.2 kg (21 lbs.) of potassium dichromate, 3.6 kg of sulphuric acid (without specifying concentration) and 8 kg (17 lbs.) of water. Potassium dichromate is, unfortunately, a highly toxic product, mortal if inhaled, and demanding special treatment after use. In addition, working on it without wearing protective clothing and a mask, even in the open air, was formally discouraged. It made the engineers question how Trouvé managed originally. Although Sequana hoped to continue their investigations with firefighters and laboratories specialized in handling hazardous materials laboratories, this would have proved too costly, so the project was temporarily shelved.

In a similar way, the author contacted an association dedicated to building working replicas of flapping-wing flying machines or mechanical birds. Details of Trouvé's 1891 experiment were published in their on-line magazine and a challenge made to members to build and fly a replica of Trouvé's prototype. There were no takers.

Quite independently from this author's quest, in February 2014, faculty members of the University of Victoria in British Columbia presented a project called "Debuting Our Early Wearables." They created a kit focused on Gustave Trouvé's electric jewelry. Through this kit, they used

Trouvé's work to unravel and historicize the very notion of "wearables" or "wearable technologies." The kit, which they placed in a typical Trouvé presentation box, replicated the parts required to construct a simple, battery-powered circuit that uses a small LED to illuminate a filigree hairpin. They also included supplementary materials, such as pictures of women modeling Trouvé's pieces, a handbill for a production of *Faust* (for which Trouvé created light-up swords), and instructional materials that explain the basic principles of circuitry.

In May 2014, an electric boat went into service on the River Seine in central Paris, this time solar-powered. A 17-metre Aquabus C60, made by Grove Boats at Yverdon-les-Bains, Switzerland, became part of the Batostar fleet, offering 40-minute trips around the Ile Saint-Louis and up to the Eiffel Tower. Departures are from the foot of the Pont-Marie. It is called the *Felix de Azara* after an eighteenth century Spanish naturalist. In September 2014, Budsin Woodcraft of Marshallberg, North Carolina, specializing in electrically powered day boats, decided to call their new 19-footer *Trouvé* in honor of the French pioneer.

In 2012, the City of Paris was approached for official permission to put up and officially unveil a commemorative plaque on the wall outside N° 14 rue Vivienne, in the second arrondissement—where the inventor resided, conceiving and building his dazzling array of instruments over some 24 years. This is a long administrative process.

In January 2015, after considerable deliberation, the special Historical Commission gave its "feu vert" (green light) for a plaque to be unveiled later that year.

The French Postal Service has been approached for a possible philatelic first-day cover stamp illustrating the inventor, and this has also joined a long waiting list for consideration.

But indubitably, as is detailed the following appendix, Trouvé's real legacy is that descendants of so many of his inventions are being used in the twenty-first century.

Appendix I: Trouvé's 75 Inventions and Innovations

1864	electro-spherical motor
1865	electric gyroscope
1865	electro-medical apparatus
1865	electro-mobile jewelry
1865	"Lilliputian" sealed battery
1866	electric rifle
1867	electro-medical kit
1869	liquid-fuelled pantoscope
1870	device imitating the flight of birds
1872	portable military telegraph
1873	improved dichromate battery
1874	explorer-extractor of bullets
1875	electric almanac or calendar
1875	oxygen spacesuit for balloonists
1875	portable dynamo-electric machine
1877	electric paperweight
1877	simulation of muscle contraction
1878	exploratory polyscopes for cavities of the human body
1878	improvements of the telephonic microphone.
1880	improved Siemens motor
1881	electric boat
1881	electric tricycle
1881	luminous electric jewels
1881	manufacture of magnets
1881	marine outboard motor
1881	miniaturized dental drill
1883	electric vehicle headlamp
1883	Trouvé-Hélot frontal headlamp

1883	underwater lighting
1884	electric safety lamp
1885	electrical apparatus for lighting physiology and chemistry laboratories
1885	underwater lighting used during the Suez Canal construction
1886	electric siren as an alarm signal
1886	new system for constructing propellers
1887	electric auxanoscope (image projector)
1887	working model electric helicopter (tethered)
1889	dynamo electric demonstrator
1889	electric counter
1889	improvements to his electric rifle
1889	system for transporting plate glass sheets
1890	electric lighting for horse-drawn carriages
1890	electric orygmatoscope for the inspection of geological layers
1890	mobile electric-pneumatic streetlamp lighter
1890	universal dynamometer
1891	electric horse bit
1891	improvements in luminous electric fountains
1891	second mechanical bird
1892	battery-electric massage instrument for hernia
1892	electric trigger mechanism for time-lapse photography
1892	hand-held medical dynamometer
1893	electric industrial ventilation system
1894	electric keyboard instrument based on Savart's wheel
1894	electric stunning lance for hunting
1894	luminous electric jewelry belt
1894	luminous electric jumping rope
1894	system for automatic fishing by night
1895	acetylene domestic lighting
1895	improved pedal bicycle
1895	manual/electric hybrid massaging machine
1895	universal AC/DC electric motor
1897	device for automatic bottling of acetylene
1897	device for hermetically sealing containers of acetylene
1897	windmill toy for hats and canes
1898	multi-task, manual-electric, industrial gyratory pump
1899	carburetor for internal combustion engines
1900	battery-powered, inflatable lifejacket
1901	phototherapy instruments
1902	propulsion of model boat or submarine by acetylene
1902	spring-loaded harpoon gun toy

Appendix II: Trouvé
in the Twenty-First Century

The right of any inventor to be included in a newly published book can be partially measured by the continuing use of his inventions in the present day. Gustave Trouvé is no exception.

In the chronology of his inventions, the first would be his carbon-zinc "Lilliputian" pocket battery (1865) as used in toys and medical instruments: Today's AA or R6 battery is manufactured in its billions by companies such as Duracell and Eveready and used in many small devices.

For a long time, his battery-electric rifle (1867) might have been considered esoteric. Although the majority of hunters still use spring-loaded rifles, a new sport has grown up, named Airsoft, in which participants eliminate opponents by hitting each other with spherical non-metallic pellets launched via replica firearms. Airsoft guns can either be spring-loaded or battery-powered (Automatic Electric Guns, or AEGs). Electric-powered Airsoft guns typically use a rechargeable battery or batteries to drive an electric motor, which cycles an internal piston/spring assembly in order to launch pellets. These AEGs often obtain muzzle velocities of 150 to 650 ft/s (46 to 200 m/s) and rates of fire of between 100 and 1,500 rounds per minute. Airsoft originated in Japan, then spread to Hong Kong and China in the late 1970s. The Japanese company Tokyo Marui dominates the market. In a Tokyo Marui, AEGs are powered primarily by nickel metal hydride (NiMH) batteries with varying voltages and milliampere hours ratings. Recently, however, Lithium-Polymer, or Li-po, batteries are becoming more popular in the Airsoft world.

In February 2012, the U.S. Navy fired its first successful test shots from its 32-megajoule, half-power, prototype electromagnetic railgun at a range in Dahlgren, Virginia. Developed at a price of $30 million, this weapon uses electromagnetic fields to fling projectiles at speeds of up to 5,000 mph. The laser system was deployed in 2014, two years ahead of schedule, aboard the USS *Ponce*.

Trouvé's explorer-extractor (1869) to find and extract metal bullets may have been replaced by the ubiquitous x-ray scanner, but millions of metal-detectors are used by professional and amateur archeologists all over the world.

Trouvé's polyscope (1873) remains in almost daily universal use in and beyond the medical world. Among the major manufacturers of endoscopes are Karl Storz GmbH of Tuttlingen, and Richard Wolf GmbH of Knittlingen, both headquartered in Germany, and U.S. Endoscopy, headquartered in northeast Ohio. Such companies have been innovating and manufacturing in their millions a very wide range of instruments, running into the hundreds, for medical, industrial or veterinary use, each device ending with the suffix "-scope."

The legacy of Trouvé's suggestions for a space suit and enclosed pressurized flight cabin made in a letter written in 1875 have already been outlined in this book. Two high points so far are the 17-year-old International Space Station and its astronauts at an orbital height of 370 km and Felix Baumgartner who, wearing a pressurized suit, set the world record for skydiving an estimated 39 km. (24 mi.), reaching an estimated speed of 1,357.64 km/h (843.6 mph), on 14 October 2012.

Trouvé's artificial muscle (1877) was just a tiny element in the growing twenty-first century burgeoning robotics industry.

His battery-powered tricycle and boat (1881) have had a checkered life. On 2 January 1939, the centenary of Trouvé's birth, there were very few electric vehicles in operation in a world dominated by the internal combustion engine. Mention of electric vehicles had come to mean forklift trucks, short distance delivery vehicles, and golf carts, but little more. There were one or two survivors from fleets of electric passenger boats that had once seen regular service on the lakes in Austria, but no more.

With the German Occupation of France in 1940, the scarcity of petrol provoked a great deal of engineering ingenuity. Perhaps most interesting was the aluminum CGE-Tudor electric automobile as designed by Jean Grégoire, with a normal range of 90 km per electrical charge. Production of the Grégoire was authorized by the Germans on condition that the majority were exported to Germany. Though two cars a week were made for nearly two years, so far as is known none are left France. One was offered to the director of a biscuit factory in exchange for his weight in biscuits, and everyone was happy with the transaction!

Forty years later, by 1979, following the energy crisis, a growing number of companies had begun to invest many millions of dollars in producing electric automobiles with recently innovated batteries. There were only a handful of electric boats, most of them in California, but there were one or two isolated examples on the inland waterways of England and one on a French canal.

Thirty-six years later, 2015, the world of transport is now fully concerned with continuingly increasing oil prices, the excess consumption of fuel-inefficient SUVs, and the need to curb greenhouse gas emissions. This has resulted in over 15 of the major automobile companies developing and manufacturing at least one hybrid-electric or battery-electric vehicle.

Since 2004, Tesla Motors of California has sold more than 2,500 of its Roadsters in 31 countries. By February 2011, the Mitsubishi i MiEV became the first electric car to sell more than 10,000 units, including the models badged in Europe as the Citroën C-Zero and Peugeot. During that year, the Smart electric drive, Wheego Whip LiFe, Mia electric, Volvo C30 Electric, and the Ford Focus Electric were launched for retail customers. The BYD e6, released initially for fleet customers in 2010, began retail sales in Shenzhen, China, that October. By 2013, the Nissan Leaf had passed the milestone of 50,000 units sold worldwide. Models released to the market in 2012 and 2013 include the BMW ActiveE, Coda, Renault Fluence Z.E., Tesla Model S, Honda Fit EV, Toyota RAV4 EV, Renault Zoe, Roewe E50, Mahindra e2o, Chevrolet Spark EV, Fiat 500e, Volkswagen e-Up! and BMW i3.

In Paris, where Trouvé had tested the world's first electric vehicle 130 years before, the Bolloré Bluecar was released in December 2011 and deployed for use in the Autolib's car-sharing service in Paris.

Alongside an already out-of-date total number of 160,000 electric four-wheelers can be added several commercially produced electric motorcycles available in markets around the world, including the Brammo Empulse, Zero S, Energica EGO, Quantya Strada, Yamaha EC-03, Electric Motorsport GPR-S, Hollywood Electrics, Yo Exl, and the Lito Sora.

Given that Trouvé's prototype was a three-wheeler, one example worth citing here is the Philippines. There are approximately 3.5 million conventional combustion-engine tricycles operating in the Philippines, contributing millions of tons of carbon dioxide emissions to the environment every year. The Asian Development Bank, with the Philippine government and the Department of Energy, hopes to transform the public transportation sector by widely adopting electric tricycles throughout the Philippines.

Finally, the e-bike, used worldwide, has experienced rapid growth since 1998. It is estimated that there were roughly 120 million e-bikes in China as of early 2010, and sales are expanding rapidly in India, the United States of America, the Netherlands, and Switzerland. A total of 700,000 e-bikes were sold in Europe in 2010, up from 200,000 in 2007 and 500,000 units in 2009. Today, China is the world's leading producer of e-bikes. According to the data of the China Bicycle Association, a government-chartered industry group, in 2004 China's manufacturers sold 7.5 million e-bikes nationwide, which was almost twice the year 2003 sales; domestic sales reached 10 million in 2005, and 16 to 18 million in 2006.

Although with a more gentle sales curve than electric four-wheelers and two-wheelers, battery-electric boats and hybrid-electric boats are making steady and very positive progress around the world. Ranging from car ferries to fishing dinghies, both inboard and outboard craft worldwide have passed the 50,000 fleet mark. Since 1968 the Duffy Electric Boat Company of California has mass-produced over 10,000 electric powered boats, while since 2005, the German company Torqeedo has sold some 40,000 electric outboards. In February 2014, IDTechEx predicted that the global market for electrically powered watercraft—including those that operate on and under the water—would grow from $2.6 billion in 2014 to $7.3 billion in 2024.

At the time of this writing, on the River Seine in Central Paris, where Trouvé carried out his pioneer experiments in 1881, there is one solar-powered passenger catamaran taking tourists on 40-minute round trips from the foot of the Pont-Marie around the Ile Saint-Louis and up towards the Eiffel Tower. This is a 17-metre Aquabus C60, made by Grove Boats at Yverdon-les-Bains, Switzerland. It is called the *Felix de Azara*, an eighteenth century Spanish naturalist, not the *Gustave Trouvé*. Other than that there are two electric commuter ferryboats and 15 hire-boats on the Paris canal system. Further downstream on the Seine, at Chatou, where Trouvé once entertained his Impressionist painter friends with the multicolored lights on his electric launch, an electric boat called *le Dénicheur* gives regular rides to tourists showing them the landscapes Monet and Renoir painted in the 1880s.

At the 1881 International Electric Exhibition, Trouvé's little engine also powered a sewing machine. Among the several manufacturers who mass produce electric and electronic sewing machines—such as Singer and Janome—there is Brother Industries Ltd., a Japanese multinational electronics and electrical equipment company headquartered in Nagoya, Japan. With a turnover in excess of $100 million, it is the fourth biggest company under the Brother Industries Ltd. umbrella of organizations. Brother Industries manufactures mechanical sewing machines in Zhuhai,

China, and computerized sewing and embroidery machines in Taiwan. A new sewing machine factory was opened in 2012 in Dong Nai Province, Vietnam, which is the largest single-brand sewing machine factory in the world. In September 2012, Brother Industries manufactured their 50-millionth home electric sewing machine.

The principle of the frontal headlamp, which Trouvé pioneered with Hélot in 1883, is more popular than ever, simply by considering the number of speleologists enjoying and exploring the dark caverns of the world and the mountaineers scaling its mountain peaks who would not be without one. Since the end of the 1960s, Petzl of Switzerland has invested in the field of the frontal headlamp. The founder, Fernand Petzl, developed models for speleology, his passion. In 1972, Petzl developed the first "all on the head" model, with a combined light and energy source. From this model was developed the famous Zoom lamp, which has equipped speleologists and mountaineers. In 2000 Petzl launched the Tikka, one of the first LED lamps. Sales of Petzl headlamps for the year 2006 surpassed 75 million units. Today the company is in its third generation, and tens of millions of products have been sold. It employs some 750 people in the world with a turnover in 2013 of over $167 million.

Trouvé's adaptation of the frontal headlamp to light his small fleet of Seine-based electric boats (1882) is the first known example of the use of a headlamp to give night vision *to any vehicle*. One need only reflect on the number of vehicles worldwide, on land, air, and water that are fitted with headlamps to realize the forest that grew from that seed. The same may be said for his electric klaxon. It was not until 1910 that Oliver Lucas of Birmingham, England, developed a standard electric car horn or klaxon in 1910. However, dry cells wore down quickly and had to be replaced, which was expensive. The change to electric, magneto-powered head lights and horn began in 1915. From 1919 a battery-powered horn was fitted to the electrically equipped Model T cars.

Like many of Trouvé's inventions, luminous electric jewelry receded into the shadows, even though their lights never quite died out. From the 1920s, at the Folies Bergères in Paris, multiple electric lights worn by troupes of artistes remained a regular attraction. On a more personal note, in December 1932 in an article entitled "Electric Jewelry for Milady" was published in *Modern Mechanix* magazine: "Now comes an electric light bulb to displace glowing pearls from earrings! Our photograph shows a young woman apparently wearing a large pearl earring, but in reality it is a midget electric bulb run from tiny batteries concealed in ornamental coils around it. The bulb is frosted to produce a soft light. It is particularly effective in contrast with dark hair."

Trouvé's idea of luminous electric jewels continued to be used in the decades that followed (Musée EDF Electropolis, Mulhouse).

In the 1960s, American fashion designer Diana Dew created a line of electronic fashion, including electro-luminescent party dresses and belts that could sound alarm sirens. The technology she used was made up of pliable and removable plastic lamps sewn into her clothing in segments, connected to a rechargeable battery pack worn on the hip. The batteries were good for a full five hours of flashing, and could produce 1–12 flashes per second by adjusting a control knob called a potentiometer. "They're hyperdelic transsensory experiences," said Dew in a 1967 *Time* article.

With the miniaturization of photovoltaic panels, and the introduction of the light emitting diode (LED) and the lithium-ion battery, it would not long before luminous electric jewelry would make a glowing comeback under the title of "wearable technology" or "e-textiles." Two of today's innovators are based in Europe. One of these, "Lost Values," has been created by MIT Media Lab research associate Elena Corchero: each of her accessories, be it handbag, fan or bracelet, has built-in solar cells and low-power light bulbs. By day, as the accessories are worn or carried, the solar panels charge up. At night, when the accessories no longer need to be worn, they then transform into decorative ambient light sources for the home.[1]

Since 2004, Francesca Rosella and Ryan Genz of CuteCircuit based in Shoreditch, London, have been pushing the boundaries of wearable technology. Their Kinetic Dress represents an interaction between garment and wearer's activities and mood; in fact, it lights up and changes its patterns following the person's movement. In 2008 CuteCircuit designed the M Dress, which accepts a standard SIM card and allows the wearer to make and receive calls anytime, everywhere, without having to carry a cellular phone.

At the closing ceremony of the 2014 Winter Olympics at the Fisht Olympic Stadium in Sochi, Russia, a "forest" of 204 12-meter-high LED light tubes changed color throughout, and the audience was given LED necklaces that also changed colors periodically.

Trouvé had also contributed to the use of electric special effects for the theatre. Where would the theatre be today without electricity? Not to mention the light shows used by pop musicians for their concerts. The sparkling sword fight he innovated for a Paris theatre production (1886) is of particular interest. Ninety years later, in 1977, the cinema-going public discovered the light saber used in *Star Wars* between the Jedi and the Sith. Developed by Korean Nelson Shin, an animator at the DePatie-Freleng Enterprises, the light saber has a polished metal hilt that projects a brightly lit energy blade generally about 4 feet (1.22 meters) long. In 2008, a survey of approximately 2,000 film fans found it to be the most popular weapon in film history. More recently a company called Arcadia of Bristol, England, has developed a spectacular duel called "Lords of Lightning." Two men wear protective suits and tesla coils (named after Trouvé's contemporary, Nikola Tesla) that can generate and direct high-voltage streams of electricity. Arcadia, and elsewhere a Chinese band called Thunderbolt Craziness, have developed electric light shows beyond anything Trouvé might have conceived possible.

His auxanoscope (1887) for projecting images on the wall has developed progressively. From cinema projection to simple slide shows, to Microsoft's PowerPoint (1990) and the interactive whiteboard (IWB) of 1991, the evidence is there.

Trouvé's conviction in 1891 about the heavier-than-air flying machine has also gone beyond his wildest expectations. In recent estimates, the number of aircraft in flying condition today range from 70,000 to 150,000 units, from airliners to light aircraft. It has been estimated that in peak hours, across the United States, some 12,000 aircraft including commercial, cargo, general, military and private craft, are in the sky at the same time, or some 60,000 pilots, crew and passengers are airborne over America at once. Several years ago, more than 4,000 flights a day were aloft in the Paris vicinity alone.

At the time of this writing, about half a dozen of these are electrically propelled, single-seat aircraft. One example of these is the Airbus E-Fan; each wing contains a 65-kg lithium-ion polymer battery pack that powers a 30-kW motor driving a ducted, variable-pitch fan propeller. It made its first flights in April 2014.

For those who believed in the lighter-than-air machine, there are there are just over 4,000 airships and blimps in operation, such as E-Green Technologies' 235-ft.-long *The Bullet*, which runs on algae fuel.

Again thanks to the LED-Li-ion combo, Trouvé's luminous electric walking stick/torch complete with siren has been "re-invented" by Mr. Chan King Fai of China, where it is been manufactured by Dolink Industrial Co., Ltd. in Shenzhen City, Guangdong Province, China. With the stick made of aluminum, the light made up of three LEDs has a life of more than 10,000 hours, and a range of over 20 yards; the light angle can be altered. The alarm with loudspeaker goes off when the stick is inclined to 45 degrees.

As for his decorative luminous electric fountains (1892), several companies are continuing his innovation in the twenty-first century: among these are Aquatique Show International of Strasbourg, France, and WET Design of Los Angeles, California. WET was founded in 1983 by former

Disney Imagineers Mark Fuller, Melanie Simon, and Alan Robinson. The company has designed over 200 fountains and water features using water, fire, ice, fog, and lights. It is known for creating the Dubai Fountain, the world's largest performing fountain, along with the 8-acre (3.2 ha) Fountains of Bellagio. It has designed features in over 20 countries around the world, in North America, Europe, Asia and the Middle East. WET holds more than 60 patents pertaining to lighting, water control, and specialty fountain devices that use air compression technology.

Aquatique Show International was founded in 1979 by Dominique Formhals. For over 35 years, this French company has been designing and installing prestigious synchronized water and light festivals. More than 52 countries have already applauded the firm's knowhow. When I sent details of Trouvé's fountains to Aquatique Show International, I received the following reply:

> *07/05/2007*
> Dear Sir. Thank you for your most enlightening documentation, I had not until now ever heard anyone speak about Monsieur Gustave Trouvé even though working for over 30 years in the field of fountains. The techniques used today are not so very different from those conceived by Monsieur Trouvé, except that they are more compact, lighter, less expensive ... but the results are not so very different. Yours sincerely, Dominique Formhals, Président Directeur Général Aquatique Show International."

Since 1982, Safe-Rain, based in Spain, has been manufacturing and supplying architectural fountain accessories such as kits, nozzles, lighting, water curtains.

In 1892 Trouvé had ambitiously suggested a towering luminous fountain that would be the centerpiece of the 1900 Universal Exhibition in Paris. With water jets rising to a staggering height of 250–1,000 meters, their lights would be seen from all points of the city and beyond. Their colors, as varied and as changing as so desired, could even serve as signals. His idea was ridiculed. There was simply not enough water pressure.

Trouvé may well have heard about a waterjet installed in 1886 at the Swiss factory of Coulouvrenière and used as a safety valve for a hydraulic power network. In 1891, the capacity of this Jet d'Eau to reach 30 meters (100 feet) was recognized and it was moved to its present location on Lake Geneva. Its height was increased to 90 meters (300 feet). By 1951, Geneva's Jet d'Eau was able to jet 500 liters (132 gallons) of lake water per second to a height of 140 meters (460 feet). To do this, two 500-kW pumps, operating at 2,400 V, consume over one megawatt of electricity. In 1970, the Captain Cook Memorial Jet in Canberra, Australia began jetting its water up to 147 meters (482 feet). By 1985, King Fahd's Fountain in Jeddah, Saudi

Arabia, began reaching 312 meters (1023 feet), making it the world's tallest fountain. The water it ejects can reach a speed of 375 kilometers (233 mi.) per hour and its airborne mass can exceed 18 tons. It uses over 500 spotlights to illuminate the fountain at night.

One hundred and seventeen years later, November 2009, the Dubai Fountains, set in the Burj Dubai Lake, went into action in front of "Buri Khalifa," the world's tallest building (828 m, 168 floors).

Built for $217 million by WET Design, the Dubai propels 83,000 liters (22,000 gallons) of water 150 meters (490 feet) into the air at any one time. More than 6,600 lights and 50 colored projectors, hundreds of servos, all computer-controlled, "perform" selected musical pieces in time with jets of water on the 30-acre lake. There are music-water displays every 20 minutes, with 14 nightly performances.

On 2 January 2010 in a press release it was announced that height of the Dubai fountains had been increased to 275 m due to powerful nozzles capable of shooting water higher than a 50-story building.

The electric lance (1893) has also survived into the twenty-first century. Published in 1911, *Tom Swift's Electric Rifle* was one in a succession of some 100 volumes of American juvenile science fiction and adventure stories. According to Tom Swift, for his electric rifle, "there are no batteries, but the current is a sort of wireless kind. It is stored in a cylinder, just as compressed air or gases are stored, and can be released as I need it." Fifty years later, when NASA researcher Jack Cover invented a conducted electrical weapon and was looking for a name, inspired by his childhood hero, he called it a TSER (the acronym for *Tom Swift's Electric Rifle*), soon changing it to TASER. The Taser has been manufactured in large numbers.

Trouvé's patent for a new type of musical instrument (1894) may not have even been developed in his day. But in 1990, Bart Hopkins of Experimental Musical Instruments in California came up with an idea for a musical instrument and built it, and later discovered that, as so often turns out to be the case, the idea had been explored before. He called his instrument "Savart's Wheel" in recognition of its predecessor. However, his version was more fully musical than most, having multiple wheels with a full chromatic range of two and a half octaves. It was perhaps similar to the innards of Trouvé's proposed instrument, but did not have a keyboard. The use of electricity for keyboard instruments has become a major industry, with companies such as Yamaha manufacturing their synthesizer in its millions.

At the dawn of the twentieth century, towards the abrupt end of his life, Trouvé collaborated with Foveau de Courmelles to make compact light-therapy machines to treat skin diseases. This too has given birth to a manufacturing industry, known as PUVA Therapy, used for skin infections such as psoriasis, vitiligo and eczema; even cutaneous cancers or Lichen planus. PUVA stands for "Psoralen Ultraviolet A." It is also known as photo-chemotherapy. Although many patients, unclothed and wearing protective glasses, are placed in a luminous box for 1–20 minutes, there are also smaller, more compact devices true to the Trouvé tradition.

One of the biggest manufacturers is Waldmann of Villingen-Schwenningen in Germany, who added the business of medical radiation devices to their company in 1975 and have since gained a worldwide reputation as a leading manufacturer of UV therapy systems for the treatment of skin diseases, such as psoriasis and neurodermatitis. In addition to diagnostic systems, the Waldmann range of products includes UV radiation devices for clinics and medical practices as well as special devices for home therapy. Systems for photodynamic therapy are also highly important. For partial body therapy, for example, they offer five different models the size of a small mainframe computer, using 4 UV compact lamps (PUVA) of 36 W.

With the success of the above inventions, Trouvé is doubtless an inventor and innovator whose instruments have not only survived but have also been regaining popularity in this century.

Chapter Notes

Chapter One

1. The fame of the Swedish King Gustave Adolphe (1594–1632), exemplary monarch and military strategist, drew the attention of Europe to this first name, which soon began to spread in several countries, including France. This development culminated in the nineteenth century, where "Gustave" met with a long period of popularity, illustrated in France by the painter Gustave Courbet (b. 1819), the romantic novelist Gustave Flaubert (b. 1821), engineer Gustave Eiffel (b. 1832), illustrator Gustave Doré (b. 1832) and Gustave Trouvé (b. 1839).

2. In French, the name given to an abandoned child or foundling was quite simply *Trouvé*, which means "found." The alternative was to name them after the day of the week when they were found—such as *lundi* or Monday.

3. Tourlet Ernest-Henry, *Histoire du collège de Chinon* (Paris: H. Champion, 1904), p. 205.

4. Reference ETP 812, Departmental Archives of Maine-et-Loire.

Chapter Two

1. The author has been unable to find the name of the clockmaker with whom Trouvé served his apprenticeship.

2. Archives de la Ville de Paris.

3. The Englishman Jonathan Swift's novel *Gulliver's Travels*, which includes Lemuel Gulliver's visit to Lilliput, translated into French by the Abbé Pierre-François Guyot Desfontaines as *Les voyages du capitain Lemuel Gulliver*, was published in 1727. From then on the word "lilliputien" was used to describe anything tiny.

4. George Barral, *L'histoire d'un inventeur: Exposé des découvertes et des travaux de M. Gustave Trouve dans le domaine de l'électricité* (Paris: Georges Carre, 1891), pp. 1–2.

5. His real name was Gaspard Félix Tournachon.

6. Viscount Gustave du Ponton d'Amecourt, *La conquête de l'air par l'hélice: Exposé d'un nouveau système d'aviation*, 4th ed. (Paris: E. Sausset, 1863).

7. E-mail to the author, 15 May 2007.

8. INPI Archives.

9. City of Paris archives.

10. Guillaume-Benjamin Duchenne de Boulogne, *De l'électrisation localisée et de son application à la physiologie, à la pathologie et à la thérapeutique (Localized Electrification and Its Application to Physiology, Pathology and Therapeutics)* (Paris: J.-B. Baillière, 1855).

11. *Le XIXe Siècle*, 12 August 1874.
12. Barral, *L'histoire d'un inventeur*, xx.
13. Gustave Trouvé, *Communication à la Société internationale des electriciens*, December 1885.
14. Gustave Trouvé, *Manuel théorique, instrumental et pratique, d'électrologie medicale* (Paris: O. Doin, 1893).
15. E-mail to the author, 4 June 2007.
16. INPI Archives.
17. The Exposition Universelle took place in Paris from 1 May to 31 October 1878 on the Champ de Mars.
18. Émile Zola, *Au bonheur des dames* (Paris: G. Charpentier, 1883).
19. Abbé Moigno, *Les Mondes* 40, no. 14 (1 August 1878).

Chapter Three

1. *La Nature*, no. 528 (15 September 1879).
2. *Scientific American*, 25 October 1879.
3. Gustave Trouvé, report to the Académie des Sciences, July 1880.
4. Antoine Bréguet, *Le Génie Civil*, 1 November 1880.
5. Camille Flammarion, *Le Voltaire*, 8 February 1881.
6. *La Nature*, 16 April 1881.
7. Henri de Parville, *The Official*, 20 April 1881.
8. L'Abbé Moigno, *Les Mondes*, 20 May 1881.
9. Georges Dary, *A travers l'électricité* (Paris: Vuibert et Nony, 1895), p. 456.
10. Ernest Henry Wakefield, *History of the Electric Automobile* (Warrendale, Pa.: Society of Automobile Engineers, 1993).
11. Dary, *A travers l'électricité*, p. 456.
12. Communication made by Trouvé do the Académie des Sciences de Paris, 1881.
13. Louis Figuier, *Les nouvelles conquêtes de la science*, (Paris: Girard et Boitte, 1867–1869).
14. More than 30 periodicals, French, British and American, would report on Trouvé's boat.
15. *Exposition internationale de l'électricité, Paris 1881*, Administration-jury-rapports, vol. 1, 1883 (France: Administration des postes, January 1, 1883).
16. In 1894, Trouvé would suggest electricity as the motive power for his keyboard musical instrument.
17. Letter from Mrs. Alexander Graham Bell to Mrs. Gardiner Greene Hubbard, 8 July 1881.
18. Journal kept by Wm. Schuyler Johnson, secretary to Alexander Graham Bell.
19. George Barral, *L'histoire d'un inventeur: Exposé des découvertes et des travaux de M. Gustave Trouve dans le domaine de l'électricité* (Paris: Georges Carre, 1891), xx.
20. Ibid.
21. Pantheon of the Legion d'Honneur, January 1882.
22. Letter to La grande chancellerie de la Légion d'honneur, 4 March 1882.
23. Gustave Trouvé, *Manuel théorique, instrumental et pratique, d'électrologie medicale* (Paris: O. Doin, 1893), p. 190.
24. Musical Gossip, *The Pictorial World*, 24 February 1883.

Chapter Four

1. French Patent N° 154568 was granted on the 21 July of this year; patents in Belgium and in England were granted several months later.

2. In 1849 several workshops in Paris, Duez, Duriez and Muneaux had formed the "Société confraternelle des Ouvriers Lunetiers" to cooperatively sell spectacles and mathematical instruments.

3. Adolphe Gaiffe (1830–1903), French scientific-instrument maker. In 1856, he founded the firm that bears his name. It remained in business until the early twentieth century, specializing in the production of electrotherapy apparatuses and instruments for electrical measurements.

4. The letters were kindly loaned to the author by the Hélot family.

5. Trouvé's concern over not being very patriotic was that he would be there on 14 July, Bastille Day, as important in France as the 4 July Independence Day in the United States.

6. The first time any form of powered transport used an electric headlamp.

7. Wilfrid de Fonvielle, *Obituary of Trouvé*, 1902.

8. *Gazette de France*, 18 December 1883.

9. *La Patrie*, 16 December 1883.

10. Among those publications that praised the effect: *The Illustrated Sporting and Dramatic News, The Era, The Stage, Society, Weekly Times, Lady's Pictorial, Weekly Dispatch, News of the World, Lloyd's, Daily Telegraph, Morning Post, Daily News, Pall Mall Gazette, The Echo, Daily Chronicle, Funny Folks, Modern Society, Reynold's, The London Figaro, The Queen, The Graphic,* and *The Whitehall Review.*

11. *The Illustrated and Sporting News*, 26 April 1884.

12. *The Observer*, n.d.

13. *Lloyds*, n.d.

14. *The Bazaar*, n.d.

15. *The Era*, n.d.

16. *Grey River Argus* 31, no. 5032 (8 November 1884): 1.

17. *L'Illustration* 1271 (4 October 1884).

18. *Scientific American*, 15 November 1884, p. 310.

Chapter Five

1. Trouvé, *Lampes électriques portatives*, communication to the Académie des Sciences, 10 November 1884.

2. Publicity, "Overview of the Prices of Trouvé Luminous Electric Jewels, the Sole Inventor Patented in France and Abroad," in *L'électricité au theatre, bijoux électromobiles*, ed. Trouve, G. Paris: Impr. A.L. Guillot, 1900.

3. George Barral, *L'histoire d'un inventeur: Exposé des découvertes et des travaux de M. Gustave Trouve dans le domaine de l'électricité* (Paris: Georges Carre, 1891), p. 340.

4. Trouvé, "Applications de l'électricité aux armes à feu," *Bulletin de la Société internationale des electriciens*, July 1885.

5. *La Lumière Electrique* 17, 1885.

6. Barral, *L'histoire d'un inventeur*, p. 340.

7. Le Baron B., *Le Chat Noir*, n.d.

8. Monet had arrived in Paris in 1859, the same year as Trouvé; both men were fascinated by light, natural for one, artificial for the other.

9. Barral, *L'histoire d'un inventeur*, letter from Elie Ferrand, 5 August 1887.

10. *Bulletin de la Société internationale des electriciens*, June 1888.

11. Extract from *Odontologie* on a conference entirely devoted to the description of Trouvé's instruments applied to dentistry.

12. Edouard-Alfred Martel *Les abîmes (The Abysses)* (Paris: Delagrave, 1894).

13. Jules Patenôtre, *Souvenirs d'un diplomate* (Paris: Ambert, 1913).

14. Pierre Loti, *Au Maroc* (Paris: Calmann-Lévy, 1890).

Chapter Six

1. *Bulletin de la Société internationale des electriciens*, 1892.
2. Professor Périer, communication to the Académie de Médecine, 20 April 1890.
3. Correspondence Trouvé to Hélot, 6 May 1890.
4. Gustave Trouvé, *Manuel théorique, instrumental et pratique, d'électrologie medicale* (Paris: O. Doin, 1893).
5. Corneille Cadresco, director of the *Gazette de Jassy*, today's Iasi, Rumania.
6. *Bulletin de la Société internationale des electriciens*, November 1892; French Patent N° 215819, August 1891.
7. *Bulletin de la Société d'encouragement pour l'industrie nationale*, March 1893.
8. Georges Dary, *A travers l'électricité* (Paris: Vuibert et Nony, 1895), p. 456.
9. George Barral, *L'histoire d'un inventeur: Exposé des découvertes et des travaux de M. Gustave Trouve dans le domaine de l'électricité* (Paris: Georges Carre, 1891).
10. Book review, *La Lumière Electrique*, n.d.
11. Found in a second-hand bookshop.
12. Mémoire presented by G. Trouvé, 24 August 1891, conserved at the Académie des Sciences, Paris, reference arch–2007/26.
13. *Popular Science Monthly* 40 (January 1892).
14. Science, Industry and Business Library: General Collection, The New York Public Library. "Lettre de Victor Hugo à Gaston Tissandier, à l'occasion de ses premières ascensions scientifiques avec W. de Fonvielle (1869)." New York Public Library Digital Collections.

Chapter Seven

1. Foveau de Courmelles, *L'indépendance luxembourgeoise*, 1 August 1902.
2. *Le Phare du Littoral*, 28 January 1893.
3. *Le Phare du Littoral*, 9 February 1893.
4. *Le Mentonnais*, 1 March 1893.
5. Julian Lefèvre, *Electricity at the Theatre*. Paris: n.p., 1894.
6. Gustave Trouvé, *Manuel théorique, instrumental et pratique, d'électrologie medicale* (Paris: O. Doin, 1893).
7. French Patent N° 222,965.
8. *Bulletin de la Société d'encouragement pour l'industrie nationale*, n.d.
9. French Patent N° 233,179.
10. Gustave Trouvé, *Un nouveau système de pêche* (Paris: B. Colombier, 1894).
11. Georges Dary, *A travers l'électricité* (Paris: Vuibert et Nony, 1895), p. 456.
12. Trouvé's patent description, page 6, recorded at 3:30 a.m., 26 February 1894.
13. *L'électricien*, 8 June 1895.

Chapter Eight

1. *Journal mensuel de l'Académie nationale de l'industrie agricole manufacturière et commerciale*, December 1895.
2. *Ibid.*
3. French Patent N° 272531.
4. *Fancy Dress*, 1896.
5. On the stand "Andalusia in the Time of the Moors," Universal Exhibition, Paris.
6. Wilfrid de Fonville, "Scientific News," *Le Mois Littéraire et Pittoresque*, July–December 1900.
7. "Soirée Parisienne," *Le Radical*, 9 February 1900, p. 3.

8. Académie des Sciences, 24 December 1900.

9. Foveau de Courmelles. *Electrothérapie dentaire; cours professé à l'Ecole dentaire de Paris.* (Paris: Maloine, 1904).

10. "New Inventions," *L'Illustration,* 7 December 1901.

11. Foveau de Courmelles, *L'année électrique, électrothérapique et radiographique: revue annuelle des progrès électriques,* 1902.

12. Foveau de Courmelles, *L'année électrique, électrothérapique et radiographique: revue annuelle des progrès électriques,* 1903.

13. *L'Indépendance Luxembourgeoise,* n.d.

14. George Barral, *L'histoire d'un inventeur: Exposé des découvertes et des travaux de M. Gustave Trouvé dans le domaine de l'électricité* (Paris: Georges Carre, 1891).

15. *L'Electricien,* 23 August 1902.

16. Wilfried De Fonvielle, *L'Aérophile* n.d.

17. Georges Dary, *A travers l'électricité* (Paris: Vuibert et Nony, 1895), p. 456.

18. *L'Industrie Electrique* 255 (10 August 1902): 340.

19. Foveau de Courmelles, and A. Collombar. *L'électricité et ses applications.* (Paris: Librairie C. Reinwald, 1900).

20. De Courmelles, *L'année électrique, électrothérapique et radiographique: revue annuelle des progrès électriques,* 1903.

21. *Wiener Luftsschiffer-Zeitung,* Vienna, October 1902.

22. Marcel Cocteau, Administration de l'enregistrement des domaines et du timbre, Formule de déclaration de mutation par décès, *Succession de M Trouvé,* Paris, 1902.

23. *La Nature,* n.d.

24. Wilfrid De Fonvielle, *L'Aérophile,* 1903.

25. De Courmelles, *L'année électrique,* p. 348.

Chapter Nine

1. History presents other examples of the once famous, then forgotten and since rehabilitated: the Dutch painter Jan Vermeer (1632–75; rehabilitated from 1842); the Venetian composer Antonio Vivaldi (1648–1741; rehabilitated from 1926); and more relevant to Trouvé, French polymath inventor Denis Papin (1647–1712) and the Hollywood silent movie star Clara Bow (1905–1965; rehabilitated from 1988).

2. Georges Ribeill, *De l'objet technique a l'utopie sociale: Les ressorts de l'imaginaire technologique des ingénieurs au xixe siècle (From Technical Object to Social Utopia: The Roots of Technological Imagination by Engineers in the Nineteenth Century)* (Paris: La Découverte, 2001).

3. Letter to the author, 15 July 2014.

4. Jean-Francois Trouvé, e-mail to the author, 4 May 2007.

5. Herman Voogd, science collections manager, Teylers Museum, Haarlem, Netherlands, e-mail to author, 22 August 2014.

6. Lycée Buffon, Lycée Hoche and Lycée Sophie Germain.

Appendix II

1. Elena Corchero, elena@lostvalues.com.

Bibliography

Books

Association française pour l'avancement des sciences. *Compte-rendu de la 16e session.* Paris: au secrétariat de l'Association, 1887.

Barral, Georges. *L'histoire d'un inventeur: Exposé des découvertes et des travaux de M. Gustave Trouve dans le domaine de l'électricité.* Paris: Georges Carre, 1891.

Bonnefont, Gaston. *Le règne de l'électricité.* Tours: A. Mame, 1895.

Cardot, Fabienne, and François Caron. *Histoire générale de l'électricité en France,* vol. 1: *Espoirs et conquêtes (1881–1918).* Paris: Fayard, 1991.

Cattelin, Jacques. *Gustave Trouvé, l'Edison français?* Tours: Académie de Touraine, 2012.

Cone, John Frederick, Thomas G. Kaufman, and William R. Moran. *Adelina Patti: Queen of Hearts.* Portland, OR: Amadeus, 1993.

Dary, Georges. *La navigation électrique.* Paris: J. Baudry, 1882.

_____. *A travers l'électricité.* Paris: Vuiber et Nony, 1901.

De Courmelles, Foveau. *L'électrothérapie dentaire.* Paris: Maloine, 1904.

Deleuil, Jean-Adrien. *Catalogue des instruments de physique, de chimie, d'optique et de mathématique.* Paris: H.A. Bourdier, 1863.

De Parville, Henri. *L'électricité et ses applications: exposition de Paris.* G. Masson, 1883.

Desmond, Kevin. *Gustave Trouvé; la quête d'un génie français oublié.* Bordeaux: Editions Pleine Page, 2012.

Dictionnaire biographique illustre d'Indre-et-Loire. Paris: R. Wagner, 1895–1909.

Druilhe, Paule. *Les grandes créations de l'Opéra de Monte-Carlo: L'enfant et les sortilèges de Maurice Ravel.* Monaco: Archives monégasques, 1985.

Du Moncel, Théodore (Comte). *L'éclairage électrique.* Paris: Hatchette, 1879.

Figuier, Louis. *Les nouvelles conquêtes de la science.* Paris: Librairie illustrée, 1884.

Forissier, Maurice. *L'histoire de l'arme au fil des siècles.* Biarritz: Pecari, 2004.

Foveau de Courmelles. *Electrothérapie dentaire; cours professé à l'Ecole dentaire de Paris.* Paris: Maloine, 1904.

_____, and A. Collombar. *L'électricité et ses applications.* Paris: Librairie C. Reinwald, 1900.

Goupille, André. *La Haye–Descartes des origines à nos jours.* Tours: Chavanne, 1980.

Graffigny, Henri de. *L'électricité pour tous.* Paris: E. Bernard, 1905.

Hospitalier, Édouard, and J.A. Montpellier. *L'électricité à l'exposition de 1900.* Paris: Vve Ch. Dunod, 1902.

Irving, Laurence. *Henry Irving: The Actor and His World.* London: Faber and Faber, 1951.

Lefèvre, Julien. *L'électricité au theatre.* Paris: n.p., 1894.

Loti, Pierre. *Au Maroc.* Paris: Calmann-Levy, 1890.

Ministère des Postes et des Télégraphes. *Exposition internationale d'électricité.* Vol. 1. Paris: G. Masson, 1883.

Montillot, C.J., and L. Montillot. *La maison électrique.* Paris: A. Grelot, 1894.

Onimus, Dr. *Guide pratique de l'électrothérapie.* Paris: G. Masson, 1877.

Patenôtre, Jules. *Souvenirs d'un diplomate.* Paris: Ambert, 1913.

Planté, Gaston. *Recherches sur l'électricité.* Paris: Gauthier-Villars, 1883.

Ribeill, Georges. *De l'objet technique a l'utopie sociale: Les ressorts de l'imaginaire technologique des ingénieurs au XIXe siècle.* Paris: La Découverte, 2001.

Ségal, Alain. "Place de l'Ingénieur Gustave Trouve (1839–1902) dans l'histoire de l'endoscopie." *Histoire des Sciences Médicales* 29, no. 2 (1995): 123–132.

Sigismund, Jaccoud. *Nouveau dictionnaire de médecine et de chirurgie pratiques.* Vol. 12. Paris: J.B. Bailliere, 1871.

Stoker, Bram. *Personal Reminiscences of Henry Irving.* London: W. Heinemann, 1907.

Trouvé, Gustave. *L'électricité au théâtre: bijoux électro-mobiles.* Paris: de A.L. Guillot, 1885.

_____. *Manuel, théorique, instrumental et pratique d'électrologie médicale.* Paris: O. Doin, 1893.

_____. *Nouveaux appareils a l'usage des médecins, des chirurgiens, de l'armée et des industriels.* Paris: Impr. de Mme. Ve Bouchard-Huzard, 1872.

_____. *Un nouveau système de pêche.* Paris: G. Colombier, 1894.

_____. *Une révolution dans l'éclairage domestique... Lampe à l'acétylène.* Clermon, France: Daix frères, 1896.

_____. *Signal avertisseur universel Trouvé, à l'usage des canotiers.* Paris: A.L. Guillot and A. Julien, 1886.

Venner, Dominique. *Encyclopédie des armes de chasse.* Paris: Maloine, 1996.

Periodicals

Actualité Médicale
Bulletin de la Société Internationale des Électriciens
L'Eclairage Électrique
La Gazette de l'Électricien
L'Illustration
La Lumière Électrique: Journal Universel d'Électricité
Les Mondes
La Nature
Le Yacht

Manuscripts

Documentation concerning the Chevalier of the Legion of Honor, 1881–1882.
Letters from Gustave Trouvé to Paul Hélot (1883–1890). Collection Hellé.

Index